MASSAD AYOOB'S
GREATEST
HANDGUNS
OF THE WORLD

©2010 Krause Publications, Inc.,
a subsidiary of F+W Media, Inc.

Published by

Gun Digest® Books

An imprint of F+W Media, Inc.
700 East State Street • Iola, WI 54990-0001
715-445-2214 • 888-457-2873
www.gundigestbooks.com

Our toll-free number to place an order or obtain
a free catalog is (800) 258-0929.

Library of Congress Control Number: 2009937519

ISBN-13: 978-1-4402-0825-6
ISBN-10: 1-4402-0825-5

Designed by Tom Nelsen
Edited by Dan Shideler

Printed in China

DEDICATION

It is my pleasure to dedicate this book to Gail Pepin, the producer and editor (PrEditor?) of the Pro-Arms Podcasts (proarmspodcast.com). A state and regional IDPA Champion, Gail is my Technical Advisor, professional photographer, nurse-caregiver, and Adult Supervisor.

—Mas Ayoob

CONTENTS

FOREWORD

A number of "classic" handguns emerged from the second half of the 20th century, with lesser numbers seeing the light of day in the first half. Just to grab a few representative names (the following listing is not represented as being either complete or finite, so hold the calls and letters if I've managed to omit your personal favorite):

From a military parentage origin ... The Colt Government .45, The Browning Hi-Power and the Walther PPK. From Colt we had the Detective Special, the Diamondback and the Cadillac of their revolver line, the Python. Smith and Wesson had a prolific century that had a number of successful introductions: the Model 10 (M&P); the Model 15 (Combat Masterpiece) and its close cousins in the K-line, the Model 19 (Combat Magnum), the Model 27 (.357 Magnum) and its predecessor, the Factory Registered 357 Magnum; the Model 29 (the Dirty Harry fan club can relax, we didn't forget you); the Model 36 (Chief's Special); the Model 49 (Bodyguard); the Model 40 (Centennial); the Model 39 semi-automatic (the finest "pointing" gun I've ever used) – and right about here, boys and girls, is where we're going to stop this little litany, lest we get into the Rugers, the SIGs, the Glocks, the Kimbers, the Paras, the Berettas, the CZs, and Heaven only knows how many more ... and this Foreword as a consequence would go on for pages.

Dave Brennan, right, discusses Glock .40s with Mas Ayoob.

There have been a few books published on the topic of "great guns" but many, if not most, have attempted to cover all types of guns, be they rifles, shotguns or handguns. As a result there were a large number of guns covered in these books but the coverage was all too brief, the result of space limitations. So I was delighted to learn that Massad Ayoob, an old friend and an occasional contributor to the pages of *Precision Shooting* magazine, was to do such a book, but on handguns only. Wonderful! We'll now get some in-depth coverage of the great handguns of our era, but with personal opinions, anecdotes and relevant tales as only Mas can do. He has authored a number of handgun books and articles over the years that have been classic works – for instance, his extensive coverage of the 1986 shootout in Miami where a half dozen or so poorly armed FBI agents shot it out with two well-armed criminals who did not seemed at all inclined to surrender. The point was clearly made by Mas Ayoob that a few handguns versus a semi-automatic rifle and a pump shotgun is a hard way to earn a living and not really to be recommended.

A prolific reader and writer with an encyclopedic memory, a good sense of humor, and a genuine reverence for classic handguns and firearms history and lore... the publisher of the book that you are reading could not have made a better choice to edit this book on classic handguns than Massad Ayoob. Hopefully they will sell enough copies that some evening, when the publisher is wondering just what he should do next, the thought will cross his mind ... "Gee, we had to leave out a number of handguns that probably should have qualified for inclusion." (Note to the publisher: No charge for the strong hint that a second volume would be kind of nice ...)

Dave Brennan
Editor
Precision Shooting magazine
Manchester, CT

INTRODUCTION

The genesis of this book goes back a number of years, to when Dave Brennan, editor of *The Accurate Rifle*, called and asked me to do a handgun column for his rifle magazine. The first column was on the S&W K-22, and I began it as follows:

> *In which we begin a series on classic handguns of interest to riflemen.*
>
> *Editor Dave Brennan has for some time been threatening to introduce a handgun column to these pages. As of this issue, that alien has landed. I would say, "Take me to your leader," but I'm already there. You, the reader, do lead where a publication like this goes. If you have suggestions for this column you can write to Dave at the magazine's masthead address or to me in care of him. Until a definite reader-driven sense of direction is established, this space will be devoted to handguns that are of particular interest to rifle shooters.*
>
> *This means handguns that are accurate. Handguns that are beautifully crafted and/or brilliantly designed, with specific features that make them especially valuable for certain purposes. Guns with histories. Guns long proven to work. In short, useful handguns with class.*

It turned out that the readers liked that direction just fine, and we continued with it until *The Accurate Rifle*'s unfortunate demise, due I believe to distribution problems, a few years ago. Early on in the series, Dave mentioned that a collection of them would make a pretty cool book. I had that in mind later on, when Cameron Hopkins asked me to do a long piece on the history of the 1911 and a magnum opus on HKs in the *Combat Tactics* periodical he does for SureFire, and when Harry Kane assigned me to do a history piece on the S&W Model 27 in the Complete Book of Handguns for Harris Publications every year. Two chapters, those on the Walther and the S&W service autos, were written expressly for this book. With those exceptions, all the other chapters here appeared originally in *The Accurate Rifle*.

Harry is retired now, Dave is still putting out *Precision Rifle*, and Cameron is still doing *Combat Tactics*. All three proved

to be great editors, and I'm grateful to all three for permission to reprint here.

Each piece has been lightly edited and updated for this book. All follow a similar format. First is "pedigree," by which I mean what "role model shooters" owned the gun in question, what did they accomplish with it, and what did contemporary experts think about it after testing it and observing it extensively in use? Then, the history: where did it go? How did its design evolve? What other developments did it lead to that made it one of the great ones of its kind? Then, its shooting characteristics: how did those who used it to good effect take maximum advantages of the given model's design strengths, and compensate for its weaknesses? Finally, a personal perspective based on individual as well as collective experience with the model in question.

You'll find lots of quotes in here. I relied heavily on the perceptions of that great generation of gun experts and writers of the 20th century, the time in which many of these guns really made their bones: Askins, Cooper, Gaylord, Jordan, Keith, Stebbins, and the like. You'll also hear from the current generation, a vast pool of knowledgeable subject matter experts, some still writing and some already gone. There is much to learn from them. I quoted them as they wrote, not changing "P.38" to "P-38," for example. And, there will be occasional references to guns' use on the silver screen, which had something to do with shaping market perception of them.

The determination of greatness, whether in objects or in men, is largely a subjective one. Writer and reader may not agree on what makes the cut, and the former has an obligation to the latter to explain the choices he presents. Why, for example, a whole chapter on the S&W Model 28 Highway Patrolman, when it appears to

be simply a subset of another model introduced a score of years earlier, and lasting in the marketplace much longer? The reason is that the original .357 Registered Magnum that became the Model 27 and today's 627/327 series did indeed create one of our most popular calibers, the .357 Magnum, and set a high water mark for overall quality, but the Model 28 was far more than just a footnote in its history. By itself, the 28 set the pace for an entire genre of firearms that encompassed rifles and shotguns as well as handguns: stripped down, roughly finished, plain vanilla "economy models" that

were the same as the famous deluxe versions on the inside, and provided identical performance if not esthetics to the end user. Thus, one could argue that the Model 28 was even more important to modern firearms history and manufacture than the 27. Rather than make that value judgment, I simply included both guns here.

Why was the humble High Standard Sentinel revolver included here, but the not the splendid Smith & Wesson Model 41 target pistol? The Sentinel was neither a long-lived gun nor a much-copied one, but this brilliant Harry Seifried design broke a logjam of double action revolver design stagnation that had lasted more than half a century. In that sense, it paved the way for new double action mechanisms from Dan Wesson, Ruger, and even Colt. The Model 41, as fine a specimen of its breed as it was, simply carried on a tradition already set beforehand by High Standard with its Supermatic series: a large, finely made, super-accurate pistol with quickly interchangeable barrels. The Supermatic's influence is seen in later designs, such as the popular Browning Buckmark, but the Model 41's is not.

Thanks again to Dave Brennan, Cameron Hopkins, and Harry Kane for their assistance, and particularly to Dave for not only inspiring this book, but writing the foreword. It was a pleasure to put this book together over the years, and I learned a lot doing the research. Whether or not you and I agree on what were the greatest and most influential handgun designs during the period covered, I hope you find this book as enjoyable and instructive to read as I found it to write.

Massad Ayoob
July, 2009

The 1911
The Once – and Future? – King of Pistols

Your hand closes firmly around the slim grip-frame of the pistol, and as you slide it smoothly from the holster, your thumb closes naturally down until you feel the snick of the safety snapping into the "fire" position. The pistol seems to point itself at the target, and your finger finds the trigger at just the right spot, pressing rearward. You feel the clean, crisp release through your trigger finger, and the familiar, soft bump of the recoil through the palm of your hand. Downrange, a reaction target is slammed over by the heavy bullet you have launched, and the pistol has already cycled itself, its sights coming almost automatically back on target as you let the trigger come forward a tiny bit until you feel the click of its reset and begin the second pull.

> The 1911 is more than a magnificent legend and a classic piece of Americana – it is a splendidly functional tool of protection, sport, and combat.

In continuous production since the eponymous year of its introduction, the 1911 is a classic of design, a classic of a magnitude that extends beyond the world of the gun show.

One of the world's most recognizable silhouettes: the GI issue 1911A1 .45 caliber semiautomatic pistol. This one is by Remington-Rand, which produced more of them during WWII than Colt.

You are firing a 1911, the classic ".45 automatic." You are also experiencing a classic meeting of man and machine, the functionality of a tool intended to work as an extension of your hand. And you are steeping yourself in history, and in Americana, and in the lore of the handgun.

Perspectives

In continuous production since the eponymous year of its introduction, the 1911 is a classic of design, a classic of a magnitude that extends beyond the world of the gun. Show its silhouette to someone who has only seen guns on TV and they'll probably identify it as "a .45 automatic." Within the world of the gun, it has become absolutely iconic.

For some, this pistol literally takes on religious overtones. More than one Internet fan of John Browning's most popular design will have as a signature line, not WWJD?

("What Would Jesus Do?"), but WWJMBD?("What Would John Moses Browning Do?"). One gets the sense that not all of those posters' tongues are firmly planted in their cheeks, and that some of them don't believe John Browning's middle name was Moses for nothing.

Many die-hard 1911 fans feel that polymer pistol frames are tools of the devil, and are undecided whether buying a polymer-framed 1911 would reserve a space for the shooter's soul one ring higher or one lower on Dante's floor-plan of the Inferno than purchasing a Glock. There are those who feel that phasing out the 1911 .45 and replacing it with the Beretta 9mm in the American military was a greater act of treason than anything committed by Benedict Arnold.

Yet, in a time when modern technology has pervaded handgun design more thoroughly than any other, there are also those who would cheerfully relegate the 1911 pistol to the museum. They point out Ken Hackathorn's famous remark that this king of combat pistols is also the king of feedway stoppages, and that stock Glocks are claiming competition victories only claimed in the past by custom 1911s.

An original WWI-era 1911. Note shallow ejection port, long trigger, short grip safety tang, flat mainspring housing (bottom back of grip frame), "double diamond" cut stocks.

Praised and cursed for all the long years of its existence, this pistol has created fraternal twin cottage industries of customizing gunsmiths and of all manner of accessories. The Brownell's catalog for gunsmiths' needs has more pages of accessories and tools for 1911s than for any other handgun.

There are some who prefer the 1911 out of tradition and sentiment, but there are also those who cleave to it solely because they can find nothing better. For the latter, the proof is in the performance. At Camp Perry, the rifle ranges are now dominated by AR15s, but before that it was the M14 that ruled and before that, the bolt-action target rifle and before that, the military Springfield, all within the past century. Yet at the pistol ranges of Perry, National Championship for National Championship, it is the 1911 platform that wins the .45 event every year, and usually the centerfire event, and sometimes even the .22 event. It has been more than 50 years since a National Pistol Champion in the bullseye game has won the title without firing at least one 1911 in the course of the 270 precise shots that determine the overall winner.

Look to IPSC. There will be Glocks winning Production class and occasionally, a CZ75 or clone thereof in the open winner's circle, but most years, Limited and Limited Ten and Open will be captured with one or another high-tech 1911 derivative.

And, on the harder side, look to those at the sharpest of what British SAS always called "the sharp end." Close to a quarter century after the Beretta M9 in 9mm NATO was standardized all-service-wide, the elite Marines of MEU-SOC are issued Kimber 1911 .45s, and operators of the US Army's crack Delta Force are given an allowance to purchase their own customized 1911 .45 pistols.

The 1911, almost always in .45 ACP, is likewise still present in law enforcement circles, and indeed is undergoing a resurgence there. LAPD's role-model SWAT team has carried the 1911 as its standard sidearm for some 40 years, and today each operator carries a pair of Kimber .45s, one with and one without dedicated SureFire flashlight attached. By the 1990s, FBI's SWAT teams and elite Hostage Rescue Unit had gone to the 1911 .45 as well, acquiring both ParaOrdnance and Springfield Armory pistols with various purchase orders. A number of police departments in recent years have determined that "what's old is new," and authorized or even bought and issued one or another variation of 1911 service pistol.

It's the Ergonomics, Stupid!

Before ergonomics was a word, John M. Browning understood it. The angle of barrel to grip is well nigh perfect on his 1911 design. For most people – not all, but most – it is possible to close their eyes, raise the pistol by feel and point it blindly at a predetermined

Above: Long trigger proved too much of a reach for many doughboys with the original 1911 configuration, and square cut of frame at back of trigger guard made reach more difficult. Note how shallow the ejection port is compared to 1911s of today.

Left: 1911A1 has shorter trigger, with frame niched out behind it on both sides, for better trigger reach; arched housing to help hold muzzle upward; longer grip tang, wider rear sight notch, and slightly shorter hammer on this specimen. Plain, checkered brown plastic grips were standard GI issue.

spot, then open their eyes and find the sights dead on. In some hands, a revolver may point better; in others, the steeper grip-to-barrel angle of the Glock or the ancient Luger. But, for many, that "sweet spot" of "natural point-ability" comes with the 1911.

With its original single-stack magazine – still the most popular version, by far – the grip frame of the 1911 is slim enough to accommodate even very small hands, yet not so big that Brobdignagian paws will dig fingernails into heel of palm when the fingers take their hold.

Post-WWI studies of small arms indicated that many doughboys found the long trigger reach of the original 1911 to be too long. Remember, at that time, demographics indicated that the average American man was distinctly shorter than today, and would have had proportionally shorter fingers. The 1911A1 modifications of the 1920s included shortening the trigger markedly, and niching out the frame on either side of the trigger guard to make it that much easier for the index finger to reach.

An unfired Series '70 Colt Government Model. Author won this one at a match circa 1978, kept it as trade goods.

Top: 1911A1. **Bottom:** original 1911. Note that both have military style lanyard loops on butt.

As time went on, and prenatal care and nourishment and all of that improved sufficiently to create taller generations of Americans with longer fingers, shooters and the pistolsmiths (and later, the gunmakers) who served them went back to longer triggers. However, the 1911A1 trigger dimensions turn out to be perfect for very short fingers, using the pad or tip of the index finger as contact point, and work very well for average length adult male fingers of today if the trigger is contacted at the palmar surface of the distal joint, the spot that double action revolver shooters wisely call "the power crease." Given that a typical GI 1911A1 probably averaged about a six-pound trigger pull, this allowed more leverage that could afford more control of the trigger stroke.

Except on an egregiously bad example, the 1911 has a consistent trigger pull shot to shot. The faster the shooting gets, the more important this becomes, and in every task the 1911 has been selected for (and especially the very serious task it was designed for), there will be times when this is its most critical attribute.

The 1911 has a low bore axis, which maximizes the hand's leverage over the gun and therefore minimizes muzzle jump. It has a very fast trigger reset, something serious shooters always appreciate.

And, with proper selection, setup, care and feeding, the 1911 lives up to the repu-

Left: Popular bulls-eye shooter accessory was this extended BoMar sight rail, seen here on a target-customized commercial Colt.

Colt's attempt to make a traditional double action version of the 1911 was not a commercial success. This was the now discontinued Double Eagle…

…whose double action linkage seemed to barely skirt the Seecamp patent, and whose decocking lever was largely held in place by the grip panel.

tation for reliability that it earned in two world wars.

1911 Reliability

"The legendarily reliable 1911!" "The king of feedway stoppages!" For two such contradictory sentiments to exist, doesn't someone have to be bullshitting us?

Well...no. The simple fact is, there are enough good and bad 1911s among the millions that have been produced to live up to both the blessing and the curse.

John Browning configured his masterpiece with a 17-18 pound recoil spring on a short guide, and with a short ejector and generous tolerances between the moving parts to allow for dirty gunfire residue and the muck of the battlefield. He intended it to feed a round nose, full metal jacket 230-grain bullet in the 820-850 feet per second velocity range, with a certain overall cartridge length. That gun, with that ammunition, functioned almost flawlessly when kept even halfway cleaned and lubricated. History confirms it. Browning had to have assumed that a soldier fighting for his life with it would hold it in a death grip, hand and arm locked against the recoil so that the frame would be a firm abutment for the slide to work against.

Then, the time came when shooters and gunsmiths decided they knew more about the pistol than its designer. They tightened all the tolerances to produce pinpoint accuracy. They put in much heavier recoil springs, on full-length guide rods, and barrel bushings so tight they had to be removed with special wrenches. They extended the ejector's length. And then they loaded the gun with

Above: Smith & Wesson's copy of arch-rival Colt's most successful pistol, the SW1911, has worked out quite well. This one is nicely engraved.

Right: Bill Laughridge can't repress a smile as he shows author the ".45 Pocket Model" he builds…

…whose enclosed hammer resembles the "hammerless" design Colt and Browning popularized in 1903. Had this appeared in 1911, losing the stigma of cocked and locked appearance, gun expert Bob Schwartz believes that 1911 .45 would have been much more popular with US police, much earlier.

short cartridges that had button-nosed target semi-wadcutter configurations, or the sharp shoulders of the H&G #68 all-lead bullet, or the short 200-grain Speer hollow point that was so wide, the late 1911 expert Dean Grennell dubbed it "the flying ashtray." Some shooters and instructors decided to hold it "like a quail; just firmly enough that it doesn't fly away, but not hard enough to hurt the quail." The byword became, "Don't fight the kick, just let it recoil."

Everything had changed. A feedway angle acceptable with ball was too steep for short, wide-nose cartridges. Spring

Below: After a long hiatus, Colt's useful-size Commander reappeared in .38 Super, a useful caliber.

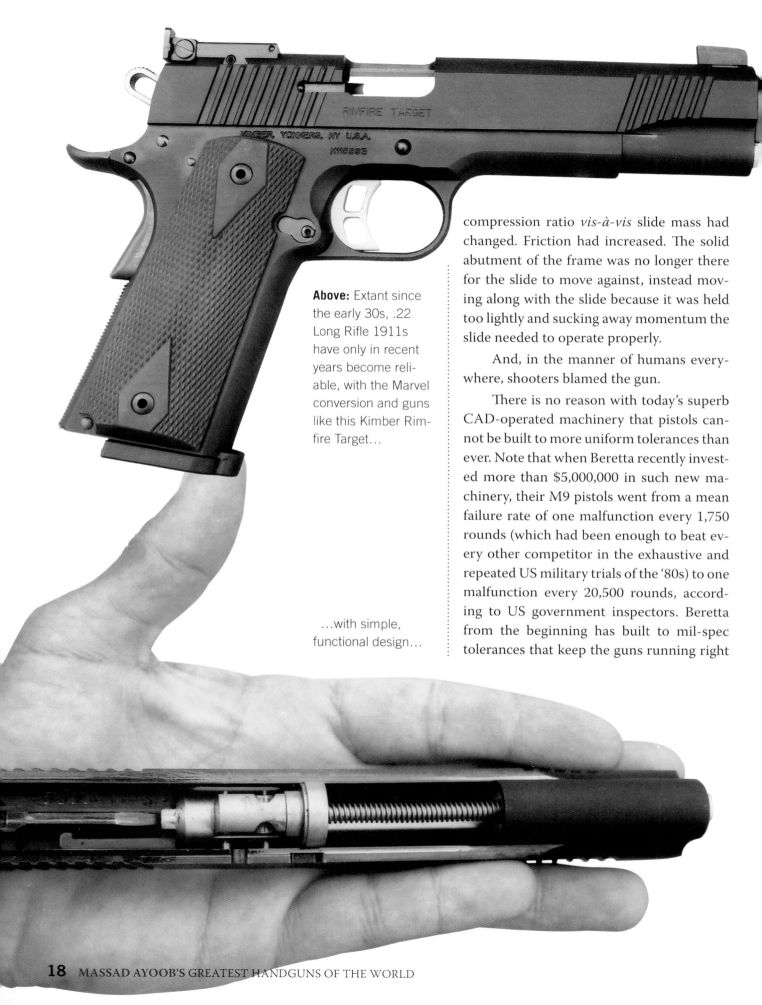

Above: Extant since the early 30s, .22 Long Rifle 1911s have only in recent years become reliable, with the Marvel conversion and guns like this Kimber Rimfire Target…

…with simple, functional design…

compression ratio *vis-à-vis* slide mass had changed. Friction had increased. The solid abutment of the frame was no longer there for the slide to move against, instead moving along with the slide because it was held too lightly and sucking away momentum the slide needed to operate properly.

And, in the manner of humans everywhere, shooters blamed the gun.

There is no reason with today's superb CAD-operated machinery that pistols cannot be built to more uniform tolerances than ever. Note that when Beretta recently invested more than $5,000,000 in such new machinery, their M9 pistols went from a mean failure rate of one malfunction every 1,750 rounds (which had been enough to beat every other competitor in the exhaustive and repeated US military trials of the '80s) to one malfunction every 20,500 rounds, according to US government inspectors. Beretta from the beginning has built to mil-spec tolerances that keep the guns running right

(unless someone buys low-bid aftermarket magazines that aren't designed to tolerate sand). Apply that engineering principle to the 1911, throat the feedway at the factory for the length and configuration of the cartridges likely to be used, and you will have a 1911 every bit as reliable as the Beretta.

Care and Feeding of the 1911

The magazine is the heart of the beast in terms of reliability, and once you get past a payload of "seven rounds of hardball," you want to be looking at the very best aftermarket products. The general rule is, "Only trust magazines that come from the manufacturer with the gun," but a singular exception seems to be the 1911. The reason is that

this pistol alone is so popular that high-tech magazines became part of the cottage industry that grew up around it, and outstripped the gun factories themselves.

Colt, McCormick, Metalform, and Wolff are among the companies that have produced 1911 magazines I trust. I prefer Wolff springs in my ParaOrdnance hi-cap magazines. That said, though, the older I get, the more I find myself using Wilson-Rogers magazines exclusively in my 9mm, 10mm, and .45 ACP 1911 pistols. As a firearms instructor, when I see those stopped 1911s in students' hands, I often am able to cure their problem simply by handing them three of my Wilson-Rogers magazines.

1911s want to be kept lubricated. Only the tightest of target pistols need to be oiled like a salad. Some lube on the rails, on the

...and serving as an economical understudy gun to larger calibers, like author's .45 Kimber Custom II above it.

barrel hood, and in a ring around the barrel where it will contact the bushing should suffice. Oh, and be sure you have stocks like Browning designed that come up and hold the plunger housing in place on the left side of the pistol.

On a defensive handgun, keep the trigger pull weight at a minimum of four pounds, and never deactivate a safety device. If you can't compress the grip safety, get a replacement part with raised bottom edge that will activate when the hand makes contact.

Shooting the 1911

"Washtub accuracy." "Wrist-wrenching recoil." Those canards came from decades of ancient, benighted military training. Men were taught to stand upright, their shoulders back, and fire with one fully extended arm. Naturally, the pistols jumped. Even after the reshaped hammers and grip safeties of the 1911A1 modification, the grip tang still bit most hands. A high-hand grasp was not encouraged for this reason, which meant that the hand was often too low, exacerbating recoil and causing the finger to pull the muzzle down as the shot broke. No ear protection worthy of the name was issued on the firing lines in those days, so naturally, men learned to cringe in the instant before the ear-splitting blast, jerking their shots even harder.

If the Marksmanship Training Units of today's American armed services could go back in time machines to the year 1911 and show their predecessors what they know today, none of that would have happened. By 1912 the 1911 would have had a beavertail grip safety that would prevent hand bite. Combatants would learn to lean into their guns, using firm grip and body mechanics to snap the gun back on target virtually the instant the slide returned to battery.

Below: 1911s in 9mm are extremely finicky, but extremely "shootable." Here Terri Strayer wins an IDPA match with hers, a Springfield Armory match grade 1911-A1.

Brian Zins, USMC, shows author the 1911 .45 he has just won the latest of many National Championships with. This ergonomic pistol has ruled bulls-eye shooting for many, many decades.

Above: The 1911 is a versatile pistol. Author's night-sighted Kimber Custom II is out of the box…

The 1911 pistol wants to be grasped high on its backstrap. By 1990, even Colt had learned that niching out the bottom of the trigger guard where it met the frame would raise the middle finger's position, allowing an even stronger grasp on the gun. The beavertail grip safety is essential to doing your best shooting, because it prevents flinch- and jerk-producing hand bite, and because when it is properly recurved at the rear of the tang, it helps to guide the drawing hand more swiftly and positively into its grasping position on the holstered gun.

…and a match-winning pistol, as he and police chief Russ Lary show off the trophies they've won at a state shoot with their 1911s.

A brief digression to serve the explanation, if you will. For generations, pistol marksmanship manuals have suggested that the pistol be grasped in the support hand around frame and slide, its muzzle up at about a 45-degree angle, and then placed carefully in the firing hand. This comes from bulls-eye shooting, and, I am largely convinced, also comes from the 1911 pistol in the days before the beavertail. Anchoring the web of the hand at the inside curve of the grip safety and then pivoting the gun down into firing grasp pulls the web of the hand and the skin behind it down taut against the rear of the grip safety. This pulls the skin down tight and away from the sharp back edge of the grip safety's tang, and minimizes the chance of "bite." It becomes unnecessary when the protective beavertail is in place, which is why all but the cheapest 1911s of today – or those built with nostalgia rather than shooting in mind – come with anything else.

The 1911 also wants to be firmly held. This is important with any gun powerful enough to generate significant recoil, which certainly applies to the .45 ACP. However, it is also important with the lesser calibers. Ray Chapman, the man Jeff Cooper called The Maestro, shot his way to fame with the Colt Government Model .45 auto, and noted that pistols always seem to work best in the caliber for which they were designed. 1911s in calibers less powerful than 10mm and .45 ACP are notoriously finicky about feeding and going into battery. (The reason the 1911 in 9mm has experienced a renaissance in PPC, NRA Action Pistol, and especially IDPA Enhanced Service Pistol division is that being heavier than the Browning, it kicks less, and its trigger lends itself to a much finer pull than the Rube Goldberg trigger mechanism of the Hi-Power. That said, classicists who want Browning-designed 9mms stay with Browning Hi-Powers, and those who want Browning-designed .45s stay with 1911s. It

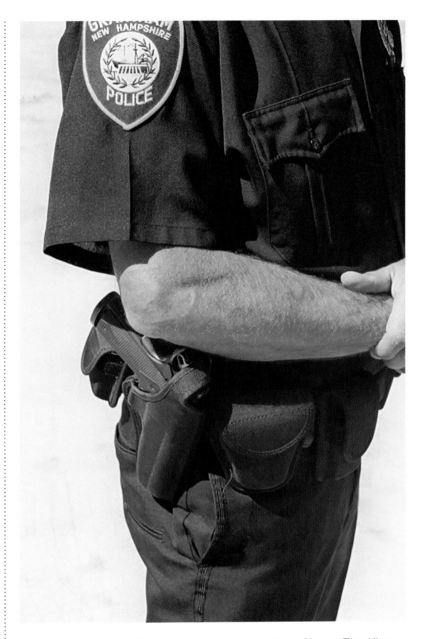

Above: The Kimber Custom II is a fine police service pistol, shown here as he carries it on duty

seems to be Nature's Way.) In any case, the more firmly the .38 Super or 9mm 1911 is held, the less it seems to malfunction. This is true to a lesser degree of the 1911 with the round Browning designed it for, the .45 ACP, but it is still true.

Trigger finger placement in firing will depend on pull weight, trigger face configuration, and perhaps more than anything else, the length and shape and range of movement of your index finger. Tip, pad (generally defined as the whorl of the fingerprint), and distal joint placement all have their advocates.

The 1911 neither began nor fossilized in its eponymous year. The history of the 1911 pistol goes back to well before that year, as surely as it continues today. Let's look at some landmarks in its development.

1896: Seeing the future, Colt's Patent Firearms signs John Browning to a contract to do developmental work on automatic pistols for them. (Semi-automatic will not become the common parlance for such designs until later.)

1899: The first Browning-designed autoloaders take form in steel, chambered for a proprietary .38 caliber round.

1902: Colt .38 automatics, in both sporting and military trim, appear on the market. Despite smooth actions and excellent workmanship, they are rickety things that resemble T-squares with triggers.

1903: Initial concept work begins on the cartridge that will be known as the .45 ACP. This same year, Colt introduces their famous Pocket Model .32 auto.

1904: The .45 Automatic Colt Pistol cartridge is born.

1905: The US Army has become insistent on a .45 caliber handgun in the wake of the Philippine Insurrection, and is somewhat open to the newfangled autoloading pistol concept, though all tested in the last five years (including early Colt .38s) have failed to prove totally adequate. Colt quietly begins production of their first .45 automatic, though the Model 1905 will not hit the market until early 1906. Like all its predecessors but the Pocket Model, it retains a nearly 90-degree grip to barrel angle. It will not please the Army for a number of reasons.

1907: An Ordnance test determines that no currently produced automatic pistol is satisfactory for US military needs but that Colt comes closest.

1908: A grip safety is developed for Colt's .45 pistol, still a work in progress.

1909: Colt's classic is now beginning to take shape. It is the first Colt to get the push button magazine release, located behind the trigger guard on the left. Its slide lock lever is a rather crude picture of what the 1911s will be. The ugly square front of the earlier guns has given way to a shorter dust cover portion of the frame, and the gracefully narrowed lower front of the slide, seen in the 1903 Pocket .32 (and the identical-in-appearance 1908 Pocket .380), as adopted on this iteration of Colt's .45 auto.

1910: The shape of John Browning's masterpiece is almost complete, but the 1910 variation lacks a thumb safety. This will be added at the insistence of the Army, which has determined it unsafe to attempt to manually decock a chamber-loaded auto pistol in the heat of battle, one-handed.

1911: The vision is complete. With long trigger and short grip tang, by today's standards, the 1911 has a safety readily accessible to a right thumb and a flat-back mainspring housing. In the climax of a long series of military handgun tests, the Colt trounces the only other remaining finalist, the Savage. In March of 1911, the United States Government officially adopts Colt Pistol, Model of 1911, as the standard sidearm of the Army, Marine Corps, and Navy. It will remain so until the mid-1980s.

1912: For the first of many, many times in its long history, production of the 1911 pistol is outsourced from Colt's. In addition to Colt's own production, the pistol is now being manufactured at the Springfield Armory in Springfield, Massachusetts. This same year, the National Rifle Association offers its members NRA-marked 1911s acquired from the Ordnance Department.

1914: Norway adopts the 1911 Colt .45 auto as its standard military sidearm. It is granted the right to produce the guns there in the following year.

1916: Argentina adopts the 1911 .45 as its standard service pistol and will soon be licensed to produce them there. Mexico will adopt the 1911 shortly after WWI.

1917: With America's entry into WWI, demand so far outstrips production that Remington becomes another licensed 1911 manufacturer, and both Colt (on their separate revolver line) and Smith & Wesson mass produce revolvers that will fire the .45 ACP cartridge with half-moon clips.

1923: A post-WWI study of small arms effectiveness determines that the 1911 needs a longer, more protective grip tang to prevent hand bite; an arched magazine housing to cure a tendency to shoot low; more visible sights; and a shorter, more easily reached trigger. These modifications combine to form the Model 1911A1, a designation that does not become official until three years later.

1929: The Colt .38 Super makes its official debut, in a Government Model format identical to the

.45. It fires a 130-grain bullet at 1300 feet per second.

1931: Colt attempts to market a blowback 1911 in .22 Long Rifle. Called the Ace model, it will prove unreliable.

1932: The National Match version is introduced. Produced in .45 and .38 Super, this handcrafted beauty will be declared by many purists to be the finest Colt automatic ever manufactured.

1935: Marsh "Carbine" Williams invents a floating chamber device that allows the 1911 to function more reliably with a .22 Long Rifle cartridge. The Colt Service Model Ace .22 pistol and the Colt .22/45 conversion unit are born.

1937: William Swartz's firing pin safety is patented. Colt buys the rights and assembles a quantity of .45s and Supers with it, eventually abandoning the concept as too difficult to machine.

1941: The outbreak of WWII creates a vast demand for 1911A1 pistols. In addition to Colt, they will be manufactured in greater or lesser quantities by such firms as Remington-Rand, Ithaca, and the Singer Sewing Machine Company.

1950: The first shortened (and the first lightened) Colt 1911, the Commander, is introduced. With aluminum alloy frame instead of steel, shortened dust cover, and barrel stubbed from the conventional 5 inches to 4.25 inches with proportional slide, it is offered in calibers .45 ACP, .38 Super, and 9mm Luger.

1957: The National Match concept is resurrected. The new pistol will be offered primarily in .45 ACP but later, briefly, in .38 Special wadcutter, and will be better known as the Gold Cup.

1970: Colt introduces their Series '70 with collet-type barrel bushing intended to improve accuracy. The collets will prove to be fragile, and this design will soon be abandoned.

1972: The United States Army officially adopts the General Officers' Pistol, a 1911 .45 shortened at muzzle and butt for issue to those with sufficient stars on their shoulders. A concept created earlier by military armorers, it has already been offered to the public as a custom Bobcat .45 by Armand Swenson and George Sheldon, separately and simultaneously, creating a new cottage industry for custom gunsmiths.

1973: Louis Seecamp offers a double action conversion of the 1911 pistol. It will later be incorporated into a short-lived, double action 1911 pistol, the ODI Viking.

1974: The Reese family founds a new gun-manufacturing firm that resurrects an old name: Springfield Armory. This firm will be the first to compete seriously with Colt in production of commercial (as opposed to military contract) 1911s, beginning in 1985.

1983: Colt introduces the Series '80/Mark IV family of 1911s, with the first passive, internal firing pin safety since the short-lived Swartz design. It is activated via trigger pull.

1985: The first commercially successful stainless 1911 is introduced by Colt in the '80 series. In the same year, Colt introduces the subcompact Officers ACP, effectively wiping out the mini-1911 market among custom gunsmiths.

1988: ParaOrdnance introduces a wide-body 1911 frame that accepts a double stack magazine, originally designed to hold 13 rounds of .45 ACP. The wide-body hi-cap platform will soon be copied by several other makers, and Para will begin producing complete 1911 pistols two years later.

1990: Colt introduces its first double action 1911, the Double Eagle, a design somewhat derivative of the Seecamp concept. It is not greeted with enthusiasm and will be discontinued in 1997.

1991: Colt introduces its first flat-finish "economy" 1911 for the commercial market, the 1991A1.

1996: Kimber introduces their aptly named Classic, a moderately priced Government Model size pistol with all the usually-custom bells and whistles. It will soon become the nation's best selling 1911.

2000: ParaOrdnance introduces the LDA, the first double action only 1911.

2003: Smith & Wesson introduces their long-awaited version, the SW1911. After a brief callback due to mismatched grip safety components, the SW1911 earns an excellent reputation.

2006: A surprisingly good, $600 1911 from Taurus hits the market. By and large, the PT1911 earns rave reviews. They sell so fast that gun dealers can't keep them in stock.

2011: John Browning's classic fighting handgun will officially celebrate its one hundredth birthday.

Try before you decide. It's what works for you that is important, not what's recommended by someone who won't be there to press the trigger for you when you need to fire.

Thumb placement is a major debate among 1911 aficionadoes. Tradition has the thumb straight to the target, and it's what you see most often in one-handed bulls-eye shooting at Championship level. This allows the index finger to come back just the least bit straighter, important in a game with 2700 points possible although no one has ever actually scored a 2700. Some recommend the thumb high on the safety, but bear in mind

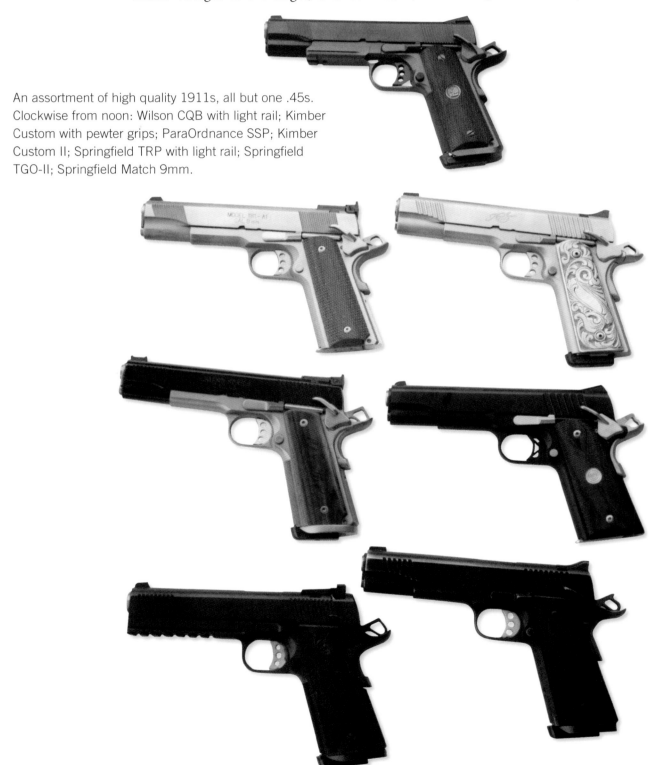

An assortment of high quality 1911s, all but one .45s. Clockwise from noon: Wilson CQB with light rail; Kimber Custom with pewter grips; ParaOrdnance SSP; Kimber Custom II; Springfield TRP with light rail; Springfield TGO-II; Springfield Match 9mm.

Gunsmiths Who Made The 1911 Better

There have been countless gunsmiths who tried for greatness and failed, because they thought they knew more about the 1911 pistol than John Browning. However, there were many whose skill allowed them to make the gun better for specific purposes as opposed to the general military work for which Browning created it...and there were a handful who actually did make it a better pistol overall.

It is generally accepted in the history of the gun that Frank Pachmayr, back in the Depression days, was the man who showed the world that by tightening frame to slide, and taking an oversize barrel and carefully mating its chamber hood to the breechface of the slide, one could make the Colt .45 automatic more accurate than it was when it left the factory. The many who have since made a living "accurizing" 1911 pistols should have lit candles to the memory of Frank Pachmayr.

Bigger, more visible sights came from King's Gun Works at about the same time Colt's was factory-installing them on the splendid National Match pistol. But there is little question that King's broke ground with a much-needed oversize thumb safety that was easier to manipulate at speed under stress, and which later became virtually standard at the higher end of the 1911-manufacturing industry.

Jim Clark, Sr., in the early 1950s pioneered the longslide 1911, through the simple expedient of cutting two slides and grafting the front of one onto the end of the other...and the much less simple expedient of making the joining appear seamless. Factory longslides would follow, much later, from AMT and other manufacturers.

As best as I can determine, Jim Hoag was the first to go the 1911A1 "one better" and create that boon to 1911 shooters, a pain-free, pinch-less, recoil-distributing grip safety in the shape of a beaver's tail. Hoag's original unit was actually flat and downward curved. It is unclear who first created the variation that swept back up at its tip, to help guide the drawing hand into position – a shape Jeff Cooper, "the high priest of the 1911," called a duckbill rather than a beavertail. Many artisans were working simultaneously on that sort of thing at that time.

Jim Boland seems to have been the first pistolsmith to craft a beavertail that also incorporated what is now called a "memory pad" and which I always thought of as a "speed bump": a raised ridge on the bottom edge of the grip safety that would allow the grasping hand to activate that part even with a weak or sloppy hold. This feature proved its work so well that, like the beavertail itself, it has become virtually standard on all but the lowest-line (or commemorative or "nostalgia" style) 1911s produced today.

The ambidextrous thumb safety for the 1911 is generally credited to Armand Swenson. Slightly oversize, Swenson's configuration was also the most ergonomic yet, curving upward in the center of the shelf so that the median joint of a curled-down thumb wouldn't inadvertently knock it upward and "on-safe" during firing, which the straighter King design was prone to do. Swenson on the West Coast and George Sheldon in New England were, roughly simultaneously, the first to offer the public 1911 .45s "chopped and channeled" to compact size. Oddly enough, both makers called their mini-.45s "Bobcats." They would be followed swiftly by such famed 'smiths as Lin Alexiou at Trapper Gun, Austin Behlert, and Charlie Kelsey at Devel. The pioneering work had been done by nameless military armorers on 1911A1s for generals, adopted officially by the Army in the early 1970s. This corner of the 1911 cottage industry was effectively nuked by Colt with their introduction of the factory Officers ACP in 1985, followed by the more accurate and more reliable Defender model and a host of subcompact clones by other makers. Such pistols are hugely popular today.

In the old days, only the Colt factory (and, oddly and little-known enough, Smith & Wesson) manufactured match-grade barrels for the 1911. Irv Stone, III, changed that, and supercharged the aftermarket auto pistol barrel industry almost single-handed. Irv also seems to have been the first to develop (and the first to discard) the collet bushing concept for improved accuracy, and to create another concept that stayed: accurate .38 Super barrels that headspaced at the case mouth as opposed to Colt's own original barrels, headspaced on the cartridge's quasi-rim, and infamously inaccurate. The Bar-Sto barrels made possible the modern renaissance of the .38 Super. Stone's genius lives today in the company he founded, still run by his son, Bar-Sto Barrels, the flagship of a cottage industry within a cottage industry.

that fleshy thumbs or gloves can cause the thumb to bind against the slide, creating a friction-induced stoppage, and the high thumb also pulls the web of the hand away from the grip safety. This is why the leading advocate of the high thumb position always recommended deactivating the grip safety, which would be Plaintiff's Counsel's Guaranteed Employment Act if you had to fire the gun in self-defense and ambulance chasers smelled the blood. If you prefer the high thumb, a grip safety with a protruding memory groove is a must.

My old friend Wayne Novak came out not long ago with a replacement backstrap that has the beavertail feature for comfort and fast grasp, but eliminates the grip safety. I think it's great for shooting, but not a cure for the civil liability aspect since having it installed puts you in the position of having a safety device removed from a lethal weapon. Not until Wayne follows the path of his brother masters of the 1911, Baer and Brown and Lauck and Wilson, and starts manufacturing his own Wayne Novak pistols – with this device in place – will its promise of civil liability protection be fulfilled.

The curled down thumb position with the firing hand creates the strongest possible one-hand grasp, and virtually guarantees activating even a mil-spec grip safety. However, some shooters find the firing hand thumb in the down position gets in the way of the drumstick of the thumb of their support hand finding its most comfortable position against the grip panel. Each shooter has to find his or her own preferred technique.

One thing on which virtually all experienced 1911 shooters agree is that cocked and locked with a round in the chamber is the fastest, most positive, and safest way to carry such a gun. Jacking the slide is a stunt when done one-handed, and one often has only one hand with which to react, draw, and fire in an emergency. The 1911's hammer is too far back to allow fumble-free cocking with the firing hand's thumb and is a nightmare to de-cock without a dedicated de-cocking mechanism, which of course does not exist on the single action 1911 pistol. The self de-cocking ParaOrdnance LDA is a sensible option for those uncomfortable with the concept or the appearance of Condition One/cocked and locked.

Cocked and locked carry with a torpedo in the launch tube pretty much mandates either an internal, passive firing pin safety, or a lightweight titanium firing pin coupled with a heavy duty firing pin spring, to make the pistol "drop-safe." Springfield Armory, and Wilson Combat in their "California Drop-Test Compliant" variation, have taken the latter approach. The trigger-activated Series '80 safety is found in all Colt 1911s made today except the "nostalgia" models, all pistols manufactured by ParaOrdnance, and in the SIGArms 1911. The Swartz concept that works off the grip safety, and is more economically feasible to manufacture with today's CAD and MIM manufacturing options, was resurrected by

Nehemiah Sirkis for the Kimber II series, and a similar design is found in the SW1911 and the Taurus PT1911.

The Future of the 1911

When I was young, the firearm in question was not referred to as "the 1911" so often as it was called "the Colt .45 automatic." Colt was the only game in town. Yeah, another armory or two had been called upon to build them for World War I, and more than that for World War II, but unless you got something that was military surplus, if you wanted to buy a new high quality .45 auto you had to buy a Colt. Period.

Things are different now. Long before the movie titled *Sleepless in Seattle*, Colt was *Clueless in Connecticut*. It was expedience that drove the Government to pressure Colt to license the design to other makers in time of national emergency. However, we cannot overlook the fact that in WWII, Remington-Rand produced more than a million 1911A1s while Colt itself manufactured fewer than half a million, and Ithaca produced only about 110,000 fewer guns than Colt.

History has repeated itself. A host of manufacturers – primarily Springfield Armory and then Kimber, and most recently Taurus – have been selling more 1911s than Colt has. Kimber has for some years led the 1911 sales parade, though Springfield Armory has

Below: This humble brown cardboard box, designed for easy storage in military armories…

…contains what many authorities believe is the finest standard issue military pistol to ever enter the battlefield: the 1911A1 .45 ACP, this specimen produced by Colt.

The 1911 is a controversial pistol, a "cult gun" if you will. There are other cult guns, and their true believers like to bash competing "ballistic belief systems." When such a topic is under discussion, the reader has a right to know where the speaker is coming from.

As a little boy, I was already fascinated with guns in general and handguns in particular. Many if not most of the adults in my life were WWII vets, many survivors of WWI were still alive, and many of the young men were freshly back from Korea. I grew up on stories of the 1911's recoil practically wrenching the shooter's arm off, and its bullet ripping the arm completely off the enemy soldier, not to mention accuracy that might not suffice to hit a washtub at 25 paces. (Yes, there were still washtubs then.)

In the late 1950s, Jeff Cooper began his famous series on the 1911 in Guns & Ammo magazine, and I pored over each segment with far more attention than I paid to my elementary school textbooks. Cooper put forth a promise of 19 one-shot stops out of 20 shots with 230-grain .45 ACP hardball. He explained the controllability of the single-action trigger, the ease of flipping off the safety between holster and target, and the speed of reloading. I already knew that accurized .45s ruled the pistol matches of the time, and Cooper explained how the same platform had come to dominate the simulated gunfighting competitions he had organized in California. The lucid logic of his argument was compelling.

It was as if a messiah had risen in the West.

I begged my dad for a Colt .45 automatic. My twelfth Christmas loomed, and that November my father took me to his favorite firearms emporium, Sprague's Gun Shop. Dad was uncertain that a boy my age could handle the mighty .45. Stan, with a knowing smile, liberated a surplus WWI-vintage 1911 from the used pistol shelf, stuffed a few lead bullet round-nose handloads into its magazine, and

took us out behind the shop. (You could do that then, too.) Bracing myself for the sprained arm I was sure would follow, I held the heavy Colt at the end of my right arm (back then they were handguns, not handsguns), and squeezed the trigger carefully, determined not to flinch in front of my father or Mr. Sprague.

I felt a gentle bump, and watched the muzzle come up a little and to the left. I settled the 1911 back on target and kept it downrange as I turned my head and said, "I like it, Dad…"

That Christmas it was under the tree, an early (1918 production) surplus Colt 1911 with flat housing, long trigger, short tang, and very worn double diamond grips. It was an ensemble present. My mother had bought me a tanker's chest holster to go with it from the local Army/Navy store, and my Uncle Whitney had purchased a yellow box of Winchester 230-grain hardball (easy to wrap, too). That afternoon, my dad drove us out in the country to a snowy field where I put 50 rounds of beige-box GI surplus hardball (five bucks a box back then; pricier Winchester would be saved for special occasions) without a hitch. That evening I set about learning to field strip it, and was soon doing so blindfolded.

Another 1911 shooter was born.

In my teen years, I experimented with various accessories. New hammer and grip safety to prevent a bitten web of hand. Bigger sights. A re-blue for its tired finish. A trigger job. A new barrel, since corrosive ammo had apparently gotten to this specimen before I did. It never occurred to me that I was ruining the collector value of a WWI artifact. They were dirt-cheap then. My father had bought this one for $37.50.

Life went on. I was a senior in college when I bought my second Colt .45 auto, a pristine 1957-series National Match that had been accurized and fitted with BoMar "hardball" sights by the USAF Marksmanship

Training Unit for the ex-airman I bought it from for $100 when he got sick of bulls-eye shooting. For many years, it would be my all-purpose 1911: it went with me in concealed carry and in police uniform, and to bullseye and PPC matches, Second Chance, and Bianchi Cup. In 1979 or so, I used it to tie the national record on bowling pins, 3.9 seconds for five pins, established by young Johnny Robbins and soon tied by Bill Wilson. That record quickly fell to Jerry Miculek and others.

Over the years, I accumulated a lot of 1911s. Some – the Vega, the Crown City – were unmitigated junk and didn't stay with me long. (The latter reminded me of the old "washtub" accuracy stories. It threw a group from a Ransom Rest too large to measure with a foot ruler, once you got it working well enough to send bullets downrange in the first place.)

There were comp guns and widebodies, .45 ACP and .45 Super. There were .38 Super, 9mm Luger, .40 S&W, .41 Avenger, .41 Action Express, 10mm Auto, 9mm Steyr, 9X23, .357 SIG, and more. (I had looked for a 7.65mm Luger barrel to put in a 1911 to bring to a South American country that would give a visitor a permit to carry, but allowed nothing larger than .32 caliber. From Colt to Bar-Sto, no such barrels were in stock, and I ended up with a Browning Hi-Power in that chambering.)

The years gave me the opportunity to own and shoot other fine 1911s besides the defining Colt: Arminex, Les Baer, Ed Brown, Jim Clark, Ithaca, Kimber, Dave Lauck, Remington-Rand, Rock River, SIG, Smith & Wesson, Springfield Armory (both Massachusetts and Illinois pedigrees), Taurus, and Wilson Combat, among others. And the custom guns of the finest master pistolsmiths: Baer, Austin Behlert, Jim Boland, Brown, Bob Chow, Ned Christensen, Jim Clark, Dick Crawford, Al Dinan, Jim Garthwaite, Al Greco, Dick Heinie, Jim Hoag, Lauck, Bill Laughridge, John Lawson, Paul Liebenberg, Ed Masaki,

D.R. Middlebrooks, Mark Morris, Wayne Novak, John Nowlin, Frank Pachmayr, Mike Plaxco, Nolan Santy, Armand Swenson, Wilson, and more.

The 1911 remains one of my favorite pistols. I shoot it better than anything else.

My current working battery includes 9mm (match grade Springfield, for Enhanced Service Pistol division of IDPA), .38 Special wadcutter (a flawless Jim Clark longslide acquired for bulls-eye and PPC, and kept "just because"), 10mm (an exquisite Mark Morris five-inch Colt Delta that almost recoils downward thanks to its efficient carry-comp design), .40 S&W (a Para P16 acquired for IPSC), and a slew of .45 ACPs.

I do not have a WWJMBD? tattoo, and I do not consider the 1911 the be-all and end-all of handgun designs. I do recognize it as a mature design that has been intelligently optimized for a number of specific purposes and that performs a remarkably wide range of purposes well. If and when I ever retire and settle on just one personal handgun to carry, I suspect it will be a minimally customized lightweight Commander .45, cocked and locked and ready to do what it has spent a century, from drawing board to battlefield to tournament range, doing amazingly well.

Above: Though many have tried to improve on it, John Browning's original barrel bushing system with short recoil spring guide is hard to beat in author's opinion.

A masterpiece of the gunsmith's craft, designed expressly for winning matches: a Colt .38 Super Government Model, converted by Clark Custom to fire .38 Special wadcutter ammunition.

closed the gap with their more affordable mil-spec models, and newcomer Taurus is coming up fast from the back of the pack with a high-featured, low-priced contestant. ParaOrdnance recently introduced their excellent GI Expert to compete in the same low price point range.

BATFE figures tell the tale, though foggily, since their production numbers are not broken down by model or even particular caliber within caliber categories. In the last year for which the Bureau had records when I wrote this, 2005, Kimber produced 47,820 pistols, almost all of them 1911s. Springfield produced 126,188. Springfield Armory believes it has surpassed Kimber as the leading vendor of 1911s today. Colt, by contrast, produced only a little over 14,000, virtually all in 1911 format, and a little less than 2,000 of their little .380s, which are 1911-ish if not true 1911s.

Thus, we see how "1911" has become a generic term.

The future tells us that the 1911 will continue to be popular. Gun dealers have different best-sellers in different parts of

the country and even in different neighborhoods, but most I talk to put "the 1911" in their top five list of best-sellers.

Taken *in toto*, the spectrum of handguns we generically call the 1911 has become more popular, and perhaps more appreciated, than ever. It will be with us well past its centennial year. There is no firearm in our military – indeed, in any army in the world – that has stayed in service longer. It is entirely possible that a modernized variation of this .45 caliber pistol may return as general issue to our military at some point.

The 1911 pistol still wins matches and wins fights and provokes controversy. It is, deservedly, timeless.

Left: The finest custom houses spare no expense. Laborious "tiger tooth" stippling by the late Jim Clark, Sr., gives shooter of this target 1911 a rock solid hold on the target 50 yards away.

The Colt Commander
(and Its Clones)

Do you own a pistol or revolver with lightweight frame of aluminum, titanium, or scandium? Do you own a modern "police style" semiautomatic service pistol? Do you own a high-powered handgun engineered for minimum weight?

If the answer is yes to any of the above, you possess a firearm that owes a debt of gratitude to a trend-setting pistol that emerged at the midpoint of the 20th century: the redoubtable Colt Commander.

Pedigree

With heavy power – usually the .45 ACP cartridge – in a light package, the aluminum framed Colt Commander got every expert's attention when

At median 20th century, this pistol ushered in the time of lightweight alloy handgun frames and changed the shape and construction of semiautomatic service pistols of the future.

The Commander as it was modified by serious shooters. This all steel Series '70 has improved sights, beavertail grip safety.

Right: Firing a mandatory one-hand-only string here, author wins an IDPA match shooting Colt CCO, a short-grip LW Commander .45, against the bigger guns. The Commanders in both weights had excellent shooting characteristics.

The Colt Commander in its original format, from Bady's book, this specimen in .38 Super. Note cheesy plastic stocks and the infamous hand-biting "stub" grip tang.

it became available in 1950. Some of them found its recoil distinctly greater than that of the pistol from which it was grafted, the full size, all steel Government Model. Elmer Keith, who was not at all sensitive to recoil himself, noted that "recoil is heavier than with the regulation weight."[1] Keith's contemporary Henry Stebbins, on the other hand, considered it a pocket gun. "Pausing only long enough to give a respectful preliminary salute to a pocket gun made in a caliber as potent as the rimless .45 Colt Auto, let's

Commander, below, was ¾ inch shorter than Government Model, right.

digress for a brief sum-up of the autoloaders as pocket guns. It is rather wonderful to have a smallish .45 that's both shootable and reasonably convenient for shoving into a pocket, to be toted for miles on end."[2]

But the most glowing praise of all came from a most unexpected quarter. Bob Nichols, for 13 years the shooting editor of *Field & Stream*, was all but fanatical in his insistence that the double action revolver beat the semiautomatic pistol hands down. He said as much in his book, *The Secrets of Double Action Shooting*, published in 1950. However, he had gotten his hands on a pre-production Commander in time to say the following in that tome: "I found it an amazing performer – definitely easier to hit with than its heavy old M1911 predecessor, which actually weighs almost exactly fifty per cent more than the new light-weight .45 automatic model. To be exact, the new gun weighs only 26-1/2 ounces, as against 39 ounces for the old model M1911....This new light-weight .45 automatic is much easier to hold on, quicker to get on with, easier to shoot, actually easier to hit with – and, of course, much more comfortable to wear."[3]

During the 1950s, Jeff Cooper was already laying the groundwork for the discipline he would come to call The Modern Technique of the Pistol. He saw a definite role for the Colt Commander. "While

the 1911 is the best fighting pistol for open wear by uniformed men, the Commander is the best sidearm available for carrying concealed," he wrote in 1961.[4]

One of Cooper's protégés was a Vietnam vet named Chuck Taylor, who would quickly become established as a combat pistol expert in his own right. Chuck would later say, "if you're in the market for a highly efficient self-defense auto, the LW (light-weight) Commander in .45 ACP provides an unbeatable combination."[5] The late, great Charles "Skeeter" Skelton was another fan of the Commander, as was survivalist guru Mel Tappan.

Indeed, the gun has become iconic among those who approach the 1911 series of pistols as something like a belief system. The rule was: all-steel 5-inch barrel Government Model for duty holster, home defense, and competition, and light-weight 4-1/4-inch barrel Commander to tuck under the blazer or concealment vest.

If imitation is the sincerest form of flattery, the Commander is flattered indeed; only its bigger brother has been copied more in the 1911 "clone wars."

MMC fixed sights, Ed Brown beavertail, and low-ride thumb safety have made this Combat Commander more shootable.

Frank Cornwall, left, shows Dave Brennan the LW Colt Commander he used to make Master on the demanding Chuck Taylor course. He found the lighter gun's faster handling helpful.

Below: Aluminum frames cracked with heavy use, but so did steel ones. Tip of Spyderco knife points to crack beginning on steel frame of Combat Commander.

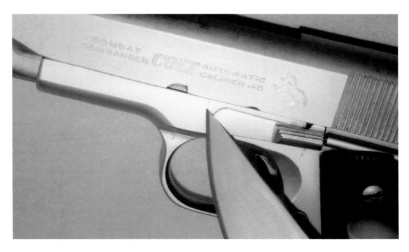

A Brief History

Shortly after WWII, the US Armed Services looked seriously at lighter-weight handguns, and also handguns that might fire the 9mm Parabellum cartridge used by nearly all our nation's allies. Colt and Smith & Wesson, then the industry leaders, took this challenge with particular seriousness.

The timeline unfolded thus:

1947: Work is already underway in Hartford. Elmer Keith, a frequent visitor to the Colt plant, would later write, "The Colt Commander was first brought out in 1947."[6] However, it was still pretty much a secret from the shooting public. Those 1947 lightweights, I suspect, would have been early prototypes for the military project, and not yet named "Commander."

1948: The new lightweight Colt .45s come to the attention of the shooting press. Chuck Taylor dug up the September 1948 issue of *American Rifleman* magazine from which he quoted in his *Gun Digest Book of Combat Handgunnery*: "Early in 1948, the Colt Company, in the course of development work for a more universal acceptance of lightweight, heavy-caliber automatic pistols, decided to see what would happen if a receiver was made from aluminum rather

Left (First): The Name Game. Original lightweight Colts were identified simply as "Commander"…

(Second): …and when the steel frame version was introduced, it was marked "Combat Commander" in the same place…

(Third): …and on the opposite side of the slide for good measure…

(Fourth): …and finally, Colt dubbed the original the "Lightweight Commander." Go figure. On new gun, note ejection port much larger than original's, for good reason.

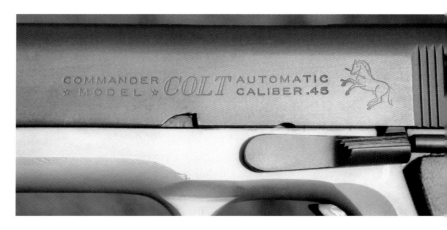

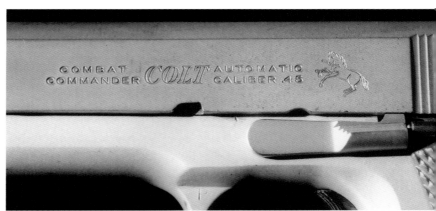

than from the standard alloy-steel forgings. Working with the Aluminum Corporation of America, it was decided, after experimentation, to try one of the high-tensile aluminum alloys. Several forgings of this amazingly light metal were specially made and issued to the Colt receiver-making department, and some 140-odd machining operations were performed on them…a new gun had been born."[7]

1950: The gun hits the market. Colt historian Donald M. Bady reports that "In 1949, it was decided to introduce the lightweight pistol for commercial sale, with a 4.25-inch barrel. Government trials continued, however…Early in 1950 the short light-weight pistol in 9 MM, .38, and .45 was introduced as a 'Commander Model.' The round hammer is used exclusively, the serial numbers continue in the 'LW' series. ALCOA continues to supply basic forgings for the frame. The material for these forgings is a special alloy, appropriately called 'COLTALLOY.'"[8]

For many years thereafter, the Commander line remained unchanged. The .45 caliber overwhelmingly outsold the .38 Super and the 9mm options. About the only noticeable upgrade in its first two decades was the eventual switch to checkered walnut grips with the Colt medallions when the decision makers in Hartford finally realized that the original Commander stocks, crappy plastic panels they called "Coltwood," were cheapening their gun's image and turning off buyers.

As time went on, the firm introduced an all-steel version they called the Combat Commander. Col. Cooper dumped on it, dubbing it neither fish nor fowl since it lacked the light weight of the original Commander and the full length sight radius of the Government Model. Yet the Combat Commander sold like hotcakes. Many serious shooters discovered that with less slide mass rocketing back and forth, the shorter all-steel Colt seemed to jump less in the hand. The center of balance also moved to the rear, which felt better in some shooters' hands. At about this time, Colt went to what may have been the handsomest grips they ever put on 1911s, plain uncheckered walnut with discreet Colt medallions inset.

In the 1980s, the Commanders got the Series '80 treatment consisting of a passive firing pin lock operated by the trigger. This added weight to the pull, and while purists shied away from the new Colts, they worked just fine for the most part, and the new design answered a genuine safety need.

In the early 1990s, Colt introduced its Enhanced series guns and gave that treatment to the Commander as well: slanted National Match style slide grooves, a flat

top, and an upscale finish. At the same time they covered the other end of the market with their plain-Jane, gray finish 1991A1 economy model, which was offered in Commander style as well as Government and subcompact Officers configurations.

By this time, Colt had finally figured out that the stubby little spur on the Commander's grip safety that had been tearing up shooters' hands for decades needed to go. It was replaced with the same slimline update of the 1911A1 grip safety, and on the upscale guns, by assorted beavertails, one reportedly designed for Colt by Ira Kay.

Along the way, the .38 Super and 9mm chamberings had been dropped. Some said hot NATO 9mm rounds and high pressure .38 Super were too much for the alloy frames, but Colt said that they did it for the simple reason that the market didn't want any caliber but .45 in that style pistol. A handful had been produced in 7.65mm Luger for the European market, and are coveted collectors' items today.

There had also been short production runs of various spinoff models. There had been a Target Commander, and there had been the CCO. The latter stood for Colt Commanding Officer, some said, while others insisted it stood for Concealed Carry Officers. Basically, it was the 4-1/4-inch Commander barrel/slide assembly atop the Lightweight Officers short-butt frame. Ray Ordorica, then at *Gun Digest*, proclaimed it the finest personal defense Colt .45 ever built. I could never argue the point.

A strange identity crisis occurred during the Commander's long run. The light model had always been known simply as the Commander, and the all-steel version was initially dubbed the Combat Commander. As time went on, Colt felt the need to distinguish the original by re-naming it the Lightweight Commander. Old heads tend to insist on the original terminology,

200-grain Speer JHP was author's choice in the Commander for many years. Note massive mushroom of bullet that killed a hog. From Ayoob's 1980s book, *The Semiautomatic Pistol in Police Service and Self-Defense.*

The shots were fired from a stubby-barreled Detonics .45 autoloader.

Note excellent expansion of this CCI Speer Inspector load, a 200-grain jacketed hollowpoint used by author to kill a hog instantly with one shot from 4¼" barrel Colt Commander .45 ACP.

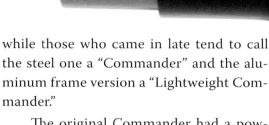

while those who came in late tend to call the steel one a "Commander" and the aluminum frame version a "Lightweight Commander."

The original Commander had a powerful influence on other gunmakers. It established two strong trends that continue today. One, of course, is the use of lightweight metals in gun frames. The other was a trend of size and shape: a compact service auto with a barrel within a half inch of the Commander's in length, but with full length grip frame and magazine.

Four or five years behind Colt, S&W entered the marketplace with its short-lived single action Model 44 (as it was later known) and the long-lived foundation of its service pistol line, the double action Model 39. Though chambered only for 9mm Parabellum, the Model 39 weighed the same 26.5 ounces, had the same kind of aluminum frame and full length single-stack magazine, and came with a 4-inch barrel.

Prior to the Commander, military service pistols with enclosed slides had barrels in the 5-inch range: the Colt Government Model, the only slightly shorter Browning Hi-Power, the Beretta Brigadier that debuted roughly concurrent with the Commander and would be the foundation of the Model 92, and the SIG P210 all fit this format. Future guns would follow the Commander with a barrel in the 4-inch range. Witness the SIG-Sauer line and the Ruger P-series. When S&W began making double action .45 automatics, they started with the Model 645 and its successor, the Model 4506, with 5-inch barrels. However, when

Smith introduced a steel Commander equivalent with 4.25-inch barrel, the Model 4566, it outstripped its big brother in sales and was adopted by such law enforcement agencies as the Syracuse (NY) Police, Chattanooga (TN) Police, and New Hampshire's state troopers. For some time, the full-size 4506 was discontinued while S&W kept the Commander-length 4566 in production. Even Beretta offered shorter barrels in their Compact and Centurion series of the 92, and in their subsequent 8000 series of rotary breech service pistols.

With its 4.5-inch barrel, the Glock 17 and the expanding line of service pistols that followed it were more in the Commander mold than the Government in terms of overall size. A Glock service gun that approximated the length of a Government Model, the Tactical/Practical series, was not produced until much later, almost as an afterthought.

No modern pistol has been more widely copied than the 1911. Most of the clonemakers have included 4 to 4.5 inch barrel versions that offer homage to the Commander. These include pistols by Kimber, Springfield Armory, Bill Wilson, Ed Brown, Les Baer, and others. The Baer version pays

With short LW Officer's frame, the Colt CCO was a great carry gun and the most compact of the Commander series. This one is stock except for Barnhart Burner grips.

the most direct homage: its model designation is intentionally spelled Commanche, with a second "m".

Meanwhile, at Colt, the Commander marches on. Unlike many other classic models of the brand, the Commander's production to my knowledge has never been interrupted in roughly 60 years. Currently available are lightweight and all-steel Commanders, and a Commander-length version of the economy grade Colt 1991A1.

Shooting the Colt Commander

The burr hammer has always been a signature Commander feature. Was it to lighten the frame? Was it ring shaped, as some discovered, to tie a string through so your friend could stand behind you during dry fire and jerk it back when you dropped the hammer, thus at once simulating recoil and recocking the gun without you having to break your hold? Was it to help shorten overall length

and make the dimensions look smaller in the catalog? Was it to keep the hammer spur from biting the hand?

Well, few people know more about 1911 pistol features than the redoubtable Bill Wilson, a famed pistolsmith, combat handgun champion, and 1911 manufacturer. He says, "A Commander hammer is mostly cosmetic."[9]

Some found the Commander slightly less reliable than the full length Government Model. This was due to three problems, all correctible. First, the shorter and faster slide cycle had to be compensated for with judicious selection of recoil spring weight. Second, the first generation of both steel and aluminum Commanders had short, narrow ejection ports, which wouldn't allow clearance of a live round. One had to clear a loaded chamber carefully, with the live round trundling down inside the grip frame instead of jumping clear of the slide mechanism. Shooters learned to have their gunsmiths open

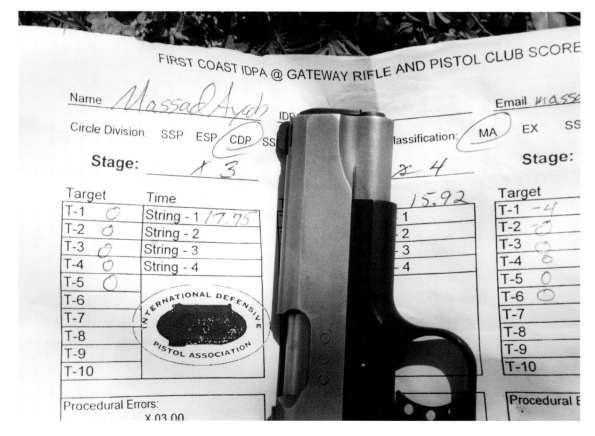

Author's scoresheet with box-stock Colt CCO and major power .45 ammo. Each "0" stands for no points down from perfect score. The CCO won the match for Mas with a "down zero" score. Commanders shoot!

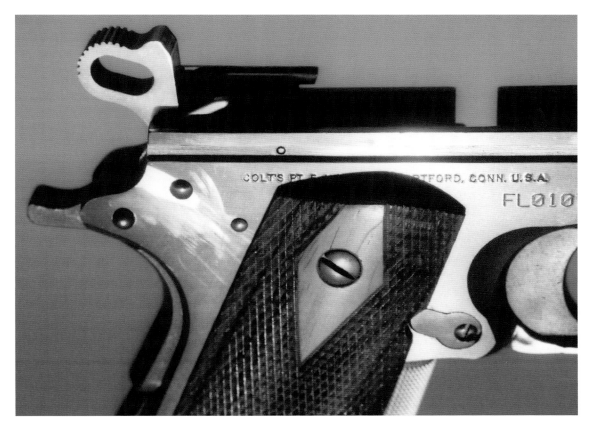

Current production Colt Commander .45s are stress-relieved at the frame rails above the slide stop.

up the ports. Colt eventually caught on and began doing the same at the factory, which solved the problem. Finally, "throating" the chamber area for hollowpoints involves taking metal off the frame, and aluminum pistol frames are hardened only at the surface. This process tended to expose soft aluminum that would get chewed up and quickly impair feeding. Only Bill Laughridge at Cylinder & Slide Shop seemed able to properly throat a lightweight Commander frame, and he never revealed his secret. By the mid-1990s, Colt had solved the problem by changing their frame forgings, producing them "factory throated" to the proper feedway dimensions and suitably hardened.

What about recoil springs? Wilson says, "You really shouldn't go over 19 pounds for hardball (in a Government Model), and in a Commander, you shouldn't go over 20. The stock spring in a Government Model is about 15 or 16 pounds, versus 18 in a Commander. Try to go up one step, but that's the limit. When you go to a big heavy spring, you cre-

ate more problems that you could possibly cure."[10]

For more than half a century, shooters feared that the powerful buffeting of .45 ACP recoil would cause accelerated wear and breakage in light frames. All things considered, the LW Commanders have stood up quite well. Taylor scoffs at Commander fragility as "a belief of the uninitiated." He says, "Several of my own LW Commanders have fired more than 30,000 rounds of full power ammo and are still going strong."[11] I've seen a lot of cracked aluminum Commander frames, but I've also seen a lot of cracked steel 1911 frames, usually in the area of the slide stop holes. Colt long ago alleviated this problem, too: they stress-relieved the area by simply cutting away the frame above the slide stop.

What of .45 ACP recoil in the powerful Lightweight Commander? The weak shooting stances of the early '50s exacerbated this, but the biggest problem was that nasty little stub of a grip tang that gouged the hand on every shot. Anyone who knew what they were do-

ing did for himself what Colt did eventually and installed a more hospitable grip safety. It is significant that when researching for an article on the Commander in a gun magazine, I couldn't find an example with the original grip safety to photograph: every single specimen in the hands of the friends and colleagues I contacted had, like all of my own Commanders, been retrofitted with a beavertail. There is no better proof that this is the accepted solution to the problem.

Nichols, while somewhat overstating the light .45's shootability in his 1950 review of the prototype, was prescient in one respect: being lighter, it was faster from holster to target. The Steel Challenge shooters (read: World Speed Shooting Championship) didn't hit on this until much later, when they realized that radically lightened 1911s would get from holster to target, and from target to target, quicker. This created a whole new subgroup of custom pistols: ultra-light "Steel

The first "Ayoob Special" by John Lawson, late 1970s. All-steel Combat Commander pre-Series '80 with Magna-Ported 5-inch barrel, fitted bushing, S&W micrometer sights, Hoag beavertail grip safety of the first generation, and a helluva good trigger job. Note hammer spur cut away to accommodate Government Model beavertail.

Challenge guns." Instructor Frank Cornwall used his daily carry gun, a customized Lightweight Commander, in lieu of one of his many full size Government Models to pass Chuck Taylor's demanding Combat Master test. "It was partly because I wanted to do it with my carry gun," Frank told me later, "but I also found I was faster to the shot with the lighter .45. Most of the multiple shot sequences in the test were multiple targets, and recoil recovery moving between targets was no real problem with the Lightweight Commander."

Once the beavertail is in place, your sight options, etc. are pretty much the same as with the bigger 1911s. Since the lighter gun does in fact want to jump a little more, the LW version may demand more attention to grasp and other elements of technique, particularly in one handed shooting. A solid hold is more important than ever. That favors a low-thumb hold, which strengthens the grasp, and those who follow the Cooper theory that the thumb should ride the manual safety may benefit from installing a low-ride safety lever of the kind pioneered by Robbie Barrkman.

Personal Experience

I didn't get into Commanders until the '70s, when beavertails became popular and made them comfortable to shoot. I won a couple of pre-Series '80s in pistol matches, one aluminum and one steel, and had them both modified. The Combat Commander went to John Lawson, who installed a Hoag beavertail and S&W micrometer sights (a popular modification to Colt autos at the time), and fitted a 5-inch barrel Magna-Ported on the exposed 3/4-inch front portion. I won my share of IPSC and bowling pin matches with it, until switching to more sophisticated "compensator guns" as they became available. The lightweight went to Bill Laughridge, who used his magic to throat the aluminum frame and the Bar-Sto barrel he expertly installed to feed the best .45 carry load of the period, the 200-grain Speer JHP that Dean Grennell dubbed "the flying ashtray." He also fitted beavertail and fixed sights from Wilson. This became my duty pistol on the police department for some time during the late '80s and I frequently carried it off duty. I shot several hogs with it, all quick one-shot kills. Each would do about an inch at 25 yards with the ammo it liked best.

As time went on, factory LW Commander accuracy got better, and I acquired three Series '80 guns: an Enhanced Commander and a pair of CCOs, one fancy and one plain-Jane. All would do about two inches at 25 yards, and all had acceptable trigger pulls out of the box, and of course relieved ejection ports, better fixed sights, and factory beavertails and throating.

I only shot a couple of matches with the LWs, but they performed well. In the late '80s, the Missouri state championships of practical police shooting required the officer to compete with the guns he carried on duty, and for me that meant the Laughridge LW Commander that particular year. I won the pistol event with it, though Ben White of Columbia (MO) PD beat us all so thor-

When Ed Brown Custom approached author to do a signature edition gun, he chose all-steel stainless in Commander configuration, with Trijicon fixed night sights, ambi safety...

...and Ed Brown's unique Bobtail butt reconfiguration. It improves concealment, and feels remarkably good in the hand.

oughly in the shotgun phase that he won the two-gun aggregate. Realizing I had no action photos of Commanders on file to use in an article on Commanders for *The Accurate Rifle*, I shot the 10/04 monthly IDPA match in Jacksonville, FL, with my stock plain vanilla CCO, and won. The fast handling Nichols had described 54 years earlier was in play, and with no more than two or three shots per target required, the slightly greater "bounce" of the aluminum .45 was no great handicap.

I'm one of many who put the lightweight Colt Commander on their list of favorite carry guns. It is exquisitely comfortable in an inside the waistband holster, and delivers big gun performance. Most of us prefer its most popular chambering, .45 ACP, but that's not unanimous. Ace firearms instructor and lawyer Tim Noe carries a Combat Commander in 9mm, and a .38 Super Commander is the preferred carry pistol of instructor and gun writer Bonnie Young.

The Colt Commander established two important precedents: lightweight handgun frames and shorter barreled service pistols with full length grip frames. Those trends, like the original modern classic itself, remain hugely evident today.

Notes

[1] Keith, Elmer, *Sixguns by Keith*, New York City: Bonanza Books, 1955.

[2] Stebbins, Henry M., *Pistols: A Modern Encyclopedia*, Castle Books, 1961.

[3] Nichols, Robert M., *The Secrets of Double-Action Shooting*, New York City: G. P. Putnam's Sons, 1950.

[4] Cooper, Jeff, *The Complete Book of Modern Handgunning*, Englewood Cliffs, NJ: Prentice-Hall, 1961.

[5] Taylor, Chuck, *The Gun Digest Book of Combat Handgunnery*, Fourth Edition, Iola, WI: Krause Publications, 1997.

[6] Keith, *op. cit.*

[7] Taylor, *op. cit.*

[8] Bady, Donald M., *Colt Automatic Pistols*, Union City, TN: Pioneer Press, 2000.

[9] Wilson, Bill, *The Combat Auto*, Berryville, AR: Innovative Products, 1991.

[10] *Ibid.*

[11] Taylor, *op. cit.*

The Colt National Match Pistol
(and Its Spiritual Descendants)

The history of the 1911 pistol's design and the nature of its many uses and special-purpose modifications are far too broad to be effectively addressed in a single book chapter ... or, indeed, in a single book. A substantial section of a firearms library could be devoted to 1911 books by Donald Bady, Dave Lauck, Tim Mullin, James Serven, Layne Simpson, Bill Wilson, Larry Wilson, et. al. Today's *Gun Digest* listing of every variation of currently produced 1911 pistol might well exceed the entire section on semiautomatic pistols in a *Gun Digest* of the early '50s.

Thus, a treatment of the topic in article length demands a specific focus, and no 1911 is more pleasing to focus on than the Colt National Match.

Considered by many aficionados to be the finest of Government Model 1911s, this tribute to the gunmaker's art has inspired imitators for more than 80 years.

In everything but glassy finish, Wilson Combat CQB equals National Match in quality and exceeds it in accuracy. The author bought this one after shooting multiple one-inch 25-yard groups with it in testing.

The Colt National Match is a timeless pistol. Here Justine Ayoob, then 19, shoots her dad's with .45 hardball.

Top: Author's pet National Match gave him some 35 years of service. BoMar sights had already been affixed by USAFMTU when he bought the accurized pistol used. Circle on rear of slide is from uniform holster's safety snap. Produced circa 1962.

Bottom: Today, Colt produces that model as the Gold Cup Trophy.

Pedigree

Tim Mullin's ode to this pistol, *American Beauty*, states boldly, "...no finer semi-automatic handgun than the prewar Colt National Match ever left the factory, and anyone who owns one of these American Beauties holds a national treasure in his or her hand."[1] In terms of appearance and workmanship, few would argue with him. There are more accurate pistols today, and more user-friendly ones, but none with the pure Quality with a capital "Q" that permeates this rare and storied handgun.

Those experts who knew the pistol during its short life had good things to say about it. Said Elmer Keith, "It was fitted with target sights, a match grade barrel and carefully honed action parts. Trigger pulls were carefully adjusted. These fine pistols were marked on the left side 'National Match Colt.' This was and is, a very fine match .45 auto...The Super Match was a fine target sighted and selected Super .38, but is no longer made. It was brought out soon after the introduction of the National Match .45 Colt."[2] Actually, most NMs wore that marking on the right side of the slide.

A contemporary of Keith was Charlie Askins, who used a Colt .45 automatic along with .38 Special revolver and .22 auto by the same maker to win the national pistol championship in the 1930s. He once wrote of the National Match .45, "This is the Government Model with target sights and a target barrel, finely fitted and finished. Heretofore the targetmen fell on this gun and felt they had the best. It is believed Colt halted the production of the National Match grade simply because it was too expensive to manufacture and it could not thereafter be offered to the public at a popular price. Hand labor is a costly proposition and a good deal of highly skilled hand effort had to go into the completion of each pistol."[3]

A Brief History

Born as an expensive gun in the depths of the Great Depression, the finely crafted National Match sold better than expected but was never destined to be a mass-market success. The addition of the Super Match, a .38 Super with the same treatment, differing only in markings, caliber, and cartridge capacity, did little to change the inevitable.

NM suffix is noted on serial number of author's pet pistol. Signature Gold Cup style trigger was later replaced with this Videcki unit. Note slanted slide grooves, relieved ejection port, both standard on second incarnation of the National Match. This gun has the controversial light slide, not externally detectable.

When production ceased with the outbreak of WWII, the epoch of the Colt National Match had come to an end. While Mullin notes that a few were assembled from left-over parts after the war's conclusion, the company chose not to make it a catalog item. However, the concept was resurrected in 1957 with the Gold Cup. The first runs were marked only "National Match" on the slide, and later "National Match Gold Cup," and finally just "Gold Cup."

According to one of the great Colt authorities, James E. Serven, "The 'National Match' first appeared in the 1933 Colt catalog. In all general specifications it resembled the standard 1911 model. However, Colt workmen gave these pistols very special attention. The action was hand-honed, a selected, carefully targetted [sic] match barrel was used, the trigger was checked and of course there was the 'hump-backed' checked arched housing."[4]

As Serven noted in his updated 1964 edition of *Colt Firearms*, "In 1957 the Colt Company resumed manufacture of a deluxe .45 automatic target pistol, naming this model the 'Colt Gold Cup National Match.' Working parts are hand-fitted; the pistol is meticulously made and super-accurate for championship shooting. Slack between the barrel and slide is automatically eliminated. The very wide, grooved trigger is fitted with an adjustable, spring-loaded trigger stop... Finish is Colt 'Royal Blue' with sandblasted areas where glare might affect aim."[5]

To Mullin and many other purists, only the prewar guns are the true American Beauties, the original National Match Colts of legend. Whether or not the Gold Cup generation measured up is a matter of debate among 1911 enthusiasts to this day. Serven seems to have been impressed with the Gold Cup incarnation. So was Charles M. Heard, a popular gun expert of the day, who described

Below: Springfield Armory's match grade guns are spiritual descendants of the National Match, author suggests. This one, in 9mm, is also an effective fight-stopper with the sort of ammo shown.

it in 1960 as the "Colt 'National Match' .45 ACP, factory accurized and custom crafted for target. Trigger pull: 4 lbs., adjustable with trigger stop. Full target sights, straight back-strap. Has all other features of Government model. REMARKS: My tests only proved this gun to be all that is claimed for it and expected of it. May be used for match target, combat, or self-defense; still the most powerful semi-auto made."[6]

The argument over the Gold Cup's right to wear the mantle of the National Match wasn't entirely nit-picking. While the original National Match was a true heavy duty Government Model .45 or .38 Super finely polished and blued and then fitted with match barrel and altogether slicked-up, the Gold Cup was seen as a lighter weight, lighter duty gun. Circa 1949, Remington had come up with a factory target load in .45 ACP that captured the bullseye shooters immediately: a 185-grain semi-wadcutter loaded to a mid-range velocity of only 770 foot-seconds velocity. It did not reliably cycle a Government Model pistol with its heavy-duty slide and full power recoil spring built for a 230-grain GI hardball round at 820 to 850 feet per second. Recognizing this, Colt lightened the slide of the 1957 series National Match/ Gold Cup .45s. NRA's technical staff writer

for *American Rifleman*, M.D. Waite, "outed" this fact in his December 1957 review of the new pistol.

Waite wrote, "Our preliminary firing tests indicated uniform functioning with both full charge and mid-range ammunition. This puzzled us a bit until we noted that the interior of the slide is cut away somewhat to reduce its weight approximately two ounces. It is thus unnecessary to change recoil springs when using factory ammunition of differing recoil potential...."[7]

Rumors spread that this made the gun weak. It certainly did not make it inaccurate, and the Gold Cup worked as advertised. Added Waite in that seminal test of the budding Gold Cup, "When machine-rest tested at 50 yards, our gun shot possible-size groups with commercial wadcutter ammunition but did not perform quite so well with government-loaded Service ammunition."[8] The very top champions kept on using Government Models that had been accurized by Chow, Clark, Dinan, Giles, Shockey, and other master pistolsmiths of the period.

Adding to the Gold Cup's bad rap for fragility were its sights. Crude by today's standards, the Stevens National Match adjustable rear sight of the prewar years at least did not break or fly off the gun. A relatively large number of original National Match pistols had sturdy fixed sights that offered a larger sight picture than the standard service pistol, the best of these being the excellent high visibility sights manufactured by the King Gun Sight Company and for some time available on the NM pistols from the Colt factory. King made a practi-

Left: Today, the mantle of the National Match has fallen on the shoulders of the custom houses. Dave Lauck at D&L Sports built this "LFI Special" to the author's specifications on a new 5-inch Colt. It will stay in an inch at 25 yards, and he can't recall its last malfunction.

Right: This Kimber Gold Match is another spiritual heir to the National Match concept. Author shot his first Master score in IDPA CDP with this one, now in the Penny Dean collection.

Below: If you enjoy fine firearms, says Ayoob, you'll enjoy reading "American Beauty" by Tim Mullin. NM's gorgeous finish is evident even in this "photo of a photo."

cal sight that was adjustable for windage but not elevation.

Alas, Colt management in the latter half of the 20th century manifested some truly egregious short-sightedness and loss of institutional history. The Gold Cup generation of the National Match series was never offered with fixed sights. Instead, it came with the Elliason adjustable rear sight and an undercut Patridge front. The front sight was not properly staked and would often depart from the slide within 500 rounds of hardball, though it lasted longer with the "softball" target loads. The Elliason rear sight proved to be superb on the Python revolver, where Colt offered it as an extra-cost option, but it did not stand up to the rocketing slide of a 1911, particularly with full power .45 ammo. Secured with hollow pins, the Elliasons often came loose when the pins cracked.

All this was a shame, because the Gold Cup was beloved by handgunners including cops of the Sixties and Seventies who wanted a gun that would feed the jacketed hollow point ammo that was becoming popular but didn't want to send their Government Model to a pistolsmith to throat its feedway for the high performance rounds. A Government Model or Commander of the period was "mil-spec" in that regard. It would feed fine with the 230-grain round-nose full metal jacket military cartridge (or, from its introduction in the early 1970s to this day, with the Remington 185-grain JHP whose nose duplicated the ogive of hardball), but would often balk at hollow-cavity projectiles with wider mouths. The Gold Cup, designed to feed the softball round, with its strangely shaped button nose and short overall length, was much more amenable to the hollow points once Lee Jurras's pioneering Super Vel ammunition company got the ball rolling in that direction in the Sixties.

Unfortunately, many of the people who wanted beautifully made Colt .45 automatics with the gorgeous Royal Blue finish, which gave the deep, rich blue-black of the prewar National Match pistols a solid run for the money, wanted heavy duty fighting handguns. The Gold Cup's reputation for fragility, to whatever degree it may or may not have been deserved, got in the way of that. By the time Colt started using the same heavy-duty slide dimensions as the Government Model, it was too late to change the Gold Cup's image. Sales of the Gold Cup were long disappointing. Colt briefly offered the Combat Elite, in essence a Gold Cup with fixed sights but without the gorgeous finish and without the advertising it should have had, and it went by the wayside. Colt produces in dribs and drabs a pistol they call the Gold Cup Trophy today.

In time, with the big resurrection of the 1911's popularity, new manufacturers came along to fill the void. The Kimber pistols, particularly the Gold Match, and the upper lines of the Springfield Armory 1911A1s, especially the TRP (Tactical Response Pistol) with fixed sights and the Trophy Match with sturdy BoMar or equivalent adjustable sights, are today's heirs to the National Match concept. They will not have the lustrous, captivating finish of the best Colts of yesteryear, however, though they'll be proportionally more affordable than the NM was when Colt introduced it in 1933. Production pistols of fine quality, like the Bill Wilson and Ed Brown lines, come closer. Perhaps most in keeping with the NM tradition are the top-line pistols from Rock River Arms and Les Baer. The latter two brands are the only out-of-the-box 1911s likely to take you to the winner's circle today at Camp Perry without aftermarket custom work. More accurate than the Springfields or Kimbers, each can be ordered in a super-tight version that guarantees accuracy on the order of 1.5

inches at 50 yards. That's more than the Colt National Match in any of its incarnations could offer. But even these fine pistols will not come with a finish that matches a prewar Colt National Match, or the best of the Gold Cups in Royal Blue.

The few thousand National Match pistols shipped out of Hartford in the less than a decade of their epoch also presaged the "combat custom" 1911 so popular today. The best of the current craftsmen, Mark Morris and Dave Lauck and Dick Heinie and a handful more, will give you today's equivalent of a National Match for several thousand dollars after a considerable wait. These guns will be much more user friendly, with lighter and cleaner triggers, beveled magazine wells, beavertail grip safeties and other amenities. But, geared for heavy duty, they will come with a finish that cannot equal the beauty of that old National Match.

Shooting the National Match and Its Successors

Way back in the Fifties, Jeff Cooper said that all the Government Model really needed was a lighter, crisper trigger; throating to feed high efficiency ammo; and more visible sights. Given that hardball was about all you could buy over the counter for a .45 auto before WWII and the NM fed it just fine, the National Match pistol had anticipated the Colonel's needs and delivered them amply when Jeff was a youngster. It is a formula that has stood the test of time.

Some say that the Gold Cup generation of National Match pistols raised the bar with its slanted slide grooves and flat top slide. Whether these truly enhance performance is an unresolved debate, but I for one just like them esthetically. The original National Match is so rare and precious today that virtually no one actually carries or shoots one anymore. If they did, they would

24. Right side closeup of the Stevens adjustable rear sight fitted to a National Match pistol, showing the elevation adjustment screw (center rear of sight body), and the larger windage adjustment screw in the slide.

fit them with beavertail grip safeties and perhaps larger-profile thumb safeties (maybe even ambidextrous), and throat them for JHP ammo. The last person I knew who carried an original National Match "for real" and used it as such was Bill Allard. Bill was the partner of the NYPD Stakeout Squad's famous Jim Cirillo, and the only man on that high-risk unit who killed more armed opponents in gunfights than Cirillo. Allard's favorite pistol – used in more than one of those shootings – was an original Colt National Match .45 with high fixed sights, a gun he had special permission to carry on duty. He has since retired his pet National Match to the gun safe, and now, in retirement, carries a Kimber .45 auto daily.

In an early Gold Cup with the lighter slide, I'd be sparing with hardball and would use no +P ammo at all. With light loads, use a light spring; with heavy loads, use a heavy spring. The 1957 concept of one spring for both helped lead to the Gold Cup getting that reputation for fragility. With a lighter spring, the slide comes back harder and hammers the frame proportionally more.

Do not expect 1-inch groups at 25 yards or 2-inch groups at 50 unless the gun has been accurized or you've paid extra for a top-line Les Baer or Rock River pistol. That degree of accuracy never seems to have been present in the original National Match, and as Waite noted was not present with ball ammo in the Gold Cup. (Even the short-lived Gold Cup factory-chambered for the .38 Special wadcutter cartridge was disappointing in its accuracy, according to most testers.) My own National Match cracks the 1-inch/25 yard mark, but only because it was accurized by the USAF Marksmanship Training Unit at Lackland AFB. In conventional configuration 1911 pistols in the National Match mold made more recently (as opposed to long-slide or compensated target guns), only my custom Colts by Morris, Lauck, et. al. will deliver that magic inch. The one exception is my Springfield TRP Operator, whose heavy extended frame with flashlight rail alters the 1911 silhouette unforgivably for the purist. It will do an inch on the nose for five shots at 25 yards with Federal Gold Medal 185 grain Match softball. The rest will do in the neighborhood of two inches at 25. For practical purposes, that's a good neighborhood, and about where the original National Match and Gold Cup dwelt with service hardball ammo. The finest "boutique .45s" from semi-custom houses such as Ed Brown's and Bill Wilson's will deliver an inch at 25 yards with the best ammo, too.

Personal Experience

Although I've shot original Colt National Match pistols, the only one I ever owned was a 1962 production Colt marked "National Match" and not "Gold Cup." It had already been accurized at Lackland and fitted with BoMar sights for the Distinguished (service pistol configuration, .45 hardball) bulls-eye matches when I got it, around 1970, for $100 from a bullseye shooter who was giving up the game and wanted to get rid of his equipment. Its gorgeous Royal Blue finish was soon marred by constant presentations from concealment leather and, before long, police duty holsters. The thumb snaps of the period did not have the cushions you see today to protect a gun's finish from metal-to-metal drag during the draw.

It never jammed until the day (at Bianchi Cup, naturally) that its extractor gave up the ghost. I pretty much wore out the trigger and Bill Laughridge at Cylinder & Slide Shop replaced it with the much better Videcki unit. I won guns with it at Second Chance, won a police combat state championship with it, and even took my share of trophies with it in the bulls-eye days of my youth. I eventually retired it to the gun safe and ultimately gave it to my ex-wife, who was my young fiancee when I bought it. My younger

The legendary J.H. Fitzgerald had a lot to do with the National Match. He's seen here adjusting a 1911 at Camp Perry circa mid-1930s in Tim Mullin's *American Beauty*.

Colt "National Match" Automatic Pistol

CALIBER .45

Equipped with Stevens Adjustable Rear Sight and Ramp Front Sight

Options and Choices 39

...BER:
...or the .45
...matic Cartridge.

...ew of Stevens
...NAL MATCH"
...ear Sight

...adjustable rear sight
...ith the "National
...d "Super Match"
...istols is the finest
...ed to an arm of this
...two-way adjusting
...trong locking screws
...sight firmly in ad-
...indage elevation is
...rning a side screw
...ide of the sight and
...t is locked in place
...the top of the sight
...tion adjustment is
...ing a single screw
...two locking screws
...e back plate that
...impossible. Guide
...rnished to aid in
...and elevation ad-

General Specifications

CAPACITY OF MAGAZINE: 7 Cartridges.
LENGTH OF BARREL: 5 inches.
LENGTH OVER ALL: 8½ inches.
STOCKS: Checked Walnut.
TRIGGER: Checked.
ARCHED HOUSING: Checked.
BARREL: Selected "Match" Barrel.
ACTION: Hand-honed, velvet smooth.
SIGHTS: Front sight fixed, ramp type with serrated face. Rear sight adjustable for both elevation and windage. (see note)
FINISH: Full Blued. Nickel finish at extra cost.
WEIGHT: 39 ounces.

NOTE—The NATIONAL MATCH can be furnished with regular fixed sights for those who do not desire the adjustable rear sight.

For many years there has been an insistent demand for the Colt Government Model Automatic Pistol — equipped for target shooting. To answer this demand the Colt Government Model is available with super-smooth, hand-honed target action — selected "Match" barrel — and two-way adjustable rear target sight. This arm is known as the Colt "National Match" Model and will appeal especially to lovers of the regulation .45 Automatic Pistol. It is equipped with all regular safety features and is identical in operation and size with the Government Model.

Special Features

...apidly increasing interest in target
...the part of shooters of the .45
...istol, the National
...el is proving un-
...lar. Military men,
...ers and members
...nal Guard have
...National Match

.45 AUTOMATIC

an arm designed especially for target shooting, and capable of producing exceptionally high scores. Its smooth action makes this model a delight to shoot and the selected "Match" barrel and adjustable Rear Sight with which it is equipped guarantee accuracy and efficiency.

Above: A contemporary ad for the Colt National Match, reproduced in the Mullin book.

daughter likes to liberate it from her mother's gun safe and take it to the range, like giving a retired racehorse some exercise.

Over the years, the deep lustrous blue of the top-line Colt finish lost its appeal. Having ruined that finish once, I was more interested in rugged gun surfaces that didn't wear and better resisted corrosion. By the late '80s I was spending more time with the new generation of National Match inspired pistols. These days, Kimbers and Springfields and "combat custom" Colts fulfill my 1911 needs, along with Ed Brown, Night-

hawk, and Wilson Custom guns. I used a Kimber Gold Match to first make Master in IDPA's single action .45 division, and shot the Springfield Trophy Match at Camp Perry one year.

Yet for me, as for anyone who appreciates handguns, the great old Colt National Match remains the *piece de resistance*. As a tool, this accurate yet reliable gun was the apotheosis of the powerful semiautomatic service pistol in its time, and it spawned generations of similar guns in the decades that followed. As an icon of fine craftsmanship, it deserves the "American Beauty" title Tim Mullin bestowed upon it. Colt's Custom Shop today has the ability to resurrect this pistol in its original glory. So does the Performance Center at Smith & Wesson, who could duplicate the original NM's old world blue-black finish that looks like liquid, on their SW1911 .45.

I really wish they would. Great beauty… unparalleled functionality in its time…that honed action that racks so smoothly, it feels like running your hand over Waterford Crystal…the Colt National Match pistol was truly one of a kind. It would find a much more receptive market if reincarnated today.

Notes

[1]Mullin, Timothy J., *American Beauty: the Prewar Colt National Match Government Model Pistol*, Cobourg, Ontario, Canada: Collector Grade Publications, 1999, p. 1.

[2]Keith, Elmer, *Sixguns by Keith*, New York City: Bonanza Books, 1955, p. 48.

[3]Askins, Charles Jr., *The Pistol Shooter's Book*, Harrisburg, PA: The Stackpole Company, 1953, Pp. 32-33

[4]Serven, James E., *Colt Firearms*, Santa Ana, CA: Foundation Press, 1954 (5th printing 12/64), p. 285.

[5]Serven, *Ibid.*

[6]Heard, Charles M., *The Complete Guidebook of Handguns*, Los Angeles: Trend Books, 1960, p. 120.

[7]"A New Colt .45" by M.D. Waite, *American Rifleman* magazine, December, 1957.

[8]Waite, *Ibid.*

The Colt Detective Special

I t was a revolver so classic in its concept that its name became a generic for others of its kind. Kleenex and Frigidaire were joined by Detective Special. Timelessly functional, it remains in wide use, even though discontinued.

A Brief History

Colt introduced the Police Positive double action small frame service revolver in .32 Long and .38 S&W in 1905. Two years later, they lengthened the frame and cylinder slightly to take the .38 Special cartridge, and the Police Positive Special variation was born. In 1927, they produced the

The first small-frame .38 Special snubnose, many connoisseurs believe, was also the best. The Detective Special spawned a family of classic protection guns, and more "firsts."

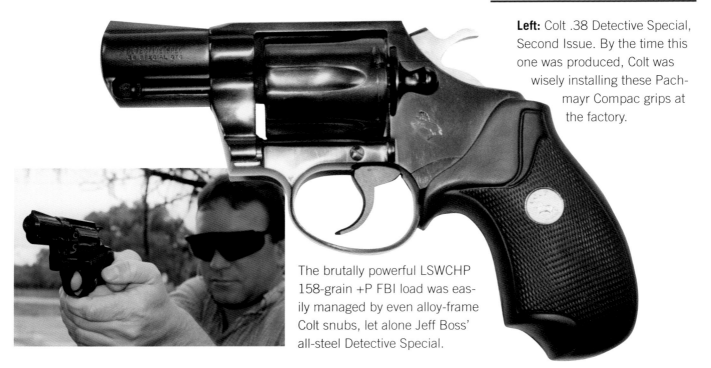

Left: Colt .38 Detective Special, Second Issue. By the time this one was produced, Colt was wisely installing these Pachmayr Compac grips at the factory.

The brutally powerful LSWCHP 158-grain +P FBI load was easily managed by even alloy-frame Colt snubs, let alone Jeff Boss' all-steel Detective Special.

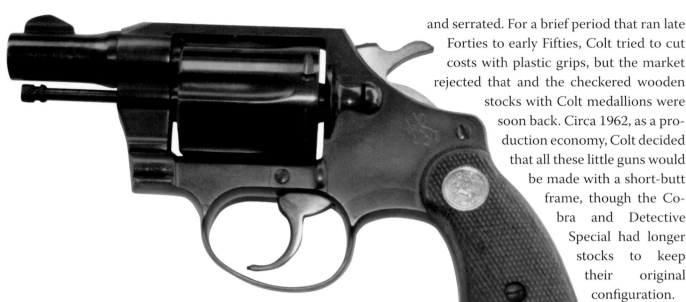

and serrated. For a brief period that ran late Forties to early Fifties, Colt tried to cut costs with plastic grips, but the market rejected that and the checkered wooden stocks with Colt medallions were soon back. Circa 1962, as a production economy, Colt decided that all these little guns would be made with a short-butt frame, though the Cobra and Detective Special had longer stocks to keep their original configuration.

Another early '50s development was the Colt Hammer Shroud, which bolted onto the frame with three screws. It shielded the hammer from snagging in pocket or clothing, leaving the tip exposed in a channel so the gun could be thumb-cocked if need be. S&W responded a couple of years later with their Bodyguard, a Chief Special with "built-in hammer shroud." That gun remains in the S&W line.

By 1972, the firm had produced some 400,000 Detective Specials alone, according to Ned Schwing.[1] The guns were given a makeover that year, and what some called the "Second Issue" was born. The chief difference was a heavier barrel, with a shroud that protected the ejector rod in the S&W Magnum style. The streamlined new front sight was steeply ramped. Agent stocks remained the same, but the Detective Special and Cobra got oversize "combat" grips. These eventually gave way to factory-installed Pachmayr Compacs, which many shooters had already determined were the most "shootable" grips for these small revolvers.

The configuration in which those of the author's generation remember the Detective Special. This First Issue specimen is circa late '50s-early '60s.

same gun with a two-inch barrel and dubbed it the Detective Special.

That's it. That simple. But so many of the great ideas are. The wee six-shooter weighed but 21 ounces, a featherweight in the time of all steel revolvers, and was the smallest and lightest .38 Special yet made in a period when that caliber utterly ruled law enforcement and had captured the civilian self defense market's attention as well. The first guns had square butts; some years later, the edges were rounded to enhance concealment.

When Colt resumed production after WWII, changes happened slowly. Checkering on the cylinder latch and trigger face was dropped. An aluminum frame clone of the Detective Special emerged from the USAF Aircrewman revolver project, and in 1950 it became the first aluminum revolver on the market. Named the Cobra, it weighed half an ounce under a pound and was an instant hit. In 1955 the Agent was added to the line, a Cobra with a shortened grip frame that concealed better and took another ounce off the weight.

In the early '50s, Colt determined that the snubby's ejector rod could stand to be a little longer for more efficient function, and it was extended almost to the muzzle. The front sight was also flattened toward the rear

In 1986, Colt was in financial trouble. The slightly smaller and lighter Smith & Wesson Chief Special and its brethren had long since been stomping the Colts in sales. Colt dropped its snub-nose .38s from production.

They returned to the market in 1996 with new lockwork and in stainless steel as the SF-VI (small frame, six shot). A year later, a subtle redesign of the mechanism was accompanied by a name change that paid homage to the original sobriquet: "DS-II." Beefed up to take the .357 round, it became the Magnum Carry. Unfortunately, none of these revolvers is currently in production.

The history of these little guns is a fascinating study. Legendary lawmen of the second quarter of the 21st century, such as Melvin Purvis and Eliot Ness, carried Colt Detective Specials. Just don't get too caught up in the terminology. Every Colt expert seems to have his own definition of the generations of this long-lived gun's complicated history.

Pedigree

Gun experts as well as the rank and file took the Detective Special to their hearts from the beginning. Few guns are so beloved as to earn nicknames; this gun garnered two. It is fondly known to many as the "Dick Special." In my circles, it was known by its initials: the "DS."

For nearly a quarter century, the DS had the small frame hideout .38 Special market to itself. The introduction of the S&W Chief Special in 1949 changed that, but the Colt was always hugely popular among the cognoscenti, and many shooters liked the small Colt better

Perfect fit to the hand made the D-frame Colt a favorite. Note forward-sitting cylinder, which with this late model's heavy barrel adds to stabilizing, muzzle-heavy feel. Trigger reach is exactly right for double action work with Pachmayrs.

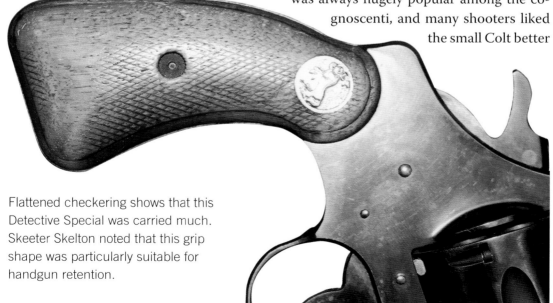

Flattened checkering shows that this Detective Special was carried much. Skeeter Skelton noted that this grip shape was particularly suitable for handgun retention.

than its big brothers. When I first toured the NYPD firearms unit in 1978, I learned that while no more than 10% of the city's cops chose the big Colt Official Police over the S&W Model 10, fully 30% or more carried the Colt instead of the Smith as their small frame off duty gun.

Mills Lane, the famous Nevada judge and boxing referee, was a Colt man. He once said, "People talk about their friends, Mr. Smith and Mr. Wesson, but I have Doctor Colt. You see, Mr. Smith and Mr. Wesson only have five shots, and Doctor Colt has six." This was, in truth, one reason so many cops liked it for off duty or backup. The one more shot meant a 20% increase in firepower when only revolvers were allowed.

John Dineen, the famous Chicago cop and police union head, carried a Detective Special inside his waistband with a Barami Hip-Grip. The current commissioner of the NYPD carries a Detective Special even now. Vern Geberth, commander of the Bronx Homicide Task Force and perhaps the nation's leading authority on homicide investigation, carried a Second Issue Detective Special. A First Issue DS was the preferred .38 snub of Bill Allard, who set the record for fatal shootings among NYPD's elite Stakeout Squad. Bill told me it was simply a more shootable gun for him than the small frame S&W. Bill's partner Jim Cirillo, no slouch in the gunfight department himself, carried a hammer-shrouded Cobra as his off duty and backup piece.

Hammer-shrouded Colt Agents were the preferred snubbies of famed combat small arms instructors Clint Smith and the late Ray Chapman. An Agent graced the cover of the first edition of Ed Lovette's excellent book on the tactical use of the short-barrel revolver. When I first met Sheriff Jim Wilson, he would no more put on his jeans without a Smith & Wesson Centennial in the front pocket than without his wallet in the back, but he recently confessed in print to having switched to a particularly nice, pre-'72 vintage Detective Special as his belly gun of choice.

Top Right:
Original front-end configuration: tapered barrel, half-disk sight, short ejector rod. This is one of the author's Dick Specials, produced in 1930.

Bottom Right:
Post-'72 barrel configuration was key change in Second Issue D-frames. Barrel is now heavy and untapered, with steep, smooth ramp sight going almost back to the frame, and fully protected ejector rod. New barrel added 2 oz.

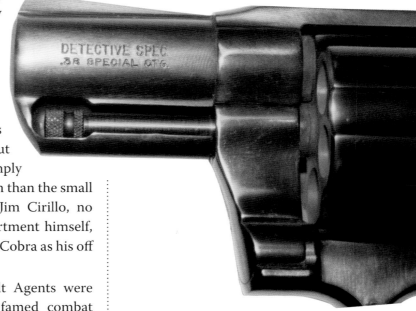

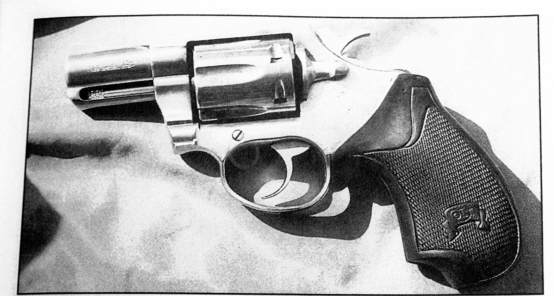

Ayoob believes Colt's top concealment revolver is this DS-II in .38 Special, and would like to see it in .357 Magnum.

"Back in the day," author called for a .357 D-frame in the pages of his *Complete Book of Handguns* …

The Detective Special was widely issued by the military to CID investigators and to senior officers. General George S. Patton carried one on days when he needed to "dress down" from the big ivory-handled sixguns that were his trademark, and General Dwight D. Eisenhower was issued a Detective Special that went with him to Europe in WWII.

If it was good enough for those real heroes, it was good enough for fictional ones; after all, it was called the Detective Special, wasn't it? Humphrey Bogart popped a 2-inch Colt .38 from a hidden dashboard compartment in his coupe to win the day as Philip Marlowe in *The Big Sleep*. Jack Webb, as Sergeant Joe Friday, had a Detective Special for the first season of *Dragnet* in the '50s, though he later switched to a 2-inch S&W M&P. In Richard S. Prather's popular series of Shell Scott private eye novels in the '60s, he armed his title character with a Colt Detective Special, carried in a "clamshell shoulder holster" presumably inspired by the real-life Berns-Martin Lightning shoulder rig. The ultimate comic strip detective, Dick Tracy, carried a post-'72 Detective Special

as a primary weapon for a while, and prior to that was known to stuff a pair of earlier model Colt Agents into twin ankle holsters.

But it was real-life shooters, not fictional characters, who pronounced the DS to be worthy of the "Special" appellation. The reason lay not just in the advantageous size, but in this classic revolver's shooting characteristics.

… and Colt complied with the Magnum Carry, the last of the breed…so far.

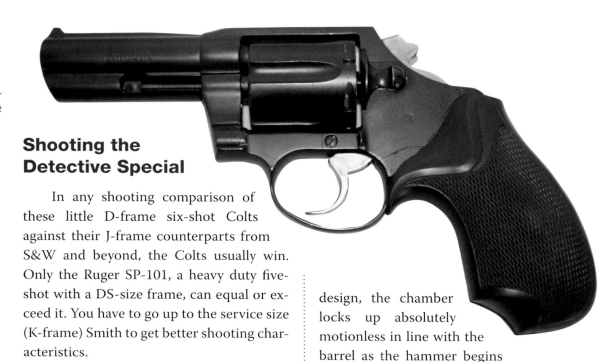

Right: Grant Cunningham tuned this 3-inch Detective Special. Note businesslike bead-blast finish, hammer bobbed in the trademark Cunningham style to retain momentum but avoid snag, and trigger polished glass smooth. Invisible is the superb action job inside. Note reshaped front sight to prevent the glare that was common on the too-steeply ramped sight of the Second Issue guns.

Bottom Left: Used in "reel life." Humphrey Bogart's hand grabs Colt .38 from secret panel in dashboard of his coupe…

Bottom Right: … and prepares to blow away a killer in *The Big Sleep*. Early D-frame snubs had short ejector rods anyway, but this prop gun appears to be missing its ejector rod head.

Shooting the Detective Special

In any shooting comparison of these little D-frame six-shot Colts against their J-frame counterparts from S&W and beyond, the Colts usually win. Only the Ruger SP-101, a heavy duty five-shot with a DS-size frame, can equal or exceed it. You have to go up to the service size (K-frame) Smith to get better shooting characteristics.

There are several reasons for this. First, the Colt has a longer trigger pull, which gives it a lighter double action stroke through simple mechanical advantage. Yes, until the sweet single-stage pulls of the DS-II and Magnum lockwork, the D-frame's V-shaped mainspring would bind or "stack" at the end of the pull, but a master gunsmith could take that out.

Some gunsmiths argue that the Colt mechanism is more fragile than the Smith's. That's debatable. It may go out of time sooner, but thanks to its "double cylinder hand" design, the chamber locks up absolutely motionless in line with the barrel as the hammer begins to fall, and is thus immune to the real-world problems of bad timing until the situation becomes truly hopeless.

By the 1960s, the Colt had better sights: a generous rear notch, and a wide 1/8-inch front. For most of that time the Smith had tiny 1/10-inch front sights with proportionally narrow rear notches, and while these were later improved, the Colt was still better. The flattened, serrated front sight from the mid-fifties through 1972 was the best; the streamlined ramp of the Second Issue was too streamlined, and too smooth. It re-

flected overhead light and "grayed out." Fortunately, gunsmiths like Bill Laughridge at Cylinder & Slide Shop (www.cylinder-slide.com), and Grant Cunningham in the Pacific Northwest (www.grantcunningham.com) can easily and inexpensively alter a post-'72 front sight into something you can see quickly and utilize effectively.

The Colt had a reputation for shooting high left with its fixed sights, particularly in the models between 1972 and 1996. The company advertised that it used lasers to sight in their fixed sight revolvers, and I can only presume that whoever sighted in the laser was cockeyed. Fortunately, it's nothing a pistolsmith can't fix for you, sometimes just with a whack of a lead babbit judiciously applied to the frame.

The D-frame Colt is one of those rare guns like the Browning Hi-Power that came out of the box with the arcane ability to be comfortable in small hand and large hand alike. It has a slightly longer trigger reach than the J-frame Smith. It's easy for hands of many sizes to reach that "sweet spot" at the crease of the distal joint of the trigger finger where that digit has the most leverage to stroke a double action trigger back.

Back in the '70s, I was a young cop on a police pistol team. The game we played was PPC, the old FBI revolver course. There were side events for snubbies called "off duty gun matches." In our part of the country, they were limited to "small frame, fixed sight" guns, defined as the J-frame Smith or the D-frame Colt, and limited to five-shot sequences to be fair to the popular S&W. We tried both…and learned real quick which was the most shootable.

I had the Chief and the DS. Liked 'em both. Shooting them both "over the course," it was no contest. Down in New Jersey, where they limited the belly gun match to 15 yards for fear of crossfires, you could get by with a Chief. But come further north where these events were shot at the 25 yard line, and the Colt would beat the Smith every time in the same shooter's hands. And

Below:
Ayoob finds the Magnum Carry very controllable even one handed, and mourns the passing of Colt's baby .357.

bigger in the grip (except for the Agent) and gave us more to hang onto. As noted, the sights were better. There may have been a smidgeon better inherent accuracy, but that was the least of it.

The D-frame Colt kicked less. A little of this had to do with the weight difference: an all-steel Chief Special Model 36 or 60 weighed 19 ounces, while a Detective Special tipped the scales at 21 ounces in its first incarnation and 23 ounces in the '72-series. Perhaps more important was that the weight distribution of the Colt brought the balance point distinctly more forward. The gun seemed to hang steadier on target, and its muzzle seemed to jump distinctly less.

Stocks? I never cared for the '72-series design. Colt did themselves and the shooters a favor when they went to Pachmayr Compacs on the DS, SF-VI, and DS-II, and Hogues on the Magnum Carry. To us baby boomers, the quintessential Detective Special is the one with the exposed ejector rod and the distinctive grip frame that is narrow at the top and wide but rounded at the bottom. The legendary Skeeter Skelton, in his very first article (*Guns* magazine, back in the '50s I think) talked about snub-nose .38s, and his preference for the DS was clear when you read between the lines. He noted that this particular grip shape was particularly suitable for hanging onto your revolver when the bad guy was trying to wrench it away from you. This was a topic Charlie Skelton had

Above:
The Colt Detective Special (left, in its first form – half-coin front sight, short ejector rod, square butt) owned the snub-nose .38 Special market for nearly a quarter century. Then the Smith & Wesson Chief Special (right, shown with Herrett stocks on square butt frame) took over sales dominance.

in New Hampshire, where for a while the 2-inch guns were shot over the same 60-shot, 7- to 50-yard course as the service revolvers, it was Colt all the way if you wanted a decent score. Later, when 2-1/2-inch and 3-inch K-frames became popular for detectives and off duty work, they of course superseded the 2-inch fixed sight Colts in turn, with the short, adjustable-sight S&W Model 19 becoming the gun of choice for the off duty gun matches.

Why was the Colt so much more shootable? The longer, lighter pull made for much better shooting than did fighting the tight little coil mainspring of the short-stroke J-frame Smith. The Colt was a little some personal street experience with, and when he talked about it, those of us who knew him listened.

In that article (one of the few that he by-lined with his given name of Charles instead of the nickname Skeeter), Skelton showed how to utilize this type of grip shape effectively. By tucking the little finger under the butt, any tendency to roll back in the hand upon recoil was mitigated.

This was particularly important when firing powerful rounds. I agree with Ed Lovette, who notes in his belly gun book that the all-lead +P semiwad-cutter hollowpoint 158-grain (aka "FBI Load," "Chicago Load," and "Metro Load") hits like a .45 hardball round out of a 2-inch barrel .38. The record is clear from decades of intensive use on the streets by police. But that round also has a nasty snap to it. A D-frame Colt, ounce for ounce, absorbs that better for the shooter than a J-frame anything, assuming similar style stocks and shooting techniques.

Speaking of which, the Colts were rated for +P before any of the competition. Back when S&W forbade +P in their aluminum frame Airweights, Colt told shooters to go ahead, and check the gun every few thousand rounds of +P and send it in for a tune-up if they were worried. In all-steel construction, it was no problem at all. The Colt cylinder's bolt cuts were off-set from the chambers, technically allowing for a stronger cylinder.

When the time of the baby Magnums came, this was proven again. S&W's first J-frame .357, the all-steel Model 640-1, was seen to lock up repeatedly with multiple specimens on our ranges when we shot it hot and heavy with full power 125-grain Magnum loads. Colt's equivalent, the all-stainless Magnum Carry, just ran and ran. Back in the '70s, a Colt executive confirmed

Engraved with a long-stemmed rose, replete with Colt Custom Shop action, this '72 series DS is owned by author's ex. It once put six shots into a silhouette target at 100 yards.

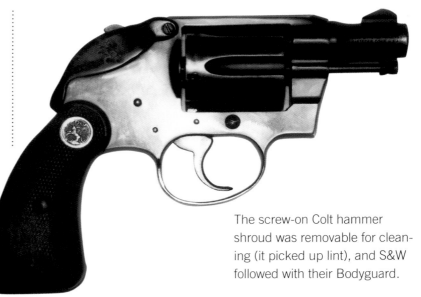

The screw-on Colt hammer shroud was removable for cleaning (it picked up lint), and S&W followed with their Bodyguard.

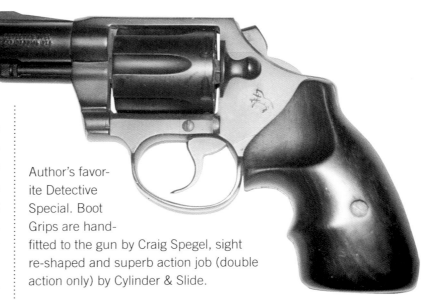

Author's favorite Detective Special. Boot Grips are hand-fitted to the gun by Craig Spegel, sight re-shaped and superb action job (double action only) by Cylinder & Slide.

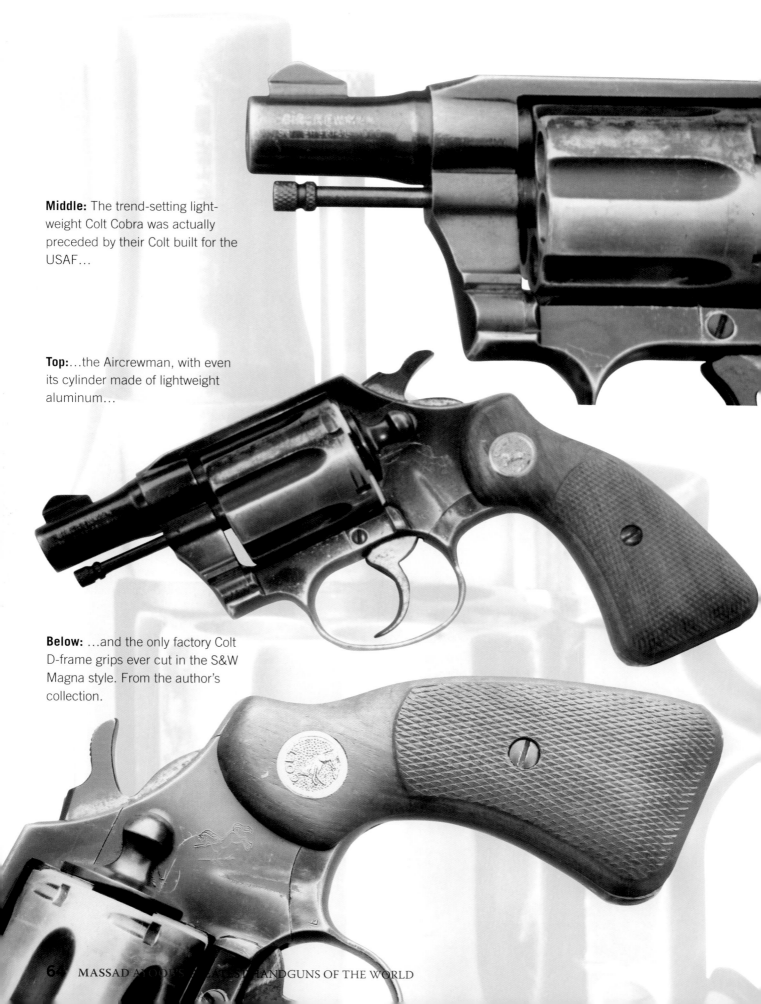

Middle: The trend-setting lightweight Colt Cobra was actually preceded by their Colt built for the USAF…

Top: …the Aircrewman, with even its cylinder made of lightweight aluminum…

Below: …and the only factory Colt D-frame grips ever cut in the S&W Magna style. From the author's collection.

what contemporary gun writer Jac Weller had written: they had indeed bored out Detective Specials to .357 Magnum and found that they'd go 5,000 rounds without a problem. They just hadn't produced the gun because they didn't think anyone could handle the brutal recoil back then.

The Detective Special and its cousins, including the finely finished Diamondback target variation with adjustable sights, are at their best with a custom action. Cunningham and Laughridge, cited above, would be my choices. There are a whole lot of folks who can do a fine S&W action job for you, and not a lot who know the arcane secrets of the more complex Colt mechanism. These guys do.

Personal Experience

My dad was a Colt man. The first handgun I ever fired was his ancient New Police .32, the predecessor of the Police Positive. I carried a gun when working in his jewelry store from the age of 12. In the early '60s, he bought me a 2-inch Cobra which we fit-

Top: The Viper, a '72 series Cobra with 4-inch barrel, is one of the rarer modern Colts.

Middle: The briefly-produced Colt Courier was produced in .22 LR (shown) and .32 Long…

Bottom: …and is desired much more by collectors now, than by users then, in the mid-1950s. This one is from the Dorothy Ayoob collection.

ted with a hammer shroud. Only trouble was, he liked it so much it soon became his gun instead of mine. That wasn't as bad as it could have been, since by then I had a 1911 under my jacket, but on hot days I still wanted a belly gun. At age 16 or so I traded my flat-top Ruger Blackhawk .44 Magnum for a Smith Bodyguard Airweight, a swap for which I kick myself to this day. The flat-top had a three digit serial number. But, I digress....

Dad gave me a Chief Special Model 36 for my 21st birthday, and I used that as my belly gun for a while, but shortly after I was married Colt announced the '72 series DS and I bought one. It supplanted the Chief on days when I figured a snubnose .38 was enough to carry. Later, I used it a lot as a backup gun. During the period when I carried a Smith & Wesson K-frame .357 Magnum as a police duty revolver, my backup was always a D-frame Colt, usually a DS or an Agent. The cylinder diameters were the same, and they would take the same HKS speedloaders. I filled the latter with .38 hot loads, either the FBI stuff or +P+, on the theory that if my service revolver was destroyed, lost, empty, or snatched, I still had 18 rounds with which to fight.

My wife became a Colt fan. I put together a hammer-shrouded Agent with Barami hip-grip that rode nicely inside the waistband of her slacks under an untucked blouse in summer. In winter, she preferred the solid Detective Special in shoulder holster or carcoat pocket. I sent one down to the Colt Custom Shop, which did an absolutely primo action tune on it. Then, I brought it to an engraver whose work at a gun show seemed good enough. I told him to cut in a long-stemmed rose, and inscribe "To Dot from Mas."

Right: Colt advertising emphasized "the all important sixth shot." HKS speedloader for S&W K-frame service revolver would fit this D-frame Colt if carried as a backup gun.

I wrote it in block capitals so there'd be no misspellings.

Unfortunately, we didn't know each other, and he figured M-A-S had to be initials. Thus, it came out reading, "To Dot From MAS". We left it that way. Well, hell, you can't grow back the steel....

She showed the gun to one of her friends one day. The friend saw my name in all caps and said sympathetically to Dot, "God, your husband *is* arrogant, isn't he?"

Notes

[1]Schwing, Ned, 2003 *Standard Catalog of Firearms*, Iola, WI: Krause Publications, 2002, P. 299.

Colt's Official Police

I n its day, the Colt Official Police was aptly named. It so dominated the market that it really was almost the official standard. Ahead of its time in some ways, it would be copied in those respects after its demise, and that very demise would leave lessons to future captains of the firearms industry.

Once America's most popular service revolver, the O.P. set trends, taught lessons, and left legacies before it faded into obscurity.

Pedigree

Some loved this revolver, and some hated it. Colt versus Smith & Wesson was one of the classic product battles of 20th century marketing, like Coke versus Pepsi and Ford versus General Motors. There were vocal partisans on both sides.

Col. Charles Askins, Jr., 1951: "This revolver is a real peach! The gun is used by more police departments than any other Colt and the splendid

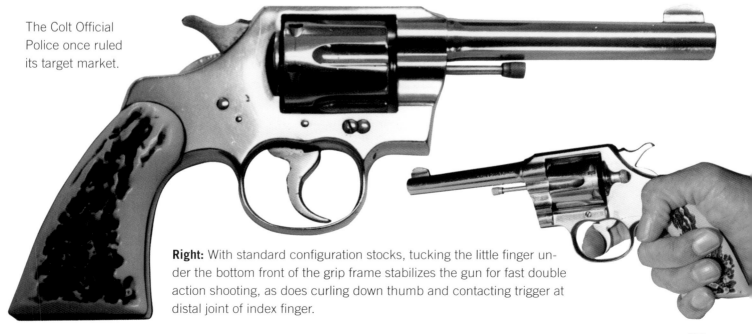

The Colt Official Police once ruled its target market.

Right: With standard configuration stocks, tucking the little finger under the bottom front of the grip frame stabilizes the gun for fast double action shooting, as does curling down thumb and contacting trigger at distal joint of index finger.

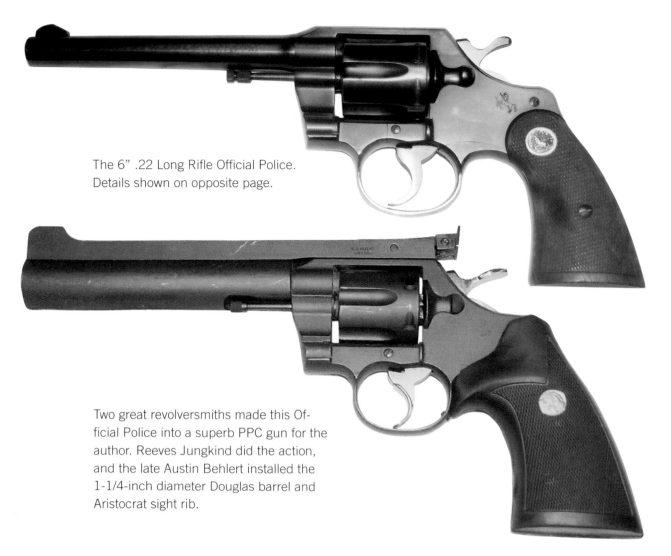

The 6" .22 Long Rifle Official Police. Details shown on opposite page.

Two great revolversmiths made this Official Police into a superb PPC gun for the author. Reeves Jungkind did the action, and the late Austin Behlert installed the 1-1/4-inch diameter Douglas barrel and Aristocrat sight rib.

reputation which it enjoys 'mongst law enforcement people is well deserved. Despite the fact that it is made as a service arm and not as a highly refined model for target panning, the Official Police will be found to have a clean quick-breaking trigger pull and a double action which is smooth and fast. Best length of barrel is 5 inches for all purposes."[1] Askins had been in a shootout with the O.P.'s predecessor, the Colt Army Special, and wrote about it much later. As a six-gun-packing youngster, he had run off with a gallon of a moonshiner's liquor, and the latter had chased him with double-ought buckshot. Wrote Charlie, "...I turned on Wild Hoss who was nicely silhouetted in the light of the open door and just in the act of cutting loose with the second barrel of his

old LeFever. I triggered off six shots from the Army Special and my intent was to kill him on the spot. However, what with poor light, and the distance, which was about 40 yards, I missed him."[2] It was just as well; had his shots struck home, one of the great lawmen and gun writers might instead have spent his life in prison.

Chic Gaylord, 1960: "As a personal defense weapon, Colt's Official Police with a four-inch barrel is as dependable a gun as you could find...The Colt Official Police revolver in .38 Special caliber with a four-inch barrel and rounded butt is an ideal service weapon for densely populated metropolitan areas. The Colt Official Police is probably the most famous police service arm in the world. It is rugged, dependable, and thoroughly tested by time. It has good sights and a smooth trouble-free action. This gun can fire high-speed armor-piercing loads. It can safely handle hand loads that would turn its competitors into flying shards of steel. When loaded with the Winchester Western 200-grain Super Police loads, it is an effective man-stopper."[3] In his *Handgunner's Guide*, we find the note, "Colt Official Police 4 inch barrel – round butt. The best designed of the .38 caliber Service weapons – the round butt enables it to be carried both in uniform and plainclothes."[4] The comment is in the form of a caption for a photo of what is clearly a Colt Marshal revolver. A mistake...unless you consider that the Colt Marshal was a round butt Colt Official Police, otherwise distinguished only by the different name on the barrel.

Henry M. Stebbins, 1961: "...it's a rugged gun with enough weight for good shooting, qualities that have made it so popular with law officers."[5] Stebbins' *Pistols: A Mod-*

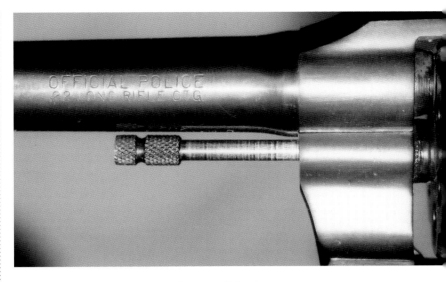

ern Encyclopedia contained one of the best and most cogently reasoned Colt-versus-Smith & Wesson discussions to ever appear in print. He agreed with Gaylord that the Colt Official Police was a stronger gun than its analog, the Smith & Wesson Military & Police.[6]

But not everyone loved the O.P. Elmer Keith, 1955: "With the adoption of the front

Cylinder of the uncommon .22 Official Police is identical to that of the Officer's Model Target in the same caliber.

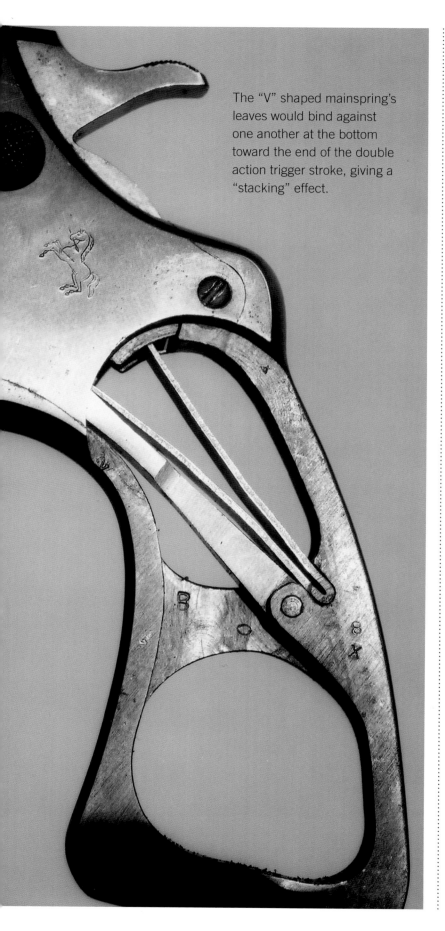

The "V" shaped mainspring's leaves would bind against one another at the bottom toward the end of the double action trigger stroke, giving a "stacking" effect.

cylinder latch on all Smith & Wesson solid frame cylinder guns, the firm forged ahead of Colt and in this respect are today superior in their cylinder locking arrangement to double action swing-cylinder Colts."[7] Keith also noted that double action Colts of more recent manufacture had "a pull that seems to increase the farther back the trigger is pulled, and this, combined with the lack of sufficient hump at the top of the grip, is not conducive to top double action shooting, on our part at least. There is no comparison between the smooth, effortless, pull of the Smith & Wesson double action as compared to the Colts, and the Smith & Wesson grip fitted our hands much the better of the two. The more pronounced hump at the top of the Smith & Wesson grip kept the gun from climbing or crawling in my hand. Many times with Colt's D.A. guns, I found before the gun was empty, that it had crawled low enough in my hand so that the hammer spur was striking the web between the first finger and thumb."[8]

A Brief History

In 1889, Colt got the jump on Smith & Wesson with the first double action revolver that had a swing-out cylinder. It combined the reloading speed of a top-break revolver with the strength of a solid frame. It was followed in 1892 by the New Army and Navy. The first gun had been chambered for .38 Colt and .41 Colt, the latter for both of those plus .32-20 and .38 S&W. In the same year Colt began making small frame pocket .32s in the same style. The four-inch square butt .32, the New Police, would be selected by Police Commissioner Theodore Roosevelt to become the first standard issue service revolver of the New York City Police Department.

S&W retaliated with their Hand Ejector series. Seeing a demand for a more powerful

.38 caliber cartridge, S&W introduced the .38 Special circa 1902. Colt resisted the urge to chamber for what they must have seen as a cartridge proprietary to their competitor, but the .38 Special proved so popular that they had no choice.

The resultant gun was the Army Special, introduced by Colt in 1908. Built on a substantial .41 caliber frame – and in fact chambered for the .41 Colt cartridge, as well as the .38 Special and .32-20 – it was a heavier and more robust-seeming gun than the graceful Smith & Wesson K-frame, which was built on a true .38 frame.

Colt also restyled and streamlined this revolver. Guns like the Navy Model and the New Police had trigger guards that looked like afterthoughts, and cheap, insubstantial looking square cylinder latches. The restyling, also applied to the large frame New Service and the small frame gun now called the Police Positive, and Police Positive Special in .38 Special, included a trigger guard that flowed into the frame in one seamless and handsome line, and a much more attractive and stronger-looking rounded cylinder latch. The lockwork, however, was little changed from the guns of the Gay Nineties.

Sales went well. In 1927, Colt apparently realized that the name "Army Special" was incongruous to a revolver sold primarily to the police, not the military. They changed the name to Official Police.

During World War II, Colt produced this revolver with brown plastic grips and a Parkerized finish for the war effort, dubbing the wartime model the Colt Commando. It was purchased by the US Government in much smaller quantity than the analogous Smith & Wesson Victory Model. Most of the Commando revolvers seem to have gone to security personnel at war materiel plants. An estimated 50,000 of these guns were built during WWII. By contrast, more than ten times that many S&W Victory Models

Top: Two of the uncommon 2-inch Colt Official Police barrels. Prewar model has "Official" and "Police" on two lines, sports round "half coin" shaped front sight…

Bottom: …while postwar version differs with "Official Police" in one line, and semi-ramped front sight. Note also different configuration of ejector rod head.

were manufactured just for Great Britain (in caliber .38/200, a.k.a. .38 S&W), and almost a quarter million .38 Special Victory Models were made for US forces.

By the war's conclusion, Colt's longtime dramatic lead over S&W in police sales was coming to an end. A generation of WWII vets were coming back to America's police departments, many of them appreciatively familiar with the Smith & Wesson Military & Police in its Victory Model format, standard issue for many Navy personnel and for fliers such as future President George H. W. Bush, who had a Smith & Wesson .38 in his shoulder holster when he parachuted from his stricken warplane in the Pacific.

In his 1950 book *The Secrets of Double Action Shooting*, Bob Nichols slammed the Colt and extolled the Smith & Wesson, particularly the old long action design that S&W had just cashiered in favor of the short action redesign that continues today. He

Three generations of Official Police. Top, early model with gutta percha Colt grips and round front sight. Center, postwar model has partially ramped front sight, slimmer and more ergonomic hammer spur, Colt target stocks not yet cut for speedloaders. Below, late production 4-inch O.P. w/Pachmayr aftermarket grips.

noted that Colt was far and away the most popular service revolver in America, which he felt was an injustice both to the cops and to the Smith & Wesson Military & Police.

The cops were starting to agree. Before, most police firearms training had involved single action bulls-eye shooting. This had favored the Colt revolver, whose mechanism allowed easier and faster thumb cocking. But now, influenced by more modern training, cops were going to reality-based double action combat shooting. The shorter, more straight-through trigger pull, as well as the grip shape, favored the Smith & Wesson. Elmer Keith said it in the above quote, and the cops saw and felt it.

S&W had moved into a new plant not long after the war; Colt had not. S&W made

a point of putting gun people at the helm of their company; Colt had already begun to put generic executives there. A rising young upstart in the handgun industry during that period named William B. Ruger knew many of the Colt execs of the time, and he once said that most of them would rather play golf than do anything gun-related.

The S&W revolvers of the 1950s and '60s were gorgeous things, exquisite of finish and smooth of action. They also, for the first time, began to undersell the Colt in list price as well as police department bid price. Colt's price had not only gone past their arch-competitor's, but as Keith noted above, by 1955 the once hand-honed Colt actions had become a poor second to Smith's. There had been other production economies. As early as 1940, Colt had started putting a matte finish on the top of the guns, and did so more aggressively in the '50s. It was obviously a cost-cutting measure (to save polishing), and the market saw it as a cheapening of the product. Ditto the Colt adoption in the Forties and Fifties of plastic grips, which they grandiosely called "Coltwood." The company eventually backpedaled from these poor decisions, but much of the damage to their image could not be undone.

As if that was not enough, Colt's management and marketing people insulted the collective intelligence of their loyal customers. Removing checkered walnut parts inset with gold medallions, replacing them with cheap plastic, and calling the result "(Your company's name here)-wood" is not a marketing plan likely to fool educated consumers. Colt tried to pass off the matted parts of the finish as non-glaring surfaces that wouldn't interfere with a shooter's sight picture. The market replied collectively, "Really? But if you had ever fired your own product, you would know that the top of the revolver is not visible to the shooter's eye when he has a sight picture. And how do you explain the matte finish on the underside of the frame…?"

The Fabulous Fifties ended with Smith & Wesson the leading producer of police service revolvers, a position they would continue to hold until the market's much later sea-change to the semiautomatic pistol. By 1961, the Colt Official Police would carry a suggested retail of $77.50, while the S&W M&P, now known as the Model 10, sold for $65. The handwriting was on the wall.

Colt discontinued the Official Police in 1969. They replaced it with the Mark III series of "modernized" revolvers, (which is another story in itself), and they also went the way of the dodo bird. In 1980, S&W introduced their L-frame series of new and improved heavy-duty police revolvers in .357 Magnum. They mimicked exactly the cylinder and frame dimensions of the Colt Official Police.

Smith & Wesson continues to produce the Military & Police .38 Special, announcing a new two-piece barrel system for it in the year 2005. Concurrent with that change, they announced that their popular K-frame .357 Combat Magnum would be discontinued, replaced with a seven-shot .357 revolver on the L-frame. The frame and cylinder are, again, almost exactly the dimensions of the Official Police.

Shooting the Colt Official Police

Inherently just a tad more accurate than the S&W because of its double cylinder hand locking mechanism, the Colt had a longer pull but a proportionally lighter one due to its longer throw, which gave the lockwork more "mechanical advantage." An early Army Special or Official Police, perhaps assembled at a time when Colt's skilled workers put only a few guns a day together, is the equal of any DA revolver

pull. Those of the '40s and on, unless they have received the ministrations of a skilled armorer or gunsmith, are more likely to exhibit a two-stage pull with considerable "stack" toward the end of the firing stroke. This is because the 1892 mechanism's double leaf mainspring system binds against itself at this crucial point.

Unprotected ejector rod was seen by some critics as a weak spot in the design.

Matte finish on bottom and, seen here, top of frame, was seen by the market as a cheapening of the product.

An excellent specimen of the extremely rare 2-inch Colt Marshal, from the Dorothy Ayoob collection.

Right: Note extra touches like knurling on the cylinder latch in this prewar Colt O.P., fitted later with aftermarket grips. Short barrel emphasizes the beefy ruggedness of .41 frame and cylinder.

If you have an Official Police that's a "shooter" instead of a collector's item, consider sending it to Grant Cunningham (www.grantcunningham.com). His fine work harkens back to the great Colt masterpieces of Reeves Jungkind, Jerry Moran, and Fred Sadowski. To shoot it as is, you might benefit from using a two-stage double action trigger pull. Roll the trigger back until you feel resistance, and then finish the press. In effect, you're trigger-cocking the gun.

Whatever caliber you have, your Colt is amply strong to handle it. As soon as S&W came out with their hot .38/44 round – the predecessor of the .357 Magnum, and the early version of today's +P – the Colt Company said that the gun would handle it. Still, it's always best to restrict modern +P and +P+ loadings to the O.P.s made in the Fifties or later. Most, of course, are .38 Specials. The .41 Colt and .32-20 chamberings did not survive past WWII. Interestingly, the .22 LR chambering did. Introduced in 1930 as a "training gun" for the .38 Special service revolver, the .22 caliber Official Police is something of a collector's item today, since so few were sold. Ditto the rare .38 S&W version, sometimes marked .38/200, produced for export to British Commonwealth countries.

Take heed of Keith's remarks about that low "hump" at the back of the grip. None of the calibers for which the Official Police was chambered recoil much, but you still want stocks you can hang on to. For modern shooting, you can't beat the Hogue Monogrip in my opinion; the Python size fits the O.P. For something more period correct, try an old pair of Pachmayr Presentation grips or even older Mershons.

These guns are often encountered with the target style grips of the Python and Officer's Model Match, which were erroneously considered combat grips "back in the day." They feel better in dry fire than the typical wooden "splinter grips," but still roll up in the hand when fired rapidly with hot rounds.

Particularly collectible are the round butt O.P.s Gaylord spoke of. Only some 2500 of the Colt Marshals were made, circa 1955-56, mostly with 4-inch barrels but a few with 2-inchers. However, I know for a fact that this configuration was produced earlier in the Official Police line. I bought for my then-wife's collection one of six or seven numbered 2-inch, round butt Official Police revolvers made for a Maine police department in 1941. In my own collection is a round-butt 4-incher with barrel marked Official Police, which tracks back to a special order by NYPD in the mid-'50s. NYPD by then did not issue revolvers, but bought Colts and Smiths in large quantities and let the recruits buy their choice from the department at reduced prices. That particular round butt O.P. is concurrent with Marshal production. Why not just order Colt Marshals? Probably because, in a large bureaucracy, it's harder to change a policy that says "Only Colt Official Police and Smith & Wes-

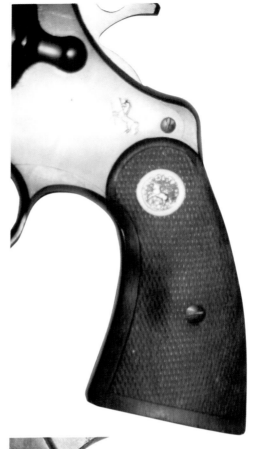

Square butt checkered walnut with inset Colt medallion was the most common factory grip for the Official Police…

…and this is the factory round butt frame and stock configuration, beloved by Gaylord and prized by collectors.

Right: This 4-inch O.P. is part of a run built for NYPD in the mid-'50s with round butt grip frame, large 1/8-inch sights. NYPD demanded blue finish, and hard chrome on this one was applied aftermarket by its owner after he retired from the force.

son Military & Police are approved" than it is to tell a gun manufacturer, "Put four-inch Official Police barrels on the round butt Marshal frames for us, and we'll buy a bunch of them."

As did S&W, Colt made their fixed sights more visible over the years. Those mid-Fifties Marshals and O.P.s, and subsequent O.P.s, had excellent 1/8-inch wide fronts and proportionally large rear sight grooves that gave the best sight pictures of the Official Police series.

Many if not most Army Specials, and some early specimens of the Official Police, will be encountered with "hard rubber" Colt grips. If you're going to shoot the gun, take these off gently and set them aside. When they age, they tend to crack and chip. Put some modern furniture on the gun for shooting.

One complaint against the Colt was that its ejector rod was thin and exposed, while the Smith's was thicker and supported by the front lug milled out of the barrel. The rod

actually was most often bent by pistol-whipping a bad guy, which is out of style these days to say the least. Colt certainly could have gotten more sales if they had protectively enclosed the O.P.'s ejector rod a'la' the Smith & Wesson Magnum style, and Colt's own Python and later Trooper Mark III. That said, the vulnerability of the naked ejector rod is not something to stay up nights worrying over.

Some will tell you that you can't pull back the cylinder latch on a Colt as fast as you can push forward the one on a Smith. That's bunk. Just catch the Colt latch with the inside edge of your right thumb – by the side of your thumb, not the tip – and you'll get a faster, more effortless release than you can

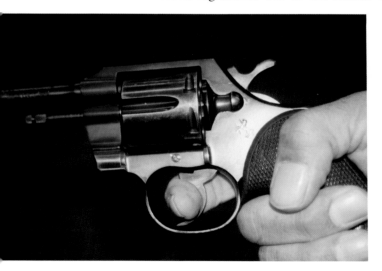

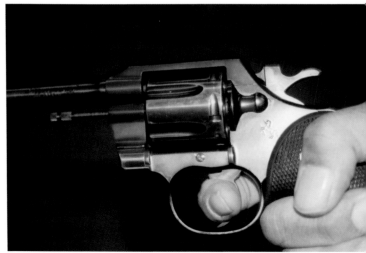

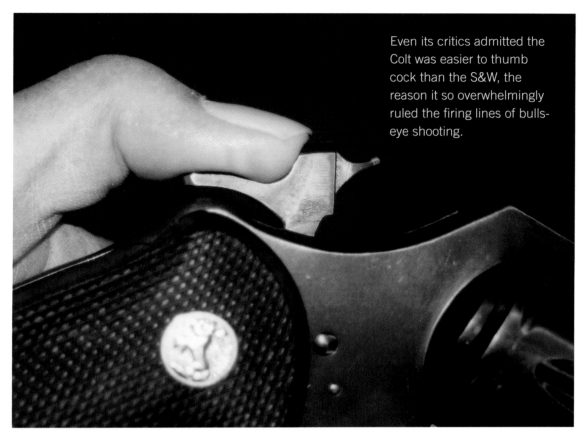

Even its critics admitted the Colt was easier to thumb cock than the S&W, the reason it so overwhelmingly ruled the firing lines of bullseye shooting.

Bottom Left to Right:

1. The controversial double action trigger pull of the Colt. Here, Official Police mechanism begins at rest…

2. …long DA pull is underway here, with hammer beginning to rise and cylinder slowly rolling clockwise…

3. …mainspring leaves are now in contact with each other, creating more resistant pull; in a two-stage Colt trigger pull, this is the second stage. Hammer is almost ready to fall, but note that cylinder doesn't come into perfect alignment…

4. …until hammer begins to fall, and second cylinder hand rises to ratchet and locks cylinder rigidly into line with barrel.

get with any other make. If you're a lefty, use the tip of your index finger. It's still faster and easier than a Smith or a Ruger.

If you're a fan of old movies, you'll see the O.P. often. It was, after all, the dominant police revolver during Hollywood's golden period. The gun the cop fires at James Stewart in *It's a Wonderful Life* is an Official Police. The gun worn on the left hip, complementing a 1911 .45 auto on the right, by Lee Marvin in

The Professionals appears to be a Colt Army Special, correct to the period. When Henry Fonda and Tyrone Power played Frank and Jesse James early in their careers, they used time-proper Colt percussion and Frontier revolvers, but on the movie poster one wielded a Colt Official Police and the other, a Smith M&P. In the first *Cape Fear*, Gregory Peck protected his family by shooting Robert Mitchum with an Official Police. Humphrey

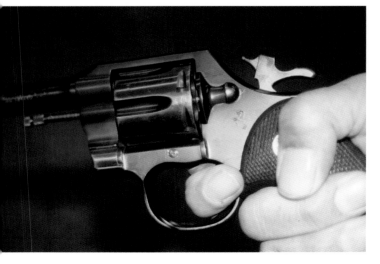

One secret of the Colt's superior accuracy. Here, with hammer cocked, the second cylinder hand (arrow) is only poised for its final movement…

…but as trigger is pulled and hammer falls, it rises to lock cylinder immobile, creating perfect alignment of chamber and barrel if gun is in proper tune.

Bogart used Colts throughout his career in preference to other guns: a Detective Special in *The Maltese Falcon*, a Pocket Model auto in *Casablanca* and *Key Largo*, and a 1911 in *High Sierra*. However, he was also often filmed holding an Official Police. Bogey and his whole gold rush crew were armed with O.P.s in *The Treasure of Sierra Madre*, and if memory serves, he also wielded that model in *The Petrified Forest* and *The Desperate Hours*, among others. In the original 1933 *King Kong*, at least one of the adventurers fires a Colt Official Police at an attacking brontosaurus, only to discover before Robert Ruark that it's necessary to "Use Enough Gun." As for TV, the O.P. was the official sidearm of Robert Stack and his entire squad of Untouchables, but try not to dwell on the fact that quintessential dumb cop Barney Fife carried an Official Police, too.

But know that the Colt Official Police is far richer in its genuine history, given the time it served "on the street" as the dominant American police handgun. It was involved in some notorious incidents. Mark David Chapman was looking down the barrel of a 4-inch Colt Official Police .38 in the hands of a New York cop when he was arrested for the murder of John Lennon. These revolvers touched the lives of Presidents. One of the would-be assassins who tried to kill Harry Truman at Blair House was cut down by a guardian's Official Police. The gun found in the dead hand of Bill Clinton appointee Vincent Foster was a 4-inch Colt Army Special.

Personal Experience

In my early teens, I had a mint Army Special 6-inch with checkered walnut grips. It was made "the old way," and I was permanently imprinted with an appreciation of what Colt craftsmanship could be. I owned many of these guns over the years. My wife liked Colts, and I helped her build

a primo collection of Official Police and Marshal rarities. Toward the end of my PPC competition days, I sent a run of the mill Official Police .38 to Austin Behlert, the man who pioneered the heavy barrel "PPC gun" concept. He installed a 1-1/4-inch diameter Douglas barrel with an Aristocrat sight rib. Then the six-gun went to Reeves Jungkind, the past master of Python actions; except for its hammer-mounted firing pin, the O.P.'s action was one with the Python's. The gorgeous result was probably the finest PPC competition revolver I ever owned.

The Colt Mark III superseded the Official Police as a service revolver, but did not prove terribly popular. This is the Trooper .357 variation with 6-inch barrel.

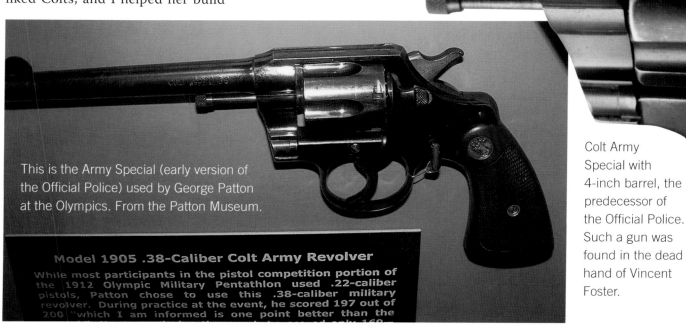

This is the Army Special (early version of the Official Police) used by George Patton at the Olympics. From the Patton Museum.

Model 1905 .38-Caliber Colt Army Revolver
While most participants in the pistol competition portion of the 1912 Olympic Military Pentathlon used .22-caliber pistols, Patton chose to use this .38-caliber military revolver. During practice at the event, he scored 197 out of 200 "which I am informed is one point better than the

Colt Army Special with 4-inch barrel, the predecessor of the Official Police. Such a gun was found in the dead hand of Vincent Foster.

As a kid, I was aware of guns, and noticed that most of the cops had Official Police .38s. Those in the capitol city where I lived, and in the state's largest city, and in the next largest community. Over the years, I watched that change until the S&W had become dominant. Spending my adult life in the firearms industry, I realized that I had been a young witness to the first symptoms of Colt's decline.

Built on what Colt called the I-frame, this .41-size revolver set the stage for the Ruger GP-100 and the Smith & Wesson L-frame that superseded it in the last days of the revolver's dominance in the American police service, guns which are still the most popular .357 Magnums today. The O.P. showed early that a stronger handgun that can stand more power is a good thing, a lesson that some other companies had to re-learn very expensively in times to come. And, in its plunge from the dominant product to discontinuance, the Colt Official Police wrote a stark lesson to the firearms in-

This is the "low hump" at upper backstrap to which Elmer Keith objected.

dustry to listen to its customers, keep its prices consistent with value, and not insult the intelligence of the end users who keep them in business.

That, in the end, is a far more valuable legacy than an old poster of Humphrey Bogart holding a Colt Official Police in the movie *Dark Passage*.

Notes

[1] Askins, Lt. Col. Charles Jr., *The Pistol Shooter's Book*, Harrisburg, PA: Stackpole, 1953, pp. 29-30.

[2] Askins, Col. Charles Jr., *Unrepentant Sinner*, San Antonio, TX: Tejano Publications, 1985, pp. 11-12.

[3] Gaylord, Chic, *Handgunner's Guide*, New York City: Hastings House, 1960, pp. 37 and 40.

[4] *Ibid.*, p. 42.

[5] Stebbins, Henry M., *Pistols: A Modern Encyclopedia*, Harrisburg, PA: Stackpole, 1961, p. 34.

[6] *Ibid.*, pp. 43-44.

[7] Keith, Elmer, *Sixguns by Keith*, New York City: Bonanza Books, 1955, pp. 38-39.

[8] *Ibid.*, pp.138-139.

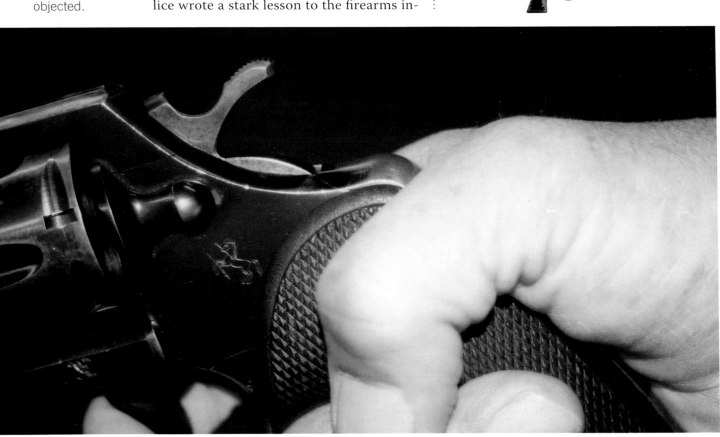

The Colt Python

There were few more iconic handguns in the latter half of the 20th century than Colt's Python. The grand old company never lavished more care on a standard catalog handgun. The Python had it all: distinctive looks, "sex appeal" (to whatever degree that term can be applied to inanimate objects, let alone firearms), and – more to the point – performance.

Pedigree

According to firearms historian Larry Wilson, "H.M. (His Majesty) Hussein I of Jordan ordered a limited number of Pythons, in 4-inch and 6-inch barrels, as gifts to his selected friends. Casing and barrel were em-

Famous for its distinctive profile and top-flight craftsmanship, the flagship of the Colt fleet also incorporated unique performance-enhancing engineering innovations.

The prestigious Python lends itself to fine engraving. This one is from the collection of Brad Lewis.

The facial expression indicates the author's satisfaction with the size of his 25-yard group. This is why a snub-nose Colt Python is worth the money.

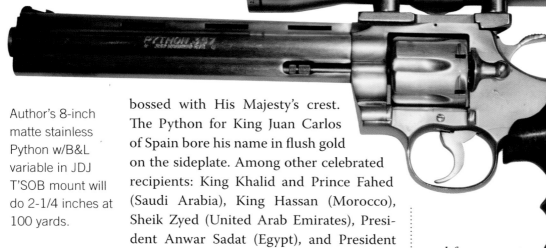

Author's 8-inch matte stainless Python w/B&L variable in JDJ T'SOB mount will do 2-1/4 inches at 100 yards.

bossed with His Majesty's crest. The Python for King Juan Carlos of Spain bore his name in flush gold on the sideplate. Among other celebrated recipients: King Khalid and Prince Fahed (Saudi Arabia), King Hassan (Morocco), Sheik Zyed (United Arab Emirates), President Anwar Sadat (Egypt), and President Hafez Assad (Syria)."[1]

Elvis Presley, a gun collector, loved Pythons. Actor David Soul used a 4-inch Python to outshoot Dirty Harry for the department championship in *Magnum Force*, a film that caused a brief spurt of Python popularity in the marketplace, and a 6-inch version as the character Hutch on TV's *Starsky and Hutch*. In the real world, Paul B. Weston, ace handgun expert of the NYPD, often used the Python in matches. He sang its praises, calling its famously smooth mechanism "a friction-free environment." Bill Jordan, well known for his preference for Smith & Wessons, owned and liked the 4-inchPython. Reeves Jungkind, pistolsmith and Texas state trooper, won numerous police combat championships with the Pythons he tuned, as did many of his customers.

A Brief History

From the beginning, reviewers called it the "Rolls-Royce of handguns," though official Colt historian Larry Wilson was a little more reserved and said, "The Python is the Rolls-Royce of Colt revolvers."[2]

In the 1953-54 *Gun Guide*, General Julian Hatcher predicted, perhaps unknowingly, this forthcoming evolution in double action Colt revolvers. "From time to time and from year to year, changes and improvements have been made in the (Colt) Officers Model target revolver," he wrote. "Some of these are minor improvements, due to new processes of manufacture or new materials available; but the major model changes have usually been the result of suggestions made to the company's experts by outstanding target shots."[3]

The firm had noticed that many serious shooters slung lead weights or welding rod under the barrels of their target revolvers to add stabilizing weight, and that King's Gun Works had made a cottage industry of installing ventilated ribs on top with target sights. Both features would be added. A re-designed mechanism done originally for the service style "Three-Fifty-Seven" revolver announced in 1954 would be integrated into the new gun, featuring a flat-faced hammer and a spring-loaded firing pin that "floated" in the frame. It would have the most deluxe finish Colt could put on a handgun, the lustrous Royal Blue.

When factory insiders gave me the scoop on the Python, they said the key to its fabulous finish was in the polishing operation, not the bluing tanks. The most skilled polishers were put to work on the Pythons

in a process that finished with 400 grit emery, which they described as roughly the texture of talcum powder. The polish showed up better on blue guns than nickel, and even better on bright stainless, such as the Python Ultimate and the exquisite limited run Double Diamond.

Almost as an afterthought, it was decided to chamber the Python for .357 Magnum. Demand for that round seemed heavy, and after all, the gun would be perfectly accurate with the shorter, milder .38 Special target ammo they expected most customers to use in it. A contest was held within the factory to name the new entry. Colt's Cobra, the first aluminum frame .38 snubnose, had

Below: Author test-drives a Grant Cunningham-tuned Python in the rare 3-inch length, from Cunningham's "private stock."

Nowhere is the topflight Colt polish job more evident than on the Double Diamond version of the Python. The camera does not do justice to this one, from the Brad Lewis collection.

been a best seller since its introduction five years before. Perhaps thinking serpentine names were lucky, the firm chose the entry of an employee whose identity seems to have since been lost to firearms history. The name was "Python."

The gun was an instant hit. While dedicated target sixgunners like Weston flocked to it, the Python had the misfortune to arrive just before the bulls-eye shooters switched *en masse* to autoloaders for the centerfire events where the .38 revolver had previously ruled. But if this market was foreclosed by changing tastes, others opened invitingly. The police saw it as a prestige service revolver, and their clamoring for a 4-inch version was soon answered. The Python had first been offered with 6-inch barrel only. Meanwhile, police combat revolver combat competition was about to start up, and the Python was virtually made for it, with the heaviest barrel then available giving more

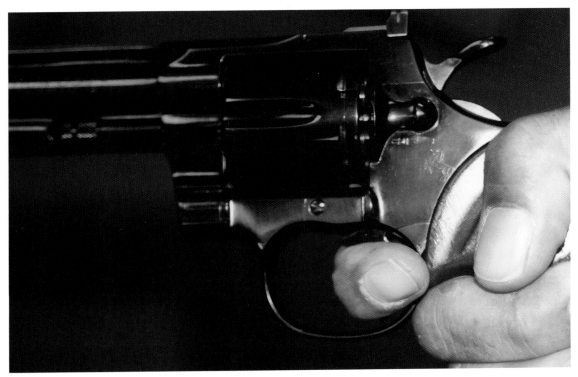

Left: The smooth trigger pull of the Python, particularly when customized by a master, gets "oohs" and "aahs" from people who try it for the first time.

Below: Flat-face hammer and floating firing pin were Python advantages from the beginning, and ahead of their time. They actually appeared first on the "357" model.

up-front weight to steady the gun against the double action pull demanded by the rules for more than half of the PPC sequence. Finally, people who loved guns were instantly taken by the obvious quality, superb workmanship, and unique appearance evinced by the Python. Despite a price tag of $125 at introduction, the guns sold as fast as Colt could produce them. In 1955, the highest priced prestige revolver on the market before the Python was S&W's big .357 Magnum, later to be designated the Model 27, which then sold for $110.

A nickel finish was soon added, and much later, the Python was offered in stainless. A small number were produced chambered for .38 Special. The market for the Python in that caliber was bifurcated. Some went to police officers who could buy their own guns but couldn't have a caliber more powerful than .38 Special. Some went to target shooters who were certain that a .38 Special chamber delivered more accuracy than a longer .357 chamber firing .38 ammo, a hypothesis that has never quite been proven or disproven since. At least one Python

Intended originally to be the *ne plus ultra* of target .38s, the Python turned out to be one of the all-time great .357 Magnums. 6-inch barrel, shown, was original and longest-produced variation. This is one of the author's, with double action only Moran tune, Magna-Port, and hardwood Hogue stocks.

each were made experimentally in .256 Winchester Magnum and .41 Magnum, but neither ever left the factory. I saw them both in Colt's so-called "black museum" in the late 1970s. (A series of Pythons gunsmith-converted to .41 Mag and re-marked in the factory style caused consternation over the years, as some unscrupulous vendors claimed them to have been factory made in that caliber.)

A 2-1/2-inch barrel version was introduced later, though it never sold well; the stubby tube seemed incongruous on the large .41-size frame. Colt had more success later when they offered an 8-inch barrel aimed at the handgun hunter market. Rarest of all was the special-run 3-inch barrel. There are rumors of a 5-inch Python, but I've never seen documentation of one leaving the Colt factory.

While it was a mark of prestige to carry one's own Python on duty, few police departments could justify its high cost when revolvers were usually bought on bid. Still,

there were exceptions. The Colorado Highway Patrol issued 4-inch blue Pythons to all troopers until their switch to the S&W .40 caliber autoloader. Georgia State Patrol and Florida Highway Patrol at various times bought small quantities of Pythons, but the deluxe Colts were never standard issue agency-wide for either. Both, like Colorado, have since adopted semiautos, the Glock for GSP and the Beretta for FHP, which at this writing is testing to determine its next generation of duty pistols.

The price continued to soar over the years. In 1980, Smith & Wesson introduced their own .41-frame .357, the Model 586, which they dubbed the L-frame. This was a brutal blow to Python sales. Copying the Python so slavishly that both brands would fit the same holster and use the same HKS speedloader, the L-frame was a Pythonized S&W with solid instead of ventilated barrel rib, and much more affordable than the Colt. Dan Wesson had copied the distinctive Python silhouette a decade earlier, and the Ruger GP100 soon shared the same configuration. The Colt Python was no longer unique.

At the end, produced as the "Python Elite," the flagship of the Colt revolver fleet sailed out of the pricey Colt Custom Shop and carried a suggested retail ten times higher than its original price. Production of the Python was discontinued in the last quarter of 1999.

Shooting the Python

"The pride of the (Colt) line is the Python, a big-frame .357 service target revolver with a distinctive ventilated sight rib. At 43 ounces, in 6-inch trim, this is a heavy pistol, excellently suited for target shooting with the .38 cartridge, or hunting with full loads. It is very popular on the PPC circuit, where target shooting is restricted to revolvers. Its single action release is usually superb, combining with its weight and fine sights to provide excellent controllability. The Python is expensive, and it should be."[4]

Those are the words of Jeff Cooper in his classic *Cooper on Handguns*, and many users saw the Python in the same light as he did. However, some others saw it as one thing more than a hunting revolver or target .38: the finest quality self-defense revolver that money could buy.

From the range to the street, the added heft at the front was appreciated by knowledgeable shooters. One of the handgun gurus of the time, Chic Gaylord, wrote in 1960, "...I rate Colt's .357 Python as the top performer in its class. The increased weight at the end of the barrel balances the gun in such a way that a very close grouping of shots can be fired with extreme rapidity. This could prove to be a lifesaver in the field."[5]

Some gunsmiths felt the Colt went out of time sooner than the S&W. I can attest from personal experience that when firing

Shooting the service revolver stage (holster is for big Power Custom S&W PPC gun), author wins three-gun aggregate of 1981 National Marksman Sports Society New England Regional PPC Championship. Revolver is Moran Custom 4-inch Python, being fired from required sitting position at 50 yards.

This Python has original Accro rear sight, Jerry Moran action job.

Mas wins a one-hand-only "wounded officer" match at Boston Gun & Rifle Club, some time in the early 1990s. Gun is 6-inch Moran Python. Respirator mask is always a good idea on an indoor range.

.357 Magnum rounds, the Python stood up better than the K-frame S&W and compared well to the bigger frame Smiths. Jerry Moran told me of one Python he owned that had passed 100,000 rounds of Magnum ammo and was still perking along with only minor tuning. Gun expert Stan Trzoniec has said in print, "The Python is an expensive revolver to be sure, but it will outlast the shooter."[6]

S&W fans hated the two-stage Colt double action pull, no matter how light and smooth. When a master 'smith could make it one-stage, even they got on board with the concept. My old friend John Taffin is a *connoisseur nonpareil* of the revolver. When others compared the Python to a Rolls, John allowed that at most it was a Cadillac. In his splendid book *Big Bore Sixguns*, the scrupulously honest Taffin readily explained how he came to upgrade his opinion of the Python. "The Colt Python is a superb sixgun to be sure," he wrote. "I have always been partial to the double action feel of Smith &

Wesson sixguns, however, a dear friend recently went Home and it was his wish that I have his prize Python, an older 6-inch .357 that Fred Sadowski tuned to perfection. My friend's family concurred and now I have a Python with a double action pull that is as fine as ever found on any slicked-up Smith & Wesson. It is all in knowing how and Sadowski certainly knew how."[7]

Fred Sadowski's breakthrough was turning the two-stage Colt DA pull into a single-stage. Joking at his own ethnic heritage, he called the secret "the Polack kink." The Colt pull "stacks" toward the end because of the way the V-shaped leaf mainspring presses against itself at that point. First using a 1911 firing pin and later special tools, Fred would insert the object between the leaves and work the trigger until the spring leaves had stretched apart and no longer pressed against one another. But that's just the tip of the iceberg: he subtly altered the geometry of the Python's insides in many other ways

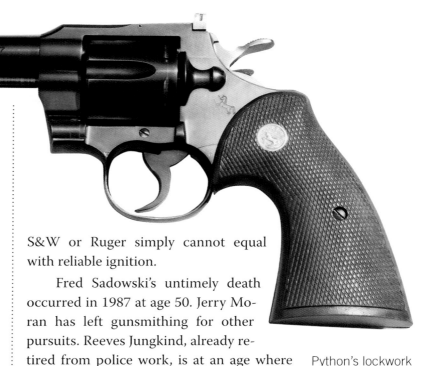

to create his extraordinary double action.

He was joined by two other 'smiths at the height of the Python customizing art: Jerry Moran of Michigan and Reeves Jungkind in Texas. These men could lighten the DA pull down to an incredible 5- or 6-pound range without compromising ignition. The secret lay in the Colt design: its longer action and longer hammer throw gave more mechanical advantage, allowing less force to be necessary to drive the trigger-cocking and firing mechanism. The floating firing pin helped, too; by lightening its spring slightly, a hammer falling more lightly (and therefore, driven by less double action trigger pressure) could still reliably ignite even Magnum primers. All of them, of course, enhanced their work with exquisite polishing of moving parts. The result is a combination of lightness and smoothness in the DA stroke that even the finest custom

S&W or Ruger simply cannot equal with reliable ignition.

Fred Sadowski's untimely death occurred in 1987 at age 50. Jerry Moran has left gunsmithing for other pursuits. Reeves Jungkind, already retired from police work, is at an age where he'll probably soon retire from pistolsmithing if he hasn't already. Today, I can personally attest to the work of one other, currently active craftsman who can equal their results on a Colt Python: Grant Cunningham at www.grantcunningham.com. I've also seen some fine Python work come out of Bill

Python's lockwork design first appeared in the Colt 357, about two years earlier.

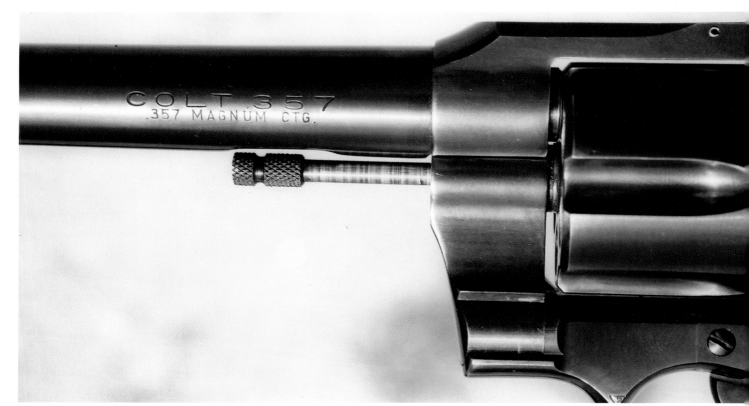

Author reveals 2-1/2-inch Junkgkind Python in Mitch Rosen Ayoob Rear Guard holster after completing Snubby Summit match, 2005. Target is 300/300, with 29 of 30 possible "X" tie-breakers.

Laughridge's Cylinder & Slide Shop, www.cylinder-slide.com.

The rumor is passed around at gun shops that Colt only nickel-plated those Pythons that came through with second-rate polish jobs. I never saw that substantiated. The few nickel plated Pythons I've handled and fired felt as good as their Royal Blue counterparts. However, this "urban gun legend" continues. Since relatively few Pythons bore the nickel finish – which tended to obscure the superb polish evident on the Royal Blue models, a big part of the whole "pride of ownership" thing – you'd think that the nickel models would command a premium price. Not so. A leading expert on the value of used guns, Ned Schwing, observes: "It is possible that the nickel-plated specimens would bring a 10 percent premium. In my experience this is not always the case as many potential purchasers have a definite preference for the blued finish."[9]

One of the big keys to the Python's popularity among serious shooters is its famous accuracy. It tends to exceed its competitors, Ruger and S&W, and is equaled only by the Dan Wesson in this regard. What makes the

Mas, left with Python snub, and Jon Strayer, right, with S&W Model 642. They won Snubby Summit shoot in six- and five-shot revolver divisions respectively. Jon beat Mas with 300-30X perfect score.

Dan Wesson so accurate is its unique barrel system, held under tension front and rear, and the tight lockup of its crane-mounted ball detent. What makes the Colt more accurate encompasses a longer list of achievements in the revolver-maker's art.

Going into the Python project, Colt already had two accuracy advantages over its arch-rival, S&W. One was a "double hand" mechanism that now goes back more than a century. As the hammer begins to fall, a second cylinder hand rises against the pawl and locks the cylinder absolutely dead-nuts solid into place. This gives more consistency in chamber-to-barrel alignment at the moment of the shot. Also, the Python kept Colt's traditional 1:14 rifling twist for .38 Special and .357 Magnum. Across the board, but particularly with .38 wadcutters used by target shooters, this seems to deliver more accuracy than the 1:18.5 rifling twist of the black powder days, used by S&W and Ruger.

In the late 1970s, I did a three part series on the Python for *American Handgunner* magazine that involved days at the factory debriefing the engineers. They told me that Python bores were tapered by .001 inch toward the muzzle, to drive the bullet deeper into the rifling. This is, if you think about

it, quite a feat of engineering. It may be one reason why for so many years, people who preferred other revolvers paid gunsmiths to install Python barrels on them, creating a "Smolt" or "Smython" when the tube was joined to an S&W and a "Cougar" when mated to a Ruger.

Sadowski would install a massive Douglas barrel if the customer insisted, but only to make it even heavier and steadier up front. He told me that his tests showed no custom barrel to be more accurate than the Python's own. By contrast, he did a land office business putting Douglas barrels on PPC Smiths, not just to weight them but to accurize them. Jungkind, Moran, and Cunningham likewise refused to put an aftermarket barrel on a Python.

How accurate? From a Ransom rest with Match ammo, the Python will generally deliver about 1-3/8-inch groups at 50 yards. This is about what you get out of a custom made PPC revolver with one-inch diameter Douglas barrel. My 8-inch matte stainless Python with Bausch & Lomb scope in J.D. Jones' T'SOB mount has given me 2-1/4-inch groups at 100 yards with Federal's generic American Eagle 158-grain softpoint .357 ammo. The same gun, with Federal

Justine Ayoob, then 17, obviously appreciates the double action pull on the 4-inch Moran Custom Python her dad won multiple state championships with. Sights are Colt-furnished Elliasons.

Match 148 grain .38 wadcutters, once put three bullets into a hole that measured .450 inch in outside diameter when calipered. That's three .38 slugs in a hole a couple of thousandths of an inch smaller in diameter than a single .45 auto bullet.

Personal Experience

I shot my first PPC match, and won my first "police combat" trophy, with a 6-inch Python borrowed from my friend Tom Stackpole in the early 1970s. In the mid-70s, I hunted at the Y-O Ranch in Texas with Hal Swiggett. Hal lent me his 6-inch Herrett-stocked Python, tuned by a young Jerry Moran. I couldn't believe the smoothness. I killed a trophy Corsican ram with two .357 slugs fired from it double action, the first through his chest as he ran and the second breaking his neck at a measured 76 yards.

I went home, ordered a brand-new Python, and sent it to Moran without even firing it.

Time went on. The 6-inch Moran gun won me First Master at the Fraternal Order of Police national shoot in Rhode Island circa 1977. A year later, I put a 4-inch barrel on it to carry on duty. It's one of the few handguns I've carried on all three police departments I served over the decades. Loaded with 125-grain Magnum hollow points, I knew it would never let me down. Soon, I owned two Morans, 4 and 6 inches, and two Jungkind Colts, 2-1/2 and 6 inches. My 8-incher was tuned by the Colt Custom Shop.

I can't say I won every match I shot with a Python, but I won a disproportionate number. Our state shoot for cops used to require a 4-inch .38 or .357 service revolver with sights and barrel produced by the gun factory, before everyone went to autos. I won the title every time I shot with a Python, once with the stubby Jungkind gun and the rest with the 4-inch Moran. All wore Elliason sights, a Colt factory option much superior to the Accro sight that came standard on the Python, let alone the sights furnished by Colt's competitors.

I found the Python to be a superbly accurate gun with functionality that went far beyond its pricey prestige. It could help mediocre shooters like me win matches, and its performance made good shooters truly great. Prices are up in the used market these days, but a Colt Python – especially when tuned by someone like Grant Cunningham – is a high performance revolver that earns its keep with far more than looks and prestige.

1978: Author in uniform with the Moran Custom Python he then carried on duty. It stood up well to lots of shooting with hot 125-grain .357 Magnum loads.

Notes

[1]Wilson, R.L., *The Colt Heritage*, New York City: Simon & Shuster, undated, p. 272.

[2]Wilson, R.L., *Colt: An American Legend*, New York City: Abbeville Press, 1985, p. 272.

[3]"Pistols and Revolvers of American Make," by Julian Hatcher, in *Gun Guide*, 1953-54 edition, published by The Gun Digest Corporation, Chicago, 1953, p. 103.

[4]Cooper, Jeff, *Cooper on Handguns*, Los Angeles, Petersen Publishing Co., 1974, p. 189.

[5]Gaylord, Chic, *Handgunner's Guide*, New York City: Hastings House, 1960, pp. 59-60.

[6]Trzoniec, Stanley W., *Modern American Centerfire Handguns*, Tulsa: Winchester Press, 1981, p. 65.

[7]Taffin, John, *Big Bore Sixguns*, Iola, WI: Krause Publications, 1997, p. 61.

[8]Schwing, Ned, 2003 *Standard Catalog of Firearms*, Iola, WI: Krause Publications, 2002, p. 302.

The Colt Woodsman

From its introduction in 1915 to its demise in 1977, the Colt Woodsman was the very definition of the discriminating shooter's .22 auto pistol. Most were bought for plinking and trail carry, yet for decades this gun ruled the .22 events at Camp Perry and some are probably still in use today. It inspired countless imitators, some very good and some in production even now. More than half a million specimens were produced.

This aptly named pistol set the standard for quality recreational handguns, and in its day ruled the target ranges.

Pedigree

The Woodsman was never a cheap gun, but for every rich movie star who liked it (Gary Cooper, a fine shot who practiced gunsmithing as a hobby, comes to mind) there were countless good, ordinary folks who appreciated this finely made pistol. It hit where you aimed it and seemed never to jam. The beautiful blue finish on its finely polished steel screamed "quality."

The classic Colt Woodsman, before the company named it that.

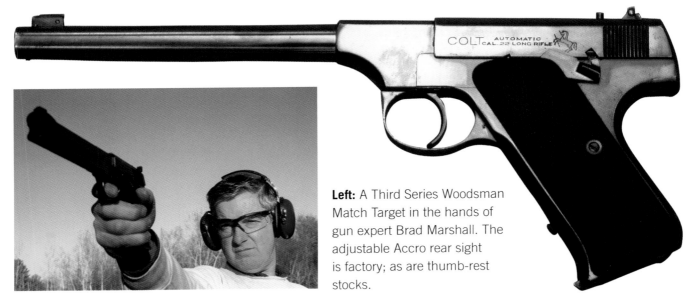

Left: A Third Series Woodsman Match Target in the hands of gun expert Brad Marshall. The adjustable Accro rear sight is factory; as are thumb-rest stocks.

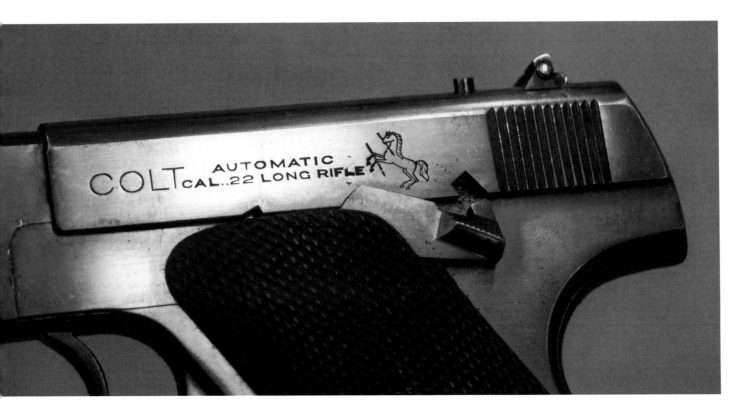

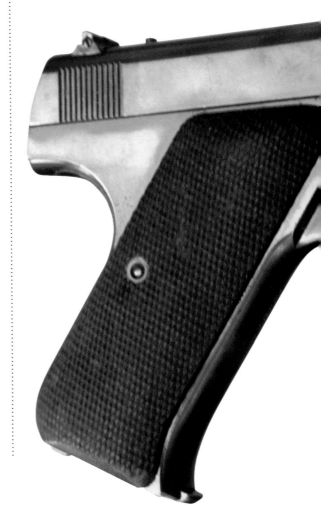

Above: This early model is simply the… "Colt Automatic Cal. 22 Long Rifle."

Right: This is the shape of the archetypal Colt Woodsman for the traditionalist. The small grip frame was handy, concealable, and fit a wide range of hand sizes. This early Target model has the slender 6.5-inch barrel of the 1915 original, and adjustable sights of the period.

So did its clean, sweet trigger press and the glassy smoothness of its slide running along the frame as you cycled the first round into its chamber.

Col. Charles Askins, Jr. was a Woodsman kind of guy. He used one to win the National Pistol Championship at Camp Perry and numerous state champion titles. Of his competition battery during his salad days, Askins wrote, "I had by this time acquired a .22 Woodsman which I had weighed with lead to make it hold a bit steadier, had the .38 Colt Shooting Master which was a splendid gun for match shooting, and a .45 auto that had been refitted and given an accuracy job by 'Buck' Buchanan who was working for Frank Pachmayr."[1]

Woodsman pistols figured in some of Askins' exploits where the excitement exceeded that of the shooting range. He told of the time he and longtime partner George Parker were picked up by "a couple of big plug-uglies in a Cadillac" for a gypsy cab ride to departure port in Honolulu which, the good colonel perceived, had turned into

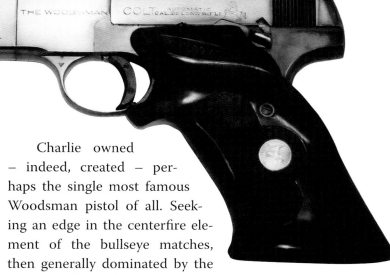

an attempted mugging of the tourists. Charlie told it thus:

"I had a Mauser HSc .380, I reckoned since I was sitting behind the driver I'd just shoot him right behind the ear when he made his play. We bowled along and the first thing I noticed was that we weren't going toward the port at all. I let this go on for a block or two and then I said to the driver, 'Turn the next corner and head for the dock, you (expletive deleted)!' This brought matters to a head right quick. I put my Mauser in my lap where the pair in the front seat could see it and Parker hauled forth his .22 Woodsman. We didn't point either gun at this pair, just left them lying in our laps."

The ride ended at Charlie's intended destination without further incident.[2]

These horizontal grooves on the mainspring housing mark a Woodsman built to take high velocity .22 LR ammo.

Charlie owned – indeed, created – perhaps the single most famous Woodsman pistol of all. Seeking an edge in the centerfire element of the bullseye matches, then generally dominated by the .38 Special revolver, Askins determined that the Colt .22 auto could be rechambered for a wildcat version of the 5.5 mm French Velo Dog cartridge. While Charlie laboriously ground the case heads of some 2,000 Remington cartridges down to fit and shortened them to .22 LR length, master gunsmith Frank Pachmayr expertly converted the Woodsman Askins sent him to centerfire and made other necessary adjustments. The result was a centerfire pistol as easy to shoot as, well, a Colt Woodsman .22, particularly advantageous at the timed and rapid fire stages. Great wails of consternation arose from Askins' competitors. As a result, NRA subsequently changed the rules to limit the centerfire handgun category to caliber .32 or larger, and Askins' supervisor on the Border Patrol ordered him not to

Above: Author got his first Colt Woodsman, this "bullseye" Match Target, in 1962. It served him well for many years.

Below: On models that didn't have a dedicated slide stop, shooters learned to lock the Woodsman slide open with the safety catch, as shown here.

Unique markings and barrel shape distinguished the 16,000 original Colt Match Target Woodsman pistols. Jeff Cooper didn't think "Match," "Target," and "Woodsman" went well together.

Pre-war adjustable sights required a screwdriver the size of a jeweler's and could have used a bigger notch by today's standards, but in their time they set national records.

In most production runs, the Woodsman had a sturdy magazine release located at the heel of the butt.

shoot the gun at any tournaments. Charlie resigned over it. "Somewhat obstinate by nature I was just be damned if I was going to let some petty bureaucrat dictate to me," he wrote later.[3] It's not every gun expert who can say that a particular firearm precipitated a career change for him, but that was exactly the case with Charlie's one of a kind "Colt Woodsman, caliber .221 Askins." He had at least one more memorable "Woodsman moment," but we'll touch on that later.

Charlie's dad, Major Charles Askins, Sr. – the nation's leading shotgun authority in his time – had been among the first to write up the Woodsman when it was new. The gun had perked through 700 rounds of UMC .22 Long Rifle ammo "without a wobble," he wrote, adding, "I am convinced that the average man will have no trouble whatsoever with this pistol."[4]

Jeff Cooper appreciated the quality of the Woodsman, writing "Colt's pride is the Match Target Woodsman, an odd series of words when you consider it, as 'Match' and 'Target' are redundant and 'Woodsman' would seem to contradict both. But that

does not detract from the pistol, which is an excellent piece for its purpose, which is winning matches."[5]

Elmer Keith waxed more enthusiastic about the little gun. He appreciated its quality and its accuracy, and recognized its proven success in the tournaments. John Lachuk sorely bemoaned its passing in the *Gun Digest Book of the .22*, and Dean Grennell flatly called it his favorite.

In his own inimitable style, Dean wrote, "Everyone is entitled to a personal opinion and it is my own tautly-clenched opinion that the Colt Woodsman represents the outermost perfection and refinement of an auto pistol ideally designed and suited to handle the .22 LR cartridge. I'll go one stubbornly-prejudiced step beyond that and claim that the pre-WWII Sport Model Colt Woodsman with its 4-1/2 inch barrel represents the high-water mark of achievement in that particular field to the present date (1983). You may not agree with that and, if so, be my guest, Edgar!"[6]

By the 50s, Colt had changed the shape of the Woodsman. As seen on this target model, adjustable sights had been updated…

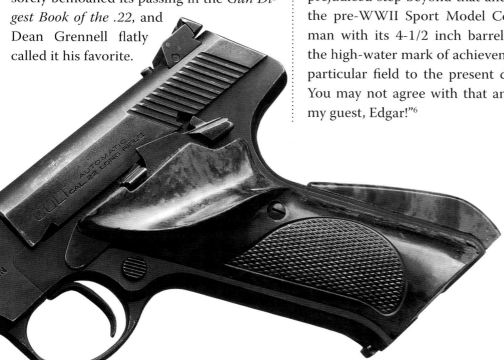

…and a separate slide hold-open lever had been added forward of the thumb safety. Note the trigger shape of the time, described by Dean Grennell as a dog leg; the push button magazine release behind the trigger guard; and the ergonomically and esthetically hideous plastic stocks.

A Brief History

"Gun histories" usually begin with the model's introduction, and what led up to it is too often ignored. For the "backstory" on this one, check out "Wanted: A .22 Automatic Pistol" by Jim Foral in the 2003 *Gun Digest*, a particularly rich edition. Foral details how, early in the 20th century, the .22 handgun was still seen by manufacturers as something that needed to be either tiny or single-shot. Sport shooters, led by the magazines *Outdoor Life* and *Outer's*, agitated for a man-size .22 with match accuracy. Realizing a demand, Colt and S&W responded respectively with the Police Positive Target and the .22/32 Bekeart revolvers on .32 frames, but the public still cried out for an autoloading pistol in that caliber.

Colt won the race in 1915 with a pistol they dubbed simply "22 Automatic Target Pistol." Weighing 28 ounces with a thin, graceful 6.5-inch barrel, it had a grip frame angled like a Luger's but much shorter, housing a 10-shot magazine held in place with a spring-loaded butt-heel release. "Hammerless" in silhouette with a curved trigger, it was one of those guns that fit the hand on first pick-up, and it was an instant hit. It remained in the catalog for 12 years before the Woodsman appellation came along, and some 54,000 were sold. Though the 2003 *Standard Catalog of Firearms* lists these guns as having checkered plastic grips,[7] ads of the period boasted "checked English Walnut stocks."

The Woodsman was officially named in 1927. The words "Colt Automatic" re-

Above: Original grip shape was a marvel of ergonomics and compactness. This is a "pre-Woodsman."

Below: If you were familiar with a cocked and locked 1911, operation of the Colt Woodsman's thumb safety would come naturally.

Above: Pre-Woodsman Colt .22 Automatic's lines are even cleaner when seen from the right side.

mained on the slide, and "THE WOODS-MAN" – both words, in caps – was stamped boldly on the left side of the frame between the permanently-affixed barrel and the relatively small slide. This gun is now known to collectors as the First Generation Woodsman. In keeping with the woodsy name, it was offered with a more holster-friendly 4-1/2-inch barrel in 1933, though the 6-1/2-inch tube remained in the line for target shooters. Indeed, the shorter gun was known as the Sport Model and the longer as the Target.

.22 Long Rifle ammo was still in the process of maturing. In 1932, the First Model Woodsman received a design/production upgrade to allow it to handle high velocity ammunition. Reports Ned Schwing, "This change took place at serial number 83790."[8] The mainspring housing along the backstrap of the grip was at this point changed from a cross-hatched surface to one with horizontal grooves. The factory recommended that no earlier gun be fired with anything hotter than standard velocity .22 LR. All told, some 112,000 of these Gen One Woodsman pistols were produced, in addition to the production tally of "pre-Woodsman" models.

The rarest factory Woodsman came next, the Match Target of 1938. It was equipped with adjustable sights and is easily distinguished by three unique features. One is its strangely shaped heavy barrel, which brought weight up to some 36 ounces. Another is its elongated "elephant ear" grips which sweep down past the short Woodsman frame to create an ample grasping surface for big-handed target shooters. Finally, a large bulls-eye logo appears at the left rear of the barrel, with the words "Match" above and "Target" below. Curiously, some production apparently continued through the years of WWII, as this gun is listed as having been produced through 1944 (Schwing, p. 326). A total of only about 16,000 left the factory. Col. Cooper's comments on the redundancy implicit in the title "Match Target" are understandable. I suspect the name was chosen to distinguish this upgraded competition gun from the standard "Target" model, which had a much slimmer barrel of equal length and less sophisticated sights.

The Second Model Woodsman appeared in 1948. Reports the *Standard Catalog*, "This is a totally redesigned pistol and is different from the preceding models. It has a slide stop, a hold-open device, and a push-button magazine release behind the trigger guard. It is blued, with brown plastic grips. There were approximately 146,000 manufactured between 1948 and 1955."[9]

The Third Series Woodsman is generally dated to 1955. The butt heel release, at the bottom of what is now a long "conventional length" grip frame, returned to replace the push button behind the trigger guard. The Match Target now had a much more conventional and esthetically pleasing heavy barrel, somewhat resembling the trick Askins and others used earlier of attaching a

Apparently on a "light day," General George S. Patton is seen carrying a Colt Woodsman .22 in the field. Elephant ear shape stocks indicate a pre-war Match Target.

stripped down version of the Woodsman became the Huntsman in 1955, further cheapened with plastic grips. It would remain in the line until the end of the Woodsman era, selling some 100,000 units.

By 1961, however, Colt no longer saw this hallmark gun as a profit center. The High Standard Supermatics and the S&W Model 41 had long since rendered it obsolete for serious bullseye competition. Among the sporting guns, High Standard's Field King and stripped down Duramatic equaled or exceeded its performance at a much lower price point. The Ruger Standard was just as accurate, and at the same $37.50 at which it was introduced 13 years before, was half the price of the Woodsman, which carried a suggested retail of $74.75 in the mainstream model and $84.50 for the Match Target.

The struggle ended in 1977. Citing the prohibitive cost of its labor-intensive high quality against heavy competition from mass-produced guns, Colt discontinued the Woodsman series. For discriminating handgunners, it marked the end of an era.

Shooting the Woodsman

Ease of operation, great reliability, and excellent inherent accuracy were the hallmarks of the Woodsman pistols. Observed Grennell, "I've encountered .22 LR pistols that were capable of better accuracy than I've been able to get from The Woodsman. High Standard's The Victor is a salient example of such designs. That presumes you've ample leisure to bed the gun into your hand with great care, sock it into a sandbag and take exquisite pains with sight picture and trigger squeeze...The great virtue of The Woodsman is that you can grab hold of its dainty butt, any old panicky which-way, stab its slender muzzle toward a selected small area, press its silky trigger through release and see the small hole turn up incredibly near the chosen point."[10]

rod of lead beneath the skinny barrel of the older Target Woodsman. Weight was now up to 40 ounces with the 6-1/2-inch barrel Match Target. For the first time, a 4-1/2-inch barrel was offered on the Match Target, with a weight of 36 ounces.

By now, Colt was feeling the heat from Bill Ruger's 1949 introduction of the gun that started his company, the Standard Model .22 auto. It dramatically undersold the Woodsman, and for the first time Colt elected to "cheapen" the gun, offering stripped down models under different names. The barebones version was called the Challenger, with cheaper grips and lacking the slide hold-open device of the contemporary Woodsman. Schwing dates its production from 1950 to 1955, with some 77,000 produced. The

Over the years, the gun went through different permutations of trigger shape. There was curved, there was very curved, and there was the relatively short-lived flat-face trigger that Grennell described as a dog-leg. This may have been the American handgun industry's first true flat-angled trigger on a target pistol, and that shape is seen today on the custom 1911s of such fine craftsmen as Ed Masaki.

How accurate was the Woodsman, really? Elmer Keith put it this way when he wrote, "These little pistols were superbly accurate and soon established an enviable reputation. We have seen one fitted with a hollow tube over the barrel some 30 inches long on which was perched a front sight and a shoulder stock, with a rear peep sight. That little gun stayed consistently in a one inch circle, at 60 yards, all day at a turkey match. It won its full share of turkeys against heavy match rifles chambered for the .22 LR, as well as many larger calibers."[11]

Sadly, great guns are sometimes like great men. While they have great strengths, they may also have great weaknesses. The big weakness I discovered over the years in the Woodsman was that it was capable of unintentionally firing when subjected to violent forward or backward inertia with a live round in the chamber, even if the thumb safety was engaged.

We turn now to the final Charlie Askins Woodsman story. I knew Charlie and greatly enjoyed his company. One day over some adult beverages we were discussing how some accidental discharges could seem terrifying at the time but funny later. He told me of the long-ago day when he was hunting rabbits with a Colt Woodsman. The gun was cocked and locked in a shoulder holster (under his right arm, since he was left-handed) and Charlie being a connoisseur of guns finely 'smithed to maximum performance, it had been given a trigger job that resulted in a very light

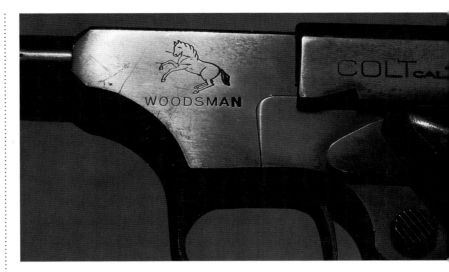

pull. Askins, a wiry and athletic man, found need to jump into an arroyo. As he landed, the impact caused the sear of the little .22 to slip from its razor-edged engagement, and the pistol discharged in its holster. The little bullet punched through the leather and created a through and through wound of the right gluteus maximus, finishing up in the dirt behind his foot.

More embarrassed than inconvenienced, Charlie made his way to the nearest medical facility, which happened to be a Catholic hospital. Not being of that religious persuasion himself, and forgetting momentarily that in the Catholic faith suicide is a mortal sin, he would never forget the expression on the face of the nun at the receiving desk when he told her, "Sister, I've shot myself." He told me later, "Now that I think about it, I probably could have phrased it better." Charlie told me that the most humorous part of the whole affair was that during the otherwise uneventful healing of the flesh wound, threads of wool from his clothing that had been carried into the wound track by the bullet worked their way out by themselves. "You know how wool can itch, Mas? I want you to picture it itching inside your butt cheek...where you can't scratch it!"

One gets the sense that John Browning designed this particular gun for the range

Woodsman! Among connoisseurs of fine firearms, the name resonates.

instead of for carry in the field with a round in the chamber. That came later. Remember that the "Woodsman" designation was an afterthought. Suffice to say that in the field, the Woodsman (and many other guns of its type) would be best carried Condition Three, i.e., with loaded magazine but empty chamber. By leaving the internal hammer pre-cocked, the hunter can cycle the topmost round into the chamber slowly and relatively quietly if he fears spooking small game.

Personal Perspective

I got my first Colt Woodsman at the age of 14 in November of 1962. My dad had picked it up from a fellow named Graves, one of his gun-trading buddies. It was a pre-war Match Target. Its signature elephant ear grips had been replaced with plastic Franzite thumb-rest stocks, and it came with hand-carved wooden grip panels in a nice floral pattern that fitted its small frame, allowing it to fit in the flap holster that was also included. It was my fourth .22 handgun. With a good two-hand hold, it would give most .22 rifles a run for their money at 100 yards.

The gun had been well used by a target shooter, but living in a gun box and receiving lavish care, it was in excellent condition. Even then I appreciated its good trigger and the feel of its slide running along the frame, which made me think of oiled ball bearings. When I got into organized match shooting five years later, this was my tournament gun for more than a year. It was already obsolete for the purpose, and the old heads teased "the kid with the antique gun," but it got me up into the 270s on the 300 point National Match Course. I shot it for more than a year before I surrendered to the superior sights, the better-holding greater weight, and the even crisper and lighter trigger of a new High Standard Supermatic Citation. By then, the old Woodsman was showing its wear. Standard velocity Remington shells would occasionally split when fired in its aging chamber. It rests today in dignified retirement in a safe deposit vault.

The Woodsman pistol left a legacy of fine craftsmanship and superb accuracy. It is one of those handguns that is widely and eternally appreciated by riflemen who cherish those same attributes.

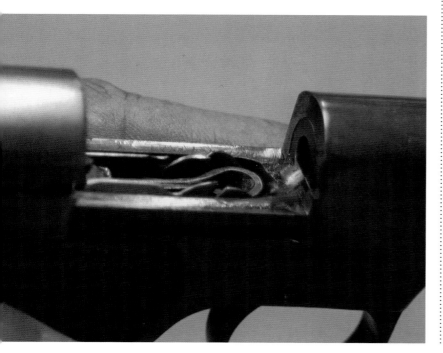

Completely open ejection area during slide operation enhanced mechanical reliability of the Woodsman series.

Notes

[1]Askins, Charles, *Unrepentant Sinner*, San Antonio, TX: Tejano Publications, 1985, p. 83.

[2]*Ibid.*, p. 250.

[3]*Ibid.*, p. 92.

[4]*Gun Digest* 2003, "Wanted: A .22 Automatic Pistol" by Jim Forey, Iola, WI: Krause Publications, 2003, p. 41.

[5]Cooper, Jeff, *Cooper on Handguns*, Los Angeles: Petersen Publishing, 1974, p. 175.

[6]Grennell, Dean A., *Gun Digest Book of Autoloading Pistols*, Northfield, IL: DBI Books, 1983, p. 63.

[7]Schwing, Ned, 2003 *Standard Catalog of Firearms*, Iola, WI: Krause Publications, 2002, p. 326.

[8]*Ibid.*, p. 236.

[9]*Ibid.*, p. 237.

[10]Grennell, *op. cit.*, p. 65.

[11]Keith, Elmer, *Sixguns*, New York: Bonanza Books, 1955, p. 49.

The Glock Pistol
Drastic, Fantastic Plastic

The Glock pistol has profoundly changed the handgun industry, creating a new generation of polymer-frame pistols, not to mention semiautomatics with uniform trigger pulls from the first shot, but usually without manual safety devices. Exquisitely light and ergonomic, easy to handle and easy to shoot well, the Glock pistols have boldly carved their own very large niche in the history of handgunning.

In a mere 20 years, a radical design became the benchmark and profoundly changed the handgun industry.

Pedigree

The Glock has been well received by the experts. "All in all, this Glock 17 has to be rated the number-one military handgun today," says Timothy

The gun that started the Glock Revolution: the first generation of the G17.

Ayoob demonstrates the G18 machine pistol on full auto. There are six spent casings in the air.

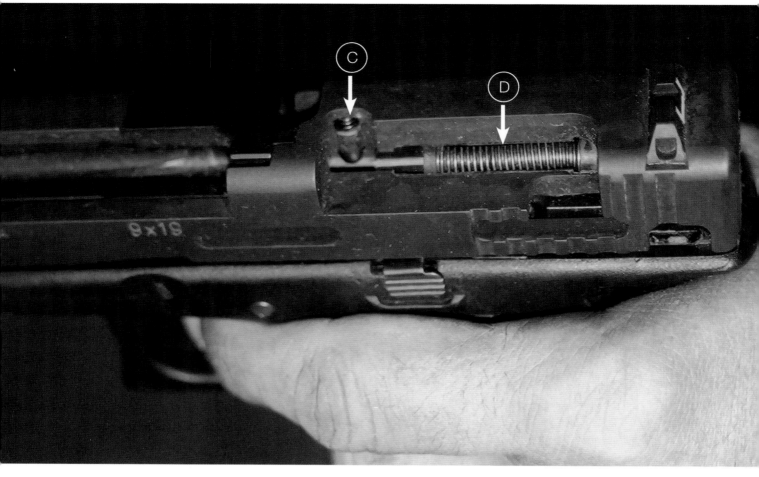

Top & Right:

Author's factory cutaway G17 shows signature Glock trigger safety and standard firing pin spring… intentional pull of the trigger will depress trigger safety (A), and pull will move trigger bar (B), simultaneously pushing firing pin safety (C) out of the way of the partially precocked striker (D).

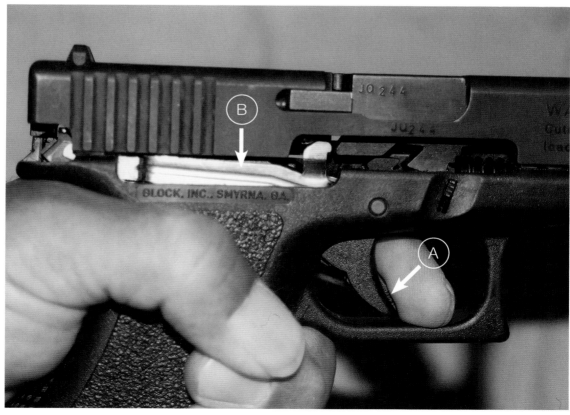

Mullin. "It is rapidly stripped, efficient to manufacture, low in cost, holds 17 rounds, has light recoil, and has an ideal safety system. The more you shoot it, the more you like it."[1]

In the second edition of the *Gun Digest Book of Combat Handgunnery*, Chuck Karwan wrote, "Though the Glock is technically a double-action-only pistol...the trigger pull does not feel like that of a double-action. For some agencies and people – including yours truly – that is the charm of the Glock. It offers the simplicity advantage of a DAO system with a crisp, easy-to-control sear release that feels like a good single-action trigger pull."[2]

When Chuck Taylor wrote the fourth edition of that title, he commented, *"The Glock is perhaps the only truly revolutionary pistol design to surface since the first two decades of this century and reflects great engineering skill. It's simple, easy to disassemble and maintain, accurate and rugged almost beyond belief. In fact, I've been trying to wear one out for over five years without success. So far, my Model 17 9mm has ingested more than 125,000 rounds of full-power ammunition and is still going strong. During the course of the test, the gun has been presented from a holster over 500,000 times, speed and tactical reloaded in excess of 100,000 times, and carried all over the world in virtually every natural environment possible. Yet it has continued to function without so much as a hiccup. In my experience, no other handgun – even the legendary Colt M1911 .45 ACP – can approach, much less duplicate or exceed, this performance."[3] Taylor concludes, "The plain facts indicate the Glock is quite safe and easy to shoot, and needs little to achieve its maximum potential. It's also tough, accurate, and utterly dependable. In my opinion, this is the best combat pistol in the world today and well worth your consideration."[4]*

More than the experts, however, threw in their lot with the Pre-eminent Polymer

Standard frame Glocks have been produced in these five sizes. From top, 6-inch longslide (G17L), 5.3-inch Tactical/Practical (G34), 4.5-inch full size (G17), 4.0-inch Compact (G19), 3.5-inch subcompact (G26). All shown are 9mm; .40s are identical in size.

Above: The FBI for more than a decade has issued choice of Glock 22 (shown) or Glock 23 to new agents.

Pistol. The rank and file went to the gun in a big way. It is issued by more police departments than any other, overwhelmingly leading in sales to law enforcement agencies with a market share claimed to be over 70%. In 1990, the FBI said that it would not approve the Glock because its short, easy trigger pull for the first shot was incompatible with their training. A decade later, the Bureau was issuing a new Glock .40 to every recruit and authorizing a broad array of Glocks for purchase by in-service agents.

The Glock may be the most publicly controversial pistol of our time. It tends to inspire either love or hate, with little ground in between, and most assuredly, not every-

one loves the Glock. Traditionalists who cleave to blue steel and checkered walnut consider the Glock anathema. Aesthetes find it ugly. Yet the Glock has inspired truly awesome levels of brand loyalty.

A Brief History

Gaston Glock had a factory in Austria where he successfully fabricated an assortment of objects from high-strength, high-impact polymer. When he was approached by firearms manufacturers about producing experimental frames for handguns, it occurred to him that a whole pistol couldn't be that hard to make. He led his engineers on a crash program that began with the prover-

Above: Glock 18 machine pistol and its 33-round magazine, which fits other 9mm Glocks. Selector switch at left rear of slide resembles safety catch on the rare G17-S variation.

Left: Author's G22, top, G27 below w/Pearce grip extender. Smaller .40 will take the larger's magazines and is actually slightly more accurate. Each is fitted with fixed night sights and NY-1 trigger.

The Gen 3 G17 has finger grooves on the front strap, and an additional pin for strength, located above trigger pivot pin. Gen 3.5 is this shape plus light rail on dust cover portion of frame.

Glocks have gone through four generations of frames. This is a G17 Gen 1, now called the "smooth" frame by enthusiasts.

bial new sheet of paper, and he unleashed the result on the firearms world in 1984.

With about the grip angle of a Luger, the low bore axis of an HK P7, and its own unique takedown system, the polymer-framed pistol was his seventeenth design and he therefore dubbed it the Glock 17. Mullin sums up best what happened next: "The Glock 17 was first adopted by the Austrian army, then by the Swedish and Norwegian armies, and now has spread throughout the world."[5]

The City of Miami Police Department was not the first American police department to adopt the Glock, but it was the highest profile one to do so to that point. A few years before, the city had ordered all its service revolvers altered to double action only after Janet Reno's State's Attorney's Office had prosecuted a Miami cop for manslaughter on the bogus theory that he had cocked the revolver and accidentally discharged it, killing a suspect. In fact, famed defense attorneys Roy Black and Mark Seiden proved to the jury that Officer Luis Alvarez had fired the single shot double action and intentionally when the suspect, Nevell "Snake" Johnson, went for his own gun while being arrested, and the jury acquitted the cop. However, "the perception was taken as reality."

Meanwhile, cops across the country were pleading with their chiefs to issue them high capacity 9mm auto pistols to replace their six-shot revolvers and give them parity with street criminals who could carry whatever illegally-obtained guns they wished. Miami's finest were no different. The chief told them, sure, they could have 9mm autos – if the guns were double action only. This was a little like telling your employees they can have a raise when horses grow wings and fly.

Members of the union approached Beretta, SIG, and S&W, who told them that double action only autos were illogical and wouldn't be profitable to make.

And then, the Bureau of Alcohol, Tobacco, and Firearms officially declared the Glock pistol to be double action only.

The undoubtedly exasperated chief was stuck with his promise, and after a torture test of monumental proportions, which the Glock 17 passed with flying colors, it became the standard issue firearm for Miami PD. Other departments followed, and Glock sales skyrocketed. Police firearms instructors reported with delight that the cops were scoring better than ever in department qualifications, because the Glocks were so easy to learn to shoot well.

Glock soon established a US headquarters in Smyrna, Georgia. In charge was Carl Walter, who brilliantly established a roving program that trained Glock instructors and armorers whenever a department adopted the guns. The polymer construction and modern manufacturing concepts adopted by Gaston Glock allowed the brand to undersell the traditional double actions by Beretta, SIG, and S&W, who only now got with the program and offered double action only

Here's Gen 2, with aggressive checkering on front and back straps for better grasp. Front strap is still straight.

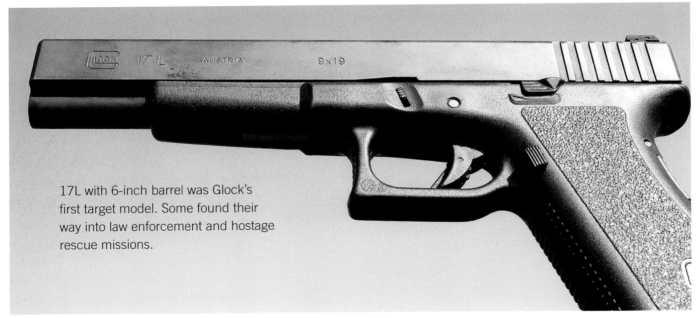

17L with 6-inch barrel was Glock's first target model. Some found their way into law enforcement and hostage rescue missions.

Glock's easy working slide makes it a favorite among those with limited upper body strength.

autos. However, their guns were still heavier, and still had longer, heavier trigger pulls that made them harder to shoot straight with limited practice. To send an officer to Smith & Wesson armorer's school, the department had to pay his salary for the duration of the five-day course; by contrast, Glock armorer's school lasted all of one day.

With a 4.5-inch barrel, the Glock 17 weighed only 22 ounces and was about the size of a Colt Lightweight Commander pistol of 1950, but lighter. Soon the company realized that Americans who liked a given gun would buy more of them in various sizes. While the second Glock was the G18, a machine pistol version of the G17, the third was destined to be much more popular. The Glock 19 was a compact: half an inch shorter in overall length than the G17 and proportionally shorter in the butt and an ounce lighter. It came out in 1988, and the same year saw the introduction of the Glock 17L, a long-slide target version with ultra-light 3.5 pound trigger pull and 6-inch barrel. "In 1990 this pistol won the IPSC (International Practical Shooting Confederation) World Stock Gun Championship," reports Ned Schwing.[6]

Development of the pistol progressed.

1990: The Glock 22 in caliber .40 S&W hits the market at the same as the Model 4006 of the eponymous company that invented that cartridge with Winchester. It will become the single most popular law enforcement sidearm in the US by the latter 1990s. It is followed by the Glock 23, a .40 in G19 size. The Glock 24 follows, chambered for .40 S&W in the 17L long-slide format.

1995 sees the introduction of the "baby Glocks," which will prove hugely popular. The G26 is an 11-shot 9mm Parabellum, while the G27 is a 10-shot in .40 S&W. Otherwise identical, they are comparable in size to snub-nose, small frame revolvers, since the baby Glocks are only 6-1/4 inches long, 20 ounces, and sporting 3.5-inch barrels with proportional slides and grip frames, the latter offering room for only two fingers unless a finger extension is installed on the magazine's floorplate.

In 1998, Glock chambers their standard frame guns for the .357 SIG. A long-slide is not offered, but the full size Glock in this cal-

Older 9mm Glocks needed but a single pin through the frame (below), but early work with the hotter .40 showed need for a second pin (above). This design made Glock frame amply strong for .40 and .357, and in 9mm, made an already strong pistol even stronger.

iber is the G31, the compact is the G32, and the subcompact is dubbed G33. This will not prove the most popular caliber, but it sells well enough to stay in the line. At about the same time, the firm introduces their Tactical/Practical line. The G34 (9mm) and G35 (.40) feature 5.3-inch barrels that give an overall length of 8.2 inches, roughly the same as a 5-inch barrel GI 1911A1. These prove so popular that they drive the longer-slide target models into interrupted production. Glock's standard frame pistol is now available in no fewer than five formats. This will multiply with the introduction of the C-series models in compact and larger sizes.

In 2003, Glock announces the G37, chambered for the company's first proprietary cartridge, the .45 Gap (Glock Auto Pistol). Delivering .45 ACP ballistics with a shorter overall cartridge length that fits in the envelope of a 9mm pistol, it is Glock's attempt to satisfy the American market's demand for a Glock .45 no larger in grip girth than the G17. The full size G37 is followed in 2005 by the compact Glock 38 and Glock 39. Like the G37, these pistols are thicker through the slide, but otherwise the same dimensions as standard Glocks of their size.

The astute reader has noticed some gaps in the chain of the model numbers. The G25 and G28 are .380s, made for markets

Top: Comminolli thumb safety is shown in the "on-safe" position; shooter operates it like that of a 1911...

Bottom: ...with a downward wipe to this "fire" position. Author's G17 also sports Heinie fixed sights, GlockWorks oversize magazine release.

where military calibers are forbidden, and are rarely seen in this country. The G20 and G29 are 10mm Auto caliber, full size and compact respectively, built on a scaled up Glock frame. That large frame is shared by two .45 ACPs, the full size G21 and the compact G30. The G36 has its own unique, slim-lined frame, and is a compact 7-shot .45 ACP. More about the larger caliber Glocks later.

By 2005, Glock was solidly in the forefront of handgun sales, the most popular in gun shops and in police holsters alike. The brand had overcome many obstacles. Anti-gun politicians had decried them as "terrorist specials" that could pass unnoticed through metal detectors and X-rays. This, of course, was balderdash. The Glocks showed up, right down to the polymer frame, on X-ray, and easily tripped metal detectors since they contained more steel than an

all-metal Smith & Wesson Airweight.

British handgun authorities Richard Law and Peter Brookesmith wrote, "Glock's lead was followed by other manufacturers when the Austrian battle pistol found a following among US law enforcement agencies, despite public misgivings about the police having firearms with no safety catches and a steady stream of negligent discharges resulting in injuries to officers."[7] While there had been unintentional discharges, these tapered off drastically in the early years, partly because of design enhancements by Glock and partly because of training, which we'll address next.

Current production Glock 19 fitted with MMC sights, and Glock's own tactical light.

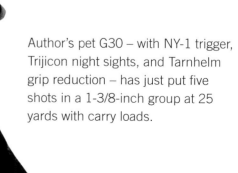

Author's pet G30 – with NY-1 trigger, Trijicon night sights, and Tarnhelm grip reduction – has just put five shots in a 1-3/8-inch group at 25 yards with carry loads.

Glocks handle recoil well with proper grasp. This is the G33 "baby Glock," loaded with 125 grain/1350 foot-second .357 SIG ammo…

…and here it is at height of recoil. Locked thumbs, crush grip, and "wedge" hold with support hand all help here.

Shooting the Glock

When it came my turn to do an edition of the *Gun Digest Book of Combat Handgunnery*, I said among other things, *"There is no easier pistol to learn to shoot well!"*[8] It's the truth, and the statement deserved the italics, then and now. The manual of arms is drastically simple. Insert magazine. Rack slide. Pistol will now shoot when trigger is pulled. End of story.

The low bore axis and the steep Luger-like grip angle make the Glock a "natural pointer." If poor light or urgent circumstances keep you from getting the sight picture you might want, the wide flat top of its slide guides the eye in coarse aim like the "BROADway" rib popularized on tournament claybird shotguns by the Browning Superposed. Caliber for caliber, it kicks less than you'd think it should, because the polymer frame is flexing very slightly with the recoil and absorbing some of the impact.

While any semiautomatic pistol can have a stoppage due to cycling failure if it is not held with a locked wrist, absent human error the Glock performs at a high order of reliability shared only by the best Beretta, HK, SIG, S&W, and Ruger products. Its durability is unexceeded.

The company's motto, "Glock Perfection," sounds rather bold. They might have better said, "Quest for Perfection," because I have to say that the company has been responsive to constructive criticism. When some felt the 5.5-pound trigger was too light for police work and self-defense, they made heavier pulls available. The first fix was an 8-pound connector between the trigger bar and the unique cruciform sear plate, but that didn't do much to mitigate unintentional discharges and just made the pistol harder to shoot accurately. At the request of the New York State Police, Glock came up with a new module to replace the trigger spring. Dubbed the New York Trigger (NY-1), it gave a firm resistance to the

Using his trademark Glock 34, David Sevigny wins another IDPA National Championship.

GLOCKS					
Model	Frame Size	Style	Caliber	Barrel (")	Capacity
G17	Standard	Full size	9X19	4.5	17
G17L	Standard	Longslide	9X19	6.0	17
G18 S	Standard	Machine pistol	9X19	4.5	33
G19	Standard	Compact	9X19	4.0	15
G20	Large	Full size	10mm Auto	4.6	15
G21	Large	Full size	.45 Auto	4.6	13
G22	Standard	Full size	.40	4.5	15
G23	Standard	Compact	.40	4.0	13
G24	Standard	Longslide .	.40	6.0	15
G25	Standard	Compact	.380	4.0	15
G26	Standard	Subcompact	9X19	3.5	10
G27	Standard	Subcompact	.40	3.5	9
G28	Standard	Subcompact	.380	3.5	10
G29	Large	Compact	10mm Auto	3.8	10
G30	Large	Compact	.45 Auto	3.8	10
G31	Standard	Full size	.357	4.5	15
G32	Standard	Compact	.357	4.0	13
G33	Standard	Subcompact	.357	3.5	9
G34	Standard	Tactical/Practical	9X19	5.3	17
G35	Standard	Tactical/Practical	.40	5.3	15
G36	Large/Slimmed	Compact	.45 Auto	3.8	6
G37	Standard	Full size	.45 GAP	4.5	10
G38	Standard	Compact	.45 GAP	4.0	8
G39	Standard	Subcompact	.45 GAP	3.5	6

trigger finger from the very beginning of the pull, and brought total pull weight up to about eight pounds while still using the 5-pound connector. NYSP adopted the Glock 17 so equipped, and kept the NY-1 when they later switched to the Glock 37. NYPD wanted an even heavier pull for the Glock 19 that was the most popular on the city's list of three approved 9mm service pistols. Glock introduced a module that raised pull weight to nearly 12 pounds, the NY-2, but it made the gun so difficult to shoot that no entities but NYPD and the New York State Parole office seem to have adopted that variation.

This, plus strong emphasis from Glock and other sectors of the police training community on keeping the finger out of the trigger guard until one has actually chosen to fire, has made the Glock pistol a safe gun in competent hands. It can be argued that no gun is safe in incompetent hands.

While I personally feel the NY-2 trigger passes a point of diminishing returns with its nearly 12-pound pull weight over a short travel, the nominally 8-pound NY-1 trigger gives a remarkably good pull, one that can satisfy the liability defense attorney and the marksman alike. I have it in all my carry Glocks, have won matches with it, and prefer it for several reasons. First, there is the liability element. It's not safer so much because it's a couple of pounds heavier; it's safer because it gives a firm resistance to the finger from the very beginning of the pull. The standard Glock trigger pull is rather like that of a classic Mauser military rifle: a long, light take-up, and then only a short space where the trigger resists the finger before giving a clean break. The vasoconstriction that accompanies fight or flight response makes us lose our sense of touch and fine motor skill, and that light

take-up can be lost under stress. The firm resistance of the New York trigger is more likely to be felt by the shooter, under these circumstances, in time to prevent an accidental discharge.

Second, the New York pull gives a crisper, cleaner break. The regular Glock trigger gives you a bit of a *sproing* like your childhood cap pistol when the shot goes, and the NY does not. It also seems to control backlash better. Finally, it is more durable. I've seen several of the little "s"-shaped springs that connect the trigger bar to the cruciform sear plate break over the years, but I've personally never seen an NY-1 fail. It's simply a stronger unit.

Early on, shooters discovered that the plastic Glock sights tended to break. Install some good metal night sights (you can order them as a factory option), and the NY-1 trig-

Above: Glock 37 holds 11 rounds of .45 GAP, and is standard issue now for state troopers in Georgia, New York, Pennsylvania, and South Carolina.

Left: Glocks ride in an estimated 70% of American police duty holsters. This is a G21 in .45 ACP.

Tinkering with Glocks is something enthusiasts can't resist. This early G23 has Caspian slide with BoMar sights installed low…

…and Will Schuemann's Hybrid recoil compensator system, which reduces muzzle jump remarkably well…

…creating, overall, a surprisingly useful custom pistol.

ger module, and you have an extraordinarily robust pistol.

The 3.5-pound trigger is, as Glock clearly states in its literature, for target shooters only. I wouldn't put it in a carry gun, and I've seen a lot of people who do better with the New York because it gives them more of a surprise break. The lighter pull will of course better survive a trigger jerk, but jerking the trigger is not how people win affairs involving pistols. Another option popular among the cognoscenti is mating the 3.5-pound connector to the NY-1 module, which gives a smooth, revolverish pull of about five pounds.

The Glock is famous for its endurance and its ability to work dry. Recently, at Frank Garcia's excellent "thousand rounds a day" shooting course (frankgarciausa@yahoo.com), I deliberately ran my G17 bone dry for the first two days. There were no malfunctions. Didn't clean it, either. I know a lot of Glocksmen who routinely go 5,000 rounds between cleanings with no problems. Neither is a good idea, but it's good to know that the gun will take it. In 2003, the trigger pivot pin broke on my G22 during the Police Combat state shoot. I didn't notice until I went to clean it when I got home; the pistol had kept working, and won the match for me. There are stories of range rental Glocks that have gone hundreds of thousands of documented rounds and kept working. In a world where many service pistols have a real-world service life of only 10,000 rounds, that's something to conjure with.

Some models, notably the G19 and G30, will occasionally eject to the rear and bounce a spent casing off your right earmuff. If that bothers you, a good gunsmith or factory-trained armorer can tweak ejector and extractor to fix that. And, for heaven's sake, use only Glock magazines! There's not an aftermarket unit out there that I'd trust.

Some find the pistol large for their hands, particularly the bigger frame models. Gaston Glock and his team designed the G17 as a military weapon, to fit the typical combat soldier, an average size adult male. Furthermore, they designed it on the assumption that the shooter would activate the trigger with the pad of the index finger. For those who prefer to make contact at the distal joint, trigger reach may also be too far.

Solution: Robbie Barrkman came up with the "Robarize" job, in which the hollow in the back of the grip is filled with epoxy, and then the whole thing is taken down, moving the rear grip-strap forward and profoundly improving trigger reach. For information reach out to www.robarguns.com. My friend Rick Devoid also does an excellent job of this, and you can reach him at www.tarnhelm.com.

For those who wish their Glock had a traditional manual safety, Devoid can handle that too. He installs the safety developed by Joe Comminolli of Syracuse, New York. Right hand only, operating with a downward swipe of the thumb like a 1911 or Browning Hi-Power's lever, it's natural, quick, and sturdy. I've carried one for months at a time and found it ergonomic and foolproof. Glock's own short-lived 17-S had its thumb safety mounted on the slide, where the selector switch is located on the G18 machine pistol.

Glock's enhancement of their products continues. More recently we've seen the SF option, a frame that is shorter front to back on the 10mm and .45 ACP versions, to better fit smaller hands. The RTF (Rough Textured Finish) option feels a little like permanent skateboard tape, factory-applied to the grips. By the time you read this, you will hopefully be able to purchase Glocks with replaceable backstrap panels to adapt grip size and trigger reach to individual shooters' needs.

Personal Experience

One day in the early 1980s, Phil Engeldrum, publisher of the wild and fun gun magazine *Pistolero*, called me after return-ing from EWA, the European firearms trade show. "Hey, Mas, you ever hear of a pistol called a 'Glock'?" Phil raved about it, and when I got my hands on one, I understood why. Sinfully light, a natural pointer, and remarkably reliable, it began making friends immediately.

It took me a while to warm up to the gun. In 1988, when my older daughter asked for a 9mm for her 11th birthday, I got her one of the first Glock 19s. In 1990, I went through Glock Instructor School and Glock Armorer School in Smyrna. That same year, I wrote a magnum opus on the pistol in *Guns* magazine that detailed what I liked about Glocks and what I didn't. Carl Walter, head of Glock USA at the time, was so furious he pulled seven figures worth of advertising out of *Guns* and its sister magazines, demanding that I be fired before the ad contract would be reinstated. Our publisher – the now deceased George von Rosen, God bless him – stood behind me and kept me there as handgun editor, where I still serve. When new people took over in Smyrna, we got along OK. The company fixed the things I had complained about.

Glock's success has led to development of other excellent pistols with polymer frames and striker-fired mechanisms, such as this Croation Springfield Armory XD and...

I've had good luck with these guns. In '99, I won Senior class in the New England Regional IDPA Championships with a Glock 17 tuned by Chris

...the Smith & Wesson Military & Police, here in .40 S&W.

Gosselin at Glockworks, and came in second Master behind Tom Yost, who was then only weeks out from winning the National Championship. I had used that same pistol to make Master in the first place on the International Defensive Pistol Association's demanding Classifier course, in the Stock Service Pistol division.

From 2001 to 2003, I won the NH state shoot for cops with the Glock 22 I carry on duty when I'm testing new security holsters for my department. (Because the standard size Glock is the most popular service pistol today, it's always the first gun they make new police holsters for.) With Black Hills' powerful and extraordinarily accurate EXP load, a 165-grain .40 Gold Dot at 1140 fps, it gives me 2- to 2.5-inch groups at 25 yards. In '03, when I went to clean the G22 after winning the shoot, I noticed a hole in the frame over the trigger guard. The trigger pivot pin had broken, and a third of it had left the pistol. Yet the gun still worked fine and won the match for me. How many other handguns could have done that?

I've become increasingly fond of its baby Glock brother, the G27 subcompact. In standard cut (but not tailored) police uniform pants, or BDUs, it rides concealably in a pocket holster, and takes the same magazines as the G22 on the duty belt. In the hottest weather, it disappears under a tucked-in shirt in a bellyband. With Winchester 155-grain .40 S&W Silvertip, it once gave me a 1.5-inch group for five shots at 25 yards, witnessed by Indiana state action shooting champion Detective Dennis Reichard.

Thus far, we've discussed primarily the standard size Glock pistols. They are the most popular and the most famous. However, there are some of us who are partial to the larger frame models. The Glock .45 and 10mm pistols have carved their own special niches in the world of working handguns. The G20 is the most popular 10mm auto in the world right now, and is mentioned in the chapter on the Bren Ten. My personal favorite of the baker's dozen Glocks I own is a G30 .45 with Tarnhelm grip trim. It has twice given me five-shot groups at 25 yards that measured under an inch, once with 185-grain Remington Match ammo and once with 230-grain Hydra-Shok.

It's hard to ask more than that of a low-price mass production pistol.

Notes

[1]Mullin, Timothy J., *The 100 Greatest Combat Pistols*, Boulder, CO: Paladin Press, 1994, p. 18.

[2]Karwan, Chuck, *The Gun Digest Book of Combat Handgunnery*, Third Edition, Northbrook, IL: DBI Books, 1992, pp. 117-118.

[3]Taylor, Chuck, *The Gun Digest Book of Combat Handgunnery*, Fourth Edition, Iola, WI: Krause Publications, 1997, p. 37.

[4]*Ibid.*, p. 38.

[5]Mullin, *op.cit.*, p. 17.

[6]Schwing, Ned, 2005 *Standard Catalog of Firearms*, Iola, WI: Krause Publications, 2004, p. 523.

[7]Law, Richard, and Brookesmith, Peter, *The Fighting Handgun*, London, England: Arms and Armour Press, 1996, p. 146.

[8]Ayoob, Massad, *The Gun Digest Book of Combat Handgunnery*, Fifth Edition, Iola, WI: Krause Publications, 2002, p. 27.

HK
A History of Innovation

Through the latter half of the 20th century and thus far into the 21st, the firm of Heckler and Koch, GmbH, has been providing sophisticated small arms to armies, law enforcement agencies, and discriminating private sector shooters all over the world. There have been a few glitches, a few less than shining stars in the firmament of HK weaponry, but remarkably few. In a real world where consistent absence of failure is often more important than occasional flashes of spectacular success, that counts for a lot.

> Quietly favored by a surprisingly large percentage of the professionally armed, Heckler and Koch products are mission-designed and built on a baseline of reliability.

A Brief History

The HK marque has a unique background. Born in the rubble of post-WWII West Germany, with little more than a national heritage of engineer-

HK's current P2000 with LEM trigger: an excellent service pistol.

Left: Modern HK pistols are very southpaw-friendly. This P7M8 rides in the off-duty holster of left-handed police chief and pistol champion Bob Houzenga.

Tip of Spyderco knife points to essential P7 cleaning area. Barrel affixed permanently to frame helped the P7 establish its excellent reputation for accuracy.

ing excellence and understanding of weapons design and realization of the importance of product quality to sustain it, HK developed with the same determined and plodding steps of the nation that gave it birth.

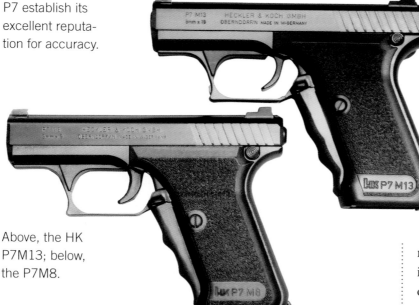

Above, the HK P7M13; below, the P7M8.

There is no better concise history of the firm than that written by Ned Schwing, for many years the author of the annual small arms encyclopedia *Standard Catalog of Firearms*. Writes Ned, "At the end of WWII, the French dismantled the Mauser factory as a part of their reparations; and the buildings remained idle until 1949, when firearms production was again allowed in Germany. Heckler & Koch was formed as a machine tool enterprise and occupied the vacant Mauser plant. In the early 1950s Edmund Heckler and Theodor Koch began to produce the G3 automatic rifle based on the Spanish CETME design and progressed to machine guns and submachine guns and eventually to the production of commercial civilian rifles and pistols. In 1990 the company got into financial difficulties because of a failed contract bid. In December 1990 the French state consortium GIAT announced the

purchase of Heckler and Koch, but a little more than a year later the contract was cancelled. Later in 1991 the company was purchased by Royal Ordnance of Britain. In 2002 the company was sold to a combined group of European investors and long-time company managers."

In a sad footnote, HK rifle design has tenuous roots in the darkest portion of German history, the Nazi years. Shortly before the end of WWII, small arms engineers of Oberndorf am Neckar came up with a "roller lock" mechanism that would theoretically provide a more controllable fully automatic assault rifle. Ludwig Vorgrimmler, late of Mauser, continued work on that design in France after WWII. He was recruited by Spain's Centro de Estudios Tecnicos de Materiales Especiales (CETME), leading the team that finalized the CETME automatic rifle in 1952. Perceiving a need for German technology, the Spaniards invited H&K to take a piece of the action, and in 1956, the Heckler and Koch selective-fire 7.62mm NATO battle rifle was born. Christened the G3, it would later be dubbed the HK91 in

its semi-automatic version. Heckler and Koch had begun its forward roll into arms-making history.

HK Pistols

Most folks think Glock innovated plastic-framed pistols. Not so. Heckler and Koch did.

In the late 1960s, Heckler and Koch introduced their P9 with plastic frame. A single action semi-auto, it was made primarily in 9mm though 7.65mm (.30 Luger) barrels were also produced for it in small numbers. It was the time of double action automatic pistols, though, and the P9 quickly gave way to the P9S.

The P7M10. Note disproportionately high slide, needed for enough mass to reduce slide velocity from the high-pressure .40 S&W cartridge.

The rare P7M10, caliber .40 S&W. From the Penny Dean collection.

Author strongly recommends this "slingshot" technique, as opposed to usual American overhand or saddle method, with P7.

Seen in the hands of its owner, gun rights attorney Penny Dean, the P7M10 demonstrates its extremely high bore axis. Author considers it the only "clunky" P7 ever made.

This was an ingenious weapon. Not only was the frame made of plastic, but the decocking mechanism actually worked off the trigger. A lever behind the trigger guard on the left side of the frame, which also served as a slide lock and slide release lever, was depressed. While the thumb held it down, the index finger pulled the trigger, and then the thumb slowly raised the lever to complete the decocking.

Was this awkward? It was, indeed, the sort of thing that would give police firearms instructors nightmares that could cause them to wake up screaming. Needless to say, the gun did not catch on in the United States. It was not totally rejected by any means, however. The conservation officers of the state of Idaho were issued .45 caliber HK P9S pistols. The 9mm P9S became standard issue for the SWAT officers of SLED, the South Carolina Law Enforcement Division.

The P9S design was "selective double action," in the same sense as the later, much more popular CZ75. In other words, while the first shot could be set to require a long, heavy double-action trigger pull, all subsequent shots would be self-cocked to fire single action – but, instead of using the scary P9S decocking mechanism, you could just leave it cocked and engage the manual safety. This was the pattern that most professionals seemed to choose once they got to know their P9S pistols.

One could write a full-length dissertation on "ergonomics and the HK P9S pistol." Yes, decocking it would make your skin crawl. Yes, the slide-mounted safety catch was "backwards" in the American judgment of the time: up for fire and down for safe, instead of vice versa as on a "real American's 1911 pistol." What made that worse was that the safety lever was a vestigial little nub that could not be activated by the normal human hand under stress. Virtually ALL of us who used these guns and carried them cocked and locked, had them fitted with oversize safety levers by custom pistolsmiths. (Nolan Santy did mine.) The magazine used a butt-heel release in the traditional European style, much slower than the push button release an American named Georg Luger had popularized three quarters of a century before, and which another American named John Browning had made his nation's standard.

However, the accuracy was phenomenal. The .45 ACP version, developed exclusively for the American market, could put five out of five in an inch at 25 yards with Match hardball. The 9mm could do the same with Federal's 115-grain JHP load. It has been postulated, though never really proven, that one reason for this superior accuracy was the fact that the P9S used a roller-lock mechanism that brought the barrel/slide assembly back into a constant relationship with the frame after every shot.

The trigger pulls were an interesting mix. If you go on the Internet, you'll find people saying the P9S had a horrible trigger, and people saying it had a great one. Neither are lying. You just have to know which trigger system they had.

The Service models of the P9S had atrocious double action trigger pulls – heavy, draggy, and lo-o-ong. Their single action pulls weren't particularly light and had so much backlash that when the sear released, the now un-resisted trigger finger would slam back against the inside of its guard on the plastic grip frame so hard that it could literally move the gun before the bullet left the barrel.

However, the Target and Sport/Target versions had single action trigger pulls that were as good as the service models were bad. A lever built into the back of the trigger guard on the polymer frame, adjustable and lockable by a set-screw, acted as a trigger stop. With it set to do its job, the double action function of the pistol was locked out

Why overhand slide manipulation can be problematic with the HK P7. For a right-handed shooter, left thumb is now in proximity to take-down button on left of frame below slide…

…and inadvertent disassembly can occur.

and the P9S became single action only. The backlash was completely eliminated.

That was only part of the trigger package in the Target and Sport/Target models. The other element was a trigger adjustable in pull weight that was simply the best of

Fat magazine plus squeeze-cock lever means the P7M13 has a lot of grip girth for fingers to get around, as seen here. Author finds the slimmer P7M8 far more ergonomic. HK sales figures showed that most other shooters felt the same.

its time, and one of the best ever. You could get the pull down into the high two pounds weight range without the gun "doubling." The adjustment was a simple slot-head screw in the trigger mechanism, readily accessible as soon as you field-stripped the barrel/slide assembly off the polymer frame.

Another polymer framed HK pistol that predated the Glock and all the rest of today's crop was the VP70Z. HK definitely made the first polymer framed pistol: whether that HK was the P9 or the VP70 may depend on which was on the drawing board first *vis-à-vis* which left the factory first. It is possible that the VP70 was indeed the first polymer handgun, though by this writer's lights the P9 would have been the first successful polymer frame pistol.

While all P9-series HKs had single stack magazines, the VP70 had a fat double stack magazine that let the gun hold 18 rounds. Originally designed as a machine pistol, it would only fire full auto when attached to its shoulder-stock. The rate of fire on full auto was stated by some experts to be over 2000 rounds per second, generally deemed too fast to control with a machine pistol. With the stock removed, and the pistol sold by itself, it became the HK VP70Z. "VP" pur-

portedly stood for *volkspistole*, or "people's pistol"; the "Z" suffix meant "zivil," a civilian model.

Having shot the VP70 both as a machine pistol and a semiautomatic handgun, this writer remains unimpressed. If it worked as a buzz gun, it would have stayed in the HK catalog. It did indeed function with ball ammo, but I found that with any hollow point except Remington, it was likely to choke. The gun had odd sights, a front that completely filled the rear notch, with the designers counting on a "shadow" concept to make the front sight visible to the shooter under stress. It didn't work well. An early striker-fired design, the VP had a horrendously heavy and difficult-to-control trigger pull. Introduced in 1970, the VP70 went under in 1989.

Every gun company that has been around a while has had a model that was to its brand what the Edsel was to Ford. For HK, I submit, that model was the VP70Z. This may be unfair to the Edsel. At least the Edsel actually worked. I've seen more than one jam-a-matic VP70Z pistol.

Perhaps the iconic HK pistol is the P7. Known to the public as the "squeeze cocker," to its advertising agency as "continuous action," and to Jeff Cooper and his acolytes as the "squirt gun" because you had to squeeze it to shoot it, the HK P7 occupies a unique place in handgun history. The lever at the front of its grip-frame had to be firmly depressed for it to work.

Originally designated PSP, supposedly for Police Self-loading Pistol, it was soon renamed the P7. These original P7s had slim, smooth grip-frames containing slim, smooth eight-shot magazines. The sights were big and blocky, much more so than most pistols of circa 1980. This contributed to a "shootability" that took advantage of their inherent accuracy, which was enhanced by a barrel solidly fixed to the frame.

A fountain of brass is airborne as Bob Houzenga fires a "Bill Drill" with HK P7M8. Named for pistol champ Bill Wilson, that means…

(Inset): …that Houzenga has reacted to a start signal, drawn, and fired six hits all in the center of this IDPA target from seven yards – all in under two seconds. P7s help the best shooters shoot their best.

Tip of Spyderco knife points to the inconspicuous lever which must be pressed rearward to manually lock back the slide of a P7 pistol.

With a very low bore axis, the P7 was also gas operated, which bled off some of the recoil impulse. With these two factors in play, the P7 had extraordinarily mild recoil. That was another big plus for the serious shooter. Soon, the P7 fan club had spread, gaining almost cult status.

The first PSPs had a butt heel magazine release. This was typical of European auto pistols, but the P7's differed in that instead of the usual set-up where the catch was pressed toward the rear of the pistol to release the mag, the P7's catch was pressed forward. This turned out to be much faster than the typical butt-catch. On most such guns, including HK's own P9S, the thumb pushed the latch to the rear and the middle and/or index finger caught the lip of the floorplate and pulled the magazine out. On the P7, a simple forward pressure caused the mag to fall free. Not so fast as the Luger/Colt/Browning push button style, it was distinctly faster than others of its kind. HK followed with a more streamlined version of the butt catch that was shielded by newly-designed grip panels so it did not protrude, thus protecting it from inadvertent dropping of the magazine when the gun butt brushed against seat cushions while sitting,

or against the ground while shooting from prone.

As butt catches go, the P7/PSP's was fast, but not fast enough for the American market. In the early 1980s, as momentum was building up for what would be a massive nationwide switch from service revolver to semiautomatic pistol in American police service, the New Jersey State Police approached H&K with a request for modification. They loved the P7, they said, but rapid reloads were seen as essential to their mission. Could they put a thumb-activated release on the gun?

Since the squeeze-cocker mechanism would have gotten in the way of a conventional magazine release button on the side of the grip-frame, HK engineers came up with an ingenious ambidextrous lever located at the rear of the trigger guard. A press downward instead of inward would dump the magazine. As an added bonus, this allowed the shooter to do so with his thumb on one side or his index finger on the other. For many, the latter was faster since the trigger finger could snap back to do the job without shifting the hand, as was often necessary to get a thumb in position to activate a side-mounted magazine release.

Because of the gas operation, it was noted that the P7 heated up quickly in the frame area during long strings of fire, as in training or competition. The updated design, called the P7M8, included a "heat shield" in this area, which also required a re-shaping of the trigger guard. NJSP adopted the P7M8, with each trooper carrying four spare eight-shot magazines. To work with the new design release, the P7M8 magazine had a sharp little projection on either side. P7 purists felt this interfered with the smooth lines of their icon, and within the P7 cult traditionalists would always favor the original style. While the P7 was officially discontinued circa 1984 in favor of the P7M8, it would occasionally be run in small lots by the factory to satisfy insistent demand from aficionadoes.

The early '80s were also the time of the JSSAP (Joint Services Small Arms Project) tests to select a 9mm service pistol to replace the 1911A1 .45 with the US Armed Forces. HK widened the grip frame and came up with a 13-shot magazine, and the result was the P7M13, following the tradition the company had established when it named the P7M8 after the magazine capacity. While it did not find favor in JSSAP circles, the P7M13 was adopted by a number of American police departments, becoming for instance standard issue for Utah's state troopers.

When Smith & Wesson and Winchester jointly announced the .40 S&W cartridge in 1990, it was accepted more quickly than any new service round since the .38 Special. Splitting the difference between 9mm Parabellums such as the P7 series and the .45 ACP of the classic Colt and some others, the .40 was recognized as a compromise that could solve debate and get past controversy so trainers could concentrate on the tactics and marksmanship under

stress that would really decide whether their officers lived or died. Demand for .40s was so great that every mainstream maker jumped on the bandwagon, and HK was no exception. The firm went in two directions: one was the USP, which we'll discuss shortly. The other was the P7M10.

This was the only "clunky" P7 to ever make it out of the factory. Since brutal slide velocity was beating up most makers' "9mms suddenly rechambered for .40," Heckler and Koch went for a massive slide that brought weight up to about two and two-thirds pounds and felt heavier than that in the hand. In the P7M10, the slimness and lithe, fast

Below: Activating the P7. Front lever is at rest, trigger finger in register unseen on opposite side of the frame. Now…

Left: …shooter's grasp tightens, squeeze cocking the pistol. Note that cocking indicator at rear of slide is now protruding. Lever must be held in (minimum pressure is required) to keep the gun firing. P7s demand firm grasp…a good thing.

handling of the original P7 was simply gone. The gun was a massive sales failure, soon discontinued, and today is a rare oddity that seems to be loved only by P7 collectors.

P7s were produced in small quantities in other calibers. A scaled down version, the P7K3, was manufactured in .380 ACP and .22 Long Rifle. It was the only true in-house HK pocket pistol design. For years the company offered the HK4 in .22 LR, .25 auto, .32 ACP, and .380, but that gun was little more than an updated Mauser HSc, another thread of the Mauser karma that runs through the history of Heckler and Koch. The rarest of P7 pistols is the P7M7, a seven-shot .45 ACP produced experimentally circa 1983. It is believed that no more than six were ever made, none leaving the possession of HK. One is occasionally displayed in the expansive HK booth at SHOT and AWA trade shows.

Today, the P7 is available only in the M8 configuration. Its high price drove it out of market competition with armies, with police departments, and with American consumers.

The mainstay of the HK pistol line today is the USP and its derivatives. Greeted by a collective yawn when they pioneered plastic pistol frames with the P9 and VP70Z, HK put all its money on the all-steel P7 to win the pistol races, only to see it eclipsed by less expensive polymer frame guns after Glock ran with the plastic ball and changed the face of the market. Priced out of the market

with the P7, HK went back to the drawing board and came up with the Universal Service Pistol in 1993.

A modular fire control system created a "Burger King" gun in the USP: you could "Have it your way." Ned Schwing lists the variants of the USP fire control system as follows:

1. DA/SA with safe position and control lever on left side of frame.
2. DA/SA with safe position and control lever on right side of frame.
3. DA/SA without safe position and decocking lever on left side of frame.
4. DA/SA without safe position and decocking lever on right side of frame.
5. DA only with safe position and safety lever on left side of frame.
6. DA only with safe position and safety lever on right side of frame.
7. DA only without control lever.
8.
9. DA/SA with safe position and safety lever on left side of frame.
10. DA/SA with safety lever on the right side of frame.

The empty spot I've left by Variant 8 is not a misprint. For some reason, HK set aside one number for a fire control system not yet planned. Just what Variant 8 was or would have been remains an unsolved mystery among HK fans.

Variant I, for most of the USP's epoch, was the most popular format. It gave the shooter choices of double action first shot, carried on safe or off, or the option of single action cocked and locked carry. A press downward on the lever brought it from "safe" to "fire," and pressing still further down decocked the pistol.

Early versions were marked "PSP," lacked the longer trigger guard/"heat shield" treatment, and had magazine release catches mounted at the butt.

Today, there is great demand for a variant not anticipated in 1993: the LEM. The Law Enforcement Module or Law Enforcement Modification came out of HK's recognition that the police market was going double action only for reasons of perceived safety. HK's own DAO variant of the USP had a trigger pull that could most charitably be described as mediocre. The ingenious LEM changed that.

In the May-June 2003 issue of *American Handgunner* magazine, Dave Anderson described the new mechanism succinctly: "Compared to the original double-action only trigger, the LEM provides a pull that is lighter, smoother, with shorter trigger travel and much quicker trigger reset. Currently it's available for law enforcement personnel only with a pull of 7.5-8.5 pounds. A variation with a 4.5-5.5 pound pull is planned which should have considerable potential for production-class competition."

Dave continued, "The LEM hammer is actually a two-piece unit with an internal cocking piece separate from the external hammer. When the shooter inserts a loaded magazine and racks the slide to chamber a cartridge, the mainspring is fully compressed. The external hammer then extends slightly from the slide, serving as a visual and tactile indicator the gun is cocked. When the trigger is pulled, instead of having to overcome the resistance of the powerful mainspring, the shooter is pulling only against the lighter resistance of the trigger return spring for the initial take-up. During this take-up the external hammer is rocked back to its full rearward position. With the test gun it took a pressure of 3.5 pounds to move the trigger through a travel of 7/16 inch. From there, pressure built smoothly and predictably to 8.5 pounds over an additional 5/16 inch of travel, at which point the sear released to fire the gun. After firing, a forward movement of the trigger of just 5/16 inch was required to reset the trig-

ger for the next shot. There is no need to let the trigger move all the way forward for follow-up shots, although the gun will function just fine if you do. Quick trigger reset is a feature competitive shooters value, as it's one of the keys to fast and accurate shooting."

The LEM vaulted into the forefront of police auto sales by HK, and became the heart of the company's superb follow-up to the USP, the P2000 series. Very accurate, and with light recoil, the P2000 guns ushered in a new feature: ambidextrous slide stop/slide release levers.

Top: This hard-chromed HK P7M8 makes an excellent carry pistol, in properly trained hands.

Bottom: Author's favorite P7 is this early generation 9mm.

The USP is available today in 9mm, .40 S&W, .357 SIG, and .45 ACP, while the P2000 and the compact P2000K are made primarily in 9mm and .40. When virtually all serious service pistols were put through the grueling ICE tests for adoption by Homeland Security a few years ago, only these HKs and the SIG made it through. No one seriously questions the endurance of today's "plastic" HK pistols.

A pioneering feature on the first USP was an integral accessory rail molded into the frame. Designed to take HK's proprietary UTL (Universal Tactical Light), it was an instant success and quickly copied by almost every other maker. Others went to the universal rail configuration to allow lights such as the superb SureFire X-series. HK followed in turn, incorporating a universal rail in the P2000 series.

Today, you'll literally find polymer frame HK pistols in police holsters in the four corners of the continental United States. Maine State Troopers have USP .45s at their hips, and the Washington State Patrol issues the USP in .40 S&W. San Bernardino, California, once the murder capitol of the nation,

Second generation of P7 butt-heel magazine release, prior to HK going to the M-series system.

selected the HK USP .40 for its city police. In humid Florida, deputy sheriffs from St. John's County on the Atlantic Coast to Leon County, surrounding the state capitol of Tallahassee on the Gulf, are issued the HK USP pistol in .45 ACP. Feds from the Border Patrol to the US Park Police now also issue modern polymer HK pistols.

The HK Legacy

Fine German workmanship has come to be so expected that it's something of a stereotype. Mercedes and Volkswagen. Leica. Zeiss and Schmidt & Bender.

And, of course, Heckler and Koch.

Machines. Machines designed precisely to do a certain job. Machines designed to work without fail with minimal maintenance. Machines designed with little subtleties of ergonomics that make them easier to use.

Call it a stereotype if you want, but HK "fits the profile."

HK Weaponry: A Personal Perspective

Every reader has a right to know where the writer of an article is coming from. "In the interest of full disclosure," as journalists are supposed to say. Fair enough.

I started working seriously with H&K firearms in the late 1970s. I was invited down to South Carolina for a bash hosted by H&K with SLED SWAT, the South Carolina Law Enforcement Division's elite Special Weapons and Tactics Team. The several days included an introduction to the then-new PSP pistol, later dubbed the PSP – I believe my article on it tied for the first published in this country, or came out a day or two ahead of the nearest competition – and a blend of Southern deer hunt and scheutzenfest. We chopped down trees with G3 .308s on full auto. We hunted deer with the G3 and its sporterized cousin, the sleek Model 770. I hunted the small South Carolina white-tails with an HK P9S .45 auto with extended barrel, though I never got close enough to take a shot. We ran the G3 full auto next to the FN FAL, and the HK33 full auto next to the M16. We shot their sniper rifles, and we shot about every pistol they had.

I left impressed. A couple of years later, when John Bressem took over marketing for HK in the USA and decided to put together an official HK pistol team, I found myself on board. My choice was the phenomenally accurate P9S Sport .45 and Sport/Target 9mm. The latter came in a kit with wooden flat grips, wooden International-style thumb-rest target stocks, barrel weight, and the whole nine yards including a short Service barrel/slide assembly that I rarely used. It sold for over $1,000 in the early 1980s. I just saw one on the Internet selling for $6000. Didn't even feel tempted. Mine is not for sale. I won High HK Shooter one year at Bianchi Cup with the 9mm Sport/Target, shooting it with the 1200-foot-second, 112-grain "saw tooth hollow point" 9mm rounds of my ammo sponsor at the time, Super Vel. I was told by the range staff who chronographed our ammo that I was shooting the single hottest load of the hundreds of competitors that year. It was no handicap in the easy-kicking, factory muzzle-weighted P9S Sport/Target, and indeed an advantage: it shot so flat I didn't have to change either sights or hold all the way out to 50 yards on Match One, the Practical, and I didn't have to lead as much as everybody else on Match Three, the Mover.

John Lawson and I were both writing for *American Handgunner* magazine back then, I as law enforcement editor and John as gunsmithing editor. John put a humongous barrel weight onto my HK .45, and Larry Kelly gave it the first trapezoidal version of MagnaPorting. John was kind enough to etch "Ayoob Special" onto the compensator, and I won a few guns with it at the Second Chance Shoot, with the 190-grain Super Vel .45 hollow points easily reefing the heavy pins back three feet off the table. I don't remember either gun ever jamming, though in fairness John had to "throat" the .45 for hollow points and Nolan Santy did the same for my 9mm.

The years went on. Briefly, I carried the P9S and the P7 on uniformed police patrol, in Gordon Davis and Safariland thumb-break duty holsters, respectively. Off duty, the P7 went many a mile with me in a variety of hideout holsters, most commonly Ted Blocker's LFI Concealment Rig. The only dedicated concealment holster I had for the P9S was a Summer Special-like IWB produced for the late, great Austin Behlert, but the 4-inch Target versions spent their time on my hip, especially in winter in the '80s because the big, Alpine-influenced Teutonic trigger guard made these guns friendly to the gloved hand.

The years went on. I had the chance one day at an IDPA match to stay late and re-enter with each of the four gun categories then in effect (the organization had not yet separated revolvers into two distinct categories). I managed to win three out of four and shot

Author set a short-lived national record with this HK P9S Sport/Target 9mm. Note long barrel with removable weight, integral adjustable trigger stop at lower rear of trigger guard, excellent sights, and oversize Nolan Santy thumb safety. Pistol is shown cocked and locked.

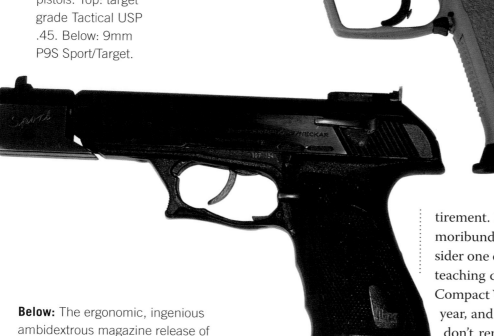

Heckler and Koch has produced some superbly accurate pistols. Top: target grade Tactical USP .45. Below: 9mm P9S Sport/Target.

Below: The ergonomic, ingenious ambidextrous magazine release of the M-series HK P7. A similar design followed in USP and P2000.

the best over-all score of the match with a P7M8 HK 9mm.

Nowadays, I still have several HKs in my gun safes. I don't shoot Bianchi Cup anymore, but if I did, I wouldn't hesitate to bring that grand old belt-carried small caliber rifle, the P9S Sport/Target, back out of retirement. Bowling pin shooting has become moribund, but if it catches back on, I'll consider one of my HK .45s. I change guns every teaching cycle and usually have my HK USP Compact Variant One .40 on for a week of the year, and still feel totally confident with it. I don't remember it ever shooting less than a perfect 300 score when I had to demonstrate the course of fire for the students. And the .45 USP is never gonna leave 'til I'm dead; it's just too big for a little guy like me to carry concealed for a week on the road.

It has been a long time since my department issue HK MP5-A3 has gone to work with me in its inconspicuous little gym bag on the floor of my patrol car. For my needs, "a bigger gun gives you more/of what you carry a big gun for." But once a year or so I teach the submachine gun, and the old MP5 comes out, and still struts its stuff with a few thousand rounds downrange with zero malfunctions and total control, so long as it's in hands that know what to do with it.

The HK remains a favorite of professionals. I personally understand, and appreciate, why.

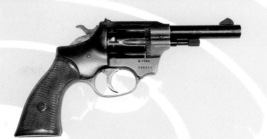

The High Standard Sentinel

I t was May of 2003. I was teaching a deadly force class at Ron Darnall's excellent shooting range in Bloomington, IL, and on break was browsing in his adjacent gunshop. I spotted a snub-nosed High Standard Sentinel .22 in a corner of the display case. "How much?" "$75," Ron answered. After checking the revolver over quickly I had only one more word to say: "Sold."

As we did the paperwork to transfer it home to another of my favorite gunshops, Lewis Arms in Bow, New Hampshire, a friend who was present smirked and asked, "Why are you buying a piece of junk like that?" "Ah, Grasshopper," I answered, "You've obviously never shot one. You wanna bet me five bucks that this little beast won't put five shots in two and a half inches at 25 yards?"

He took that bet. On my third try, Remington Thunderbolts landed in a tight cluster in the head. As we approached, I heard a smug, "Only four hits. One missed entirely." Seasoned range officer Joe Stidman was with us, and

Introduced as an inexpensive plinker and woods gun, this .22 was ahead of its time with landmark revolver design features. Perhaps most important, it broke a more than half-century logjam of design stagnation. Unfairly tarnished with a "junk gun" image, it may be the best buy in a used handgun available today.

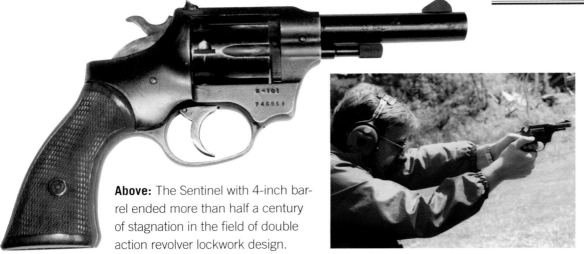

Above: The Sentinel with 4-inch barrel ended more than half a century of stagnation in the field of double action revolver lockwork design.

Left: Bob Houzenga, six time national champ, reminisces with a High Standard Sentinel like the ones with which he began his handgunning career at a tender age.

Joe Stidman, left, witnessed author, right, firing 1-1/8-inch five shot group at 25 yards with $75 Sentinel snub.

he said, "No. Look at the exits in the back. There's two through one hole." The five shot group measured 1-1/8 inches center to center. My skeptical friend was one more modern handgunner enlightened as to a little revolver that has largely become a forgotten treasure of mid-20th century firearms evolution.

The 1950s were boom times for new handgun introductions. The decade marked the return of the single action frontier style revolver once thought obsolete, the second flowering of the 1911, the introduction of the .44 Magnum, and a host of design upgrades. All but lost among them, to modern historians of handguns, was a landmark design that never received the recognition it deserved: the humble High Standard Sentinel .22 revolver.

Pedigree

The name Chic Gaylord was one to conjure with in the Fifties and Sixties. He had emerged as the dominant innovative holster maker of the time, specializing in concealment rigs, and he

Swing out cylinder, forward-sitting trigger show that the Double Nine is not the single action it pretends to be.

had also set various fast draw records. The guns he used almost exclusively in the latter endeavors were Hi-Standard Sentinels. ("Hi-Standard" was the way Gaylord wrote the manufacturer's name in his classic book, *Handgunner's Guide*, and that was how the name usually appeared on the gun barrels. Authoritative texts such as *Standard Catalog of Firearms* spell it High Standard, the way it often appeared in the company's literature. While this duality is worth about a one-beer argument among fans of the brand, most shooters including this writer use both spellings interchangeably.)

Wrote Gaylord in those pages, "Gun designer Harry Seifried dreamed up a nine-shot .22-caliber double-action revolver for Hi-Standard that has been hailed as the first 'new' gun to be designed in the past fifty years. The 'Sentinel' lists among its radical innovations a countersunk ratchet at the rear of the cylinder, a novel and sturdy locking device for the swing-out cylinder crane, a capsule action with the fastest lock time of any modern revolver, and last but not least the best balanced frame and grip since Sam Colt's famed 'hawg-leg'! This Hi-Standard Sentinel in nickel plate with a four- or six-inch barrel is in my opinion the best value for your money among the fun guns. Hi-Standard deserves kudos for putting out such a great gun for so little money."[1]

Though he recommended the longer tubes, it is said that Gaylord favored the 2-3/8-inch barrel version for fast draw, since the shorter gun cleared the holster faster. For the cowboy style that was in vogue at the time, he went to the Double-Nine, a Sentinel styled to resemble a Colt Single Action Army.

Experts of the period loved the gun. The then-new *Guns*, the first of the newsstand gun magazines, did a lavish spread on the Sentinel. The great Elmer Keith liked the gun, too. He wrote in his classic *Sixguns*:

"One revolver, entirely new in design, has appeared over the horizon in recent months – the High Standard Sentinel. It is a low priced $34.95 nine shot revolver chambering the .22 L.R. Cartridge. This gun is made in 3 inch or 5 inch barrel and was designed by my friend, Harry Sefried [sic]. It is the first radical change in revolver frame design we have seen in a great many years. The frame is in two parts, namely the frame proper, and the grip and trigger guard. The grip is one piece with a through bolt and shaped much like the early Colt Cap and Ball actions in .31 and .36 caliber and has about the same angle to the frame. It is a double action revolver holding nine rounds. The cylinder has a drilled hole ratchet and counter sunk shell heads cut out for the firing pin so it will not burr chamber rims. The cylinder latch is also an innovation and a complete change from existing models, yet it is a solid frame gun as only the crane swings out for ejection and reloading. It has simultaneous ejection, and a hardened cone shaped pin in the   rear end of the base pin that fits into a tapered hole in the aluminum alloy frame. That is the main cylinder lock but an enlargement of the extractor rod also recesses into the frame cut to hold the front end of the base pin in alignment.

"...The little gun seemed to shoot very accurately and was a very good gun for fast double action practice, either aimed fire or hip shooting...Judge Martin, to whom (the test sample) belongs, claimed it was a darn good 200 yard gun...No malfunction or misfires occurred throughout the tests. All told, it seems to be a good little gun for the price asked, and one that balances perfectly and has a remarkably well-shaped grip set at the correct angle to the frame. It is low enough behind the trigger guard so that the weight of the gun rests on the second finger, the same as the Colt, Ruger, and G.W. (Great Western brand) Single actions do. This, and its excellent pointing from the hip make it a very fine understudy for the big caliber double action revolvers. It should prove a popular and practical gun for the fisherman or camper."[2]

HI-STANDARD
.22 CAL.

Hi-Standard .22 revolvers' cylinders released by pulling forward on the ejector rod. Cylinder locking at both front and rear of frame window harkens back to the famed S&W Triple Lock, and is seen today as an accuracy-enhancing feature of the Dan Wesson and custom S&W Performance Center revolvers.

True was then the dominant "man's magazine," and its gun editor Lucian Cary was a strong voice in molding the opinions of shooters. He seemed to favor the Double-Nine version of the Sentinel, because it put a more shootable gun in the hands of those who wanted the Frontier-style revolver that was then all the rage. The caption under a photo of the Double-Nine in 1959's "Lucian Cary on Guns" said, "Nothing is more remarkable than the return of the single action revolver. Westerns of TV, and in movies and magazines, are probably responsible. But few of the millions who see TV Westerns are aware that modern double action revolvers are better weapons. The gun above, by High Standard, preserves the lines of the original Colt single action, but is really a modern double action gun."[3]

These affordable, smooth-shooting wheelguns gave many handgunners their start in the game. Bob Houzenga, who went on to win six national handgun championships and countless state titles, remembers that the first handguns he ever fired were the Sentinels owned by his father and grandfather.

A Brief History

Harry Seifried brought a lot of innovative designs to the firearms world, but the Sentinel may have been his high water mark during the time he worked for High Standard. Introduced in 1955 with glowing reviews like those above, the Sentinel caught the interest of handgun buyers. Hefting each in a gun shop, the buyer discovered that the

cost was only a little more than that of the classic economy revolvers, the Iver Johnson and the Harrington & Richardson, but the action and overall "feel" were much more in keeping with the comparatively premium-priced Smith & Wesson. Sales took off, and High Standard did the Hollywood thing: they introduced spin-offs based on the original hit.

The 6-inch barrel was added to the standard Sentinel in 1956, and a police service revolver-style 4-inch barrel in 1957. In the latter year, High Standard staged one of the most garish episodes in the history of handgunning when the aluminum anodized finish was offered in three colors that were radical for firearms: gold, turquoise, and – yes – pink. Each was set off with nickel-plated cylinder, hammer, and trigger. All wore the short barrel, and a round butt plastic stock colored white in hopes of resembling ivory. Colonel Jeff Cooper commented dryly, "This pistol may be had in nickel, gold, turquoise or pink finish in short barrels only. Prices run up to $52.50 for such attentions."[4]

The Colonel's commentary was remarkably mild. Knowing him, I would have expected him to retch if you handed him a pink .22 revolver in the shape of a fighting handgun. Indeed, the response of the red-blooded male marketplace was simi-

Above: Lacking a return spring, ejector rod remained in rear position after doing its job. Familiar with other revolvers, shooters would attempt to close an empty cylinder like, leaving the signature scars visible behind recoil shield of frame.

Above: Author's first brand new handgun was this Hi-Standard Sentinel .22, purchased for $37.50 at a Western Auto store in 1960. Sentinel embodies some interesting design features. Note tiny relief cuts at rear of chambers, to prevent damage to cylinder face from firing pin in dry fire.

lar, with the "ladies' guns" producing a response somewhere between laughter and dry heaves for the most part. Ironically, these poor sales led to discontinuance of the "color guns" in 1962, with relatively few sold, creating a scarcity such that decades later, collectors would pay triple or more the price of a regular Sentinel for the "pastel pistola."

The following year, however, saw the introduction of the most popular spin-off, the Double-Nine. By 1958, shooters wanted something that resembled what Matt Dillon, Paladin, and the rest packed on TV, but single action revolver shooting had become a lost art. High Standard had hit on something that Hollywood itself had recognized long ago. When the gun is to be wielded by someone who can't "get it" as far as thumb-cocking, disguising a double action six-shooter as a single action makes that shooter appear fast and skillful to anyone who doesn't look too close.

Long before, Stembridge Arsenal, the key supplier of prop guns to Hollywood film-makers, had figured this out. They had bolted a fake SAA style ejector rod to the side of a double action 1917 Colt .45's barrel to make it crudely resemble a Frontier model. Non-gun-oriented Dean Martin would never have been able to keep up with Sammy Davis, Jr., a genuine expert in quick draw who owned an exquisite collection of genu-

ine single action Colts. A prop gun that let Martin simply jerk the trigger while his co-star artfully manipulated a true SAA's hammer made a Rat Pack cowboy film look better to the uneducated. Similar faux cowboy revolvers had been created out of small-framed Colt Police Positive Special .38s for Dale Evans and for Gail Foster, who played Annie Oakley on TV, notes "Doc" O'Meara in his book from Krause, *Guns of the Gunfighters*.

Soon a plethora of Double-Nine variations was available. There was the long-barreled Buntline style appropriately called the Longhorn. A shorter barrel version with bird's head round butt, the Natchez, was my personal choice as the best looking. If you wanted a brass grip frame and trigger guard, there was the Posse with short barrel. Phony stag grips? The Marshall, rushed out so fast that no one checked the dictionary and realized they had given the gun a name with one "l" too many. There was also the two-tone Durango, and the rather nondescript Hombre.

Meanwhile, the ordinary Sentinel in service revolver motif was not being neglected. A deluxe version with checkered walnut stocks instead of the usual plastic emerged, appropriately called Sentinel Deluxe. An even fancier version, the Sentinel Imperial, followed.

However, all was not perfect in High Standard revolver land. The gun had started out a few dollars below what had become the benchmark for value in an affordable .22 handgun since 1949, the Ruger Standard Model autoloader at $37.50. By 1960, both guns were priced the same. By 1961, the

Sentinel was $39.50 and the Double-Nine $44.95, but the Ruger still hung in with its $37.50 price tag. The apparent value of the Sentinel, to a shooter who did comparison shopping, was going down.

It was perceived by many shooters at the time that an aluminum frame was cheap and short-lived. Even Elmer Keith had commented, "We would like to see High Standard bring this gun out in an all steel model and with higher finish and refinements even though cost would, of course, double."[5] Master revolversmith Hamilton Bowen notes in his superb book *The Custom Revolver* that even today, many shooters equate an aluminum frame with poor quality and limited longevity.

Realizing that in marketing, perception was reality, High Standard introduced steel frame versions of the Double-Nine in 1971 and the Sentinel in 1978. A .22 Magnum chambering option was added. A Mark I version with heavy barrel, shrouded ejector, and oversize grips that all strongly resembled the 1972 renovation of the Colt Detective Special was also offered. So were adjustable sights.

But steel and styling could not change one genuine problem with the Sentinel series, difficulty of disassembly. The radical two-piece

frame with removable trigger system sub-assembly was pinned together. Gun people of the time were used to sideplates and slotted screws. Elmer Keith said it best: "It is a very hard gun to disassemble or reassemble and this should be done only at the factory, as it is complicated. The barrel is simply pinned in the frame with a cross pin…The finish is rough, not highly polished. Two pins and one stock screw seem to hold the whole assembly together."[6]

In the heyday of the Sentinel, many casual shooters were less careful about using proper lubricants than they are today. A lot of 3-In-1 Oil™ and similar products got into revolver actions. With nowhere to drain, such heavy lubes would tend to eventually sludge up. Some owners perceived that the once-sweet action of their Sentinel had degraded over time, unfairly giving it the reputation of a short-lived gun.

The bloom was off the rose. Sales continued to wither. Name changes didn't work, whether it was dubbing the Sentinel the Camp Gun or putting an octagonal barrel on the Double-Nine and giving it the hubris-ridden label, "The Gun." The hokey concept

Note how far back the trigger sits in the guard, for a double action revolver at rest. The nine-shot cylinder didn't have to turn far shot to shot, and the Sentinel had a very short double action trigger pull.

of a double action dressed as a single turned off many traditionalists, let alone the gold and pink guns. In 1984, the last of these .22s left the Hamden, Connecticut production line. "The most innovative revolver of the last half century" had been discontinued after slightly less than 30 years.

Shooting the Sentinel

In the hand, your typical Sentinel feels like a J-frame Smith & Wesson with semi-square grip frame, but with more weight forward. The double action trigger pull also resembles the J-frame Smith, with which it shares a coil mainspring and a short-stroke double action trigger pull. This made the DA pull necessarily heavy; a Sentinel may have as much as 12 to 14 pounds pull weight. However, it will be a smooth pull, and that's the key to good double action shooting. In single action, the Sentinel series always offered a let-off so crisp it was virtually target grade.

The overwhelming majority of these guns are encountered with fixed sights. The rear sight sits in a dovetail that can be drifted for windage adjustment if the shooter is both adroit and gentle with a brass rod and a hammer. If the gun is not on for elevation, I've found it's more likely to shoot high than low. While higher, rounder front sights were produced on the cowboy versions and the

JC Higgins version made for Sears, Roebuck, the Sentinel is typically found with a graceful ramp that is too low rather than too high. The sight would have to be soldered up to make it higher, or a new one made. The latter would be easy to install, since that series of Sentinel front sight secured to the barrel with an Allen screw.

A swing-out cylinder that worked by pulling forward on the ejector rod was foreign to shooters of the time, though it was later widely copied by such firms as Charter Arms and RG. Unique to these new Sentinels – and uniquely irritating – was the fact that none of them had a spring loaded extractor rod like a Colt, a Smith or even a the swing-out H&R. The shooter would punch out the last nine empties, forget to manually pull the rod back forward, and attempt to close the cylinder. The result was a jarring collision of the protruding ejector star with the left side of the frame.

As a result, virtually all of these guns unless they are unfired will have characteristic and distinctive scarring on the left side of the frame behind the cylinder window. There is no doubt that the minor production economy of not putting in the self-returning ejector rod, a standard feature with every other name brand swing-out revolver, contributed to the public's impression of the Sentinel as a cheap gun. It was a time when "cheap" was often seen as a synonym for "junk." High Standard finally realized that. The 2003 *Standard Catalog of Firearms* notes, "The Sentinel revolvers begin with the R-100 design series and continue through the R-109 series...beginning with the R-102 series the ejector had a spring return."[7] The fact that the majority of Sentinels and Double-Nines I've run across don't have this feature tells me that consumer interest in the guns cooled fairly quickly. As the numeric model designations went up, sales were going precipitously downward.

Below: The Sentinel offered great feel. It dropped frame bottom was later embodied into Ruger's SP101 and Redhawk, and functioned as a built-in grip adapter. There was a built-in thumb-rest for a bulls-eye shooter's hold, and short reach to the trigger was ideal for small hands and short fingers. Curiously, built-in thumb rest for lefties like Bob Houzenga here, was smaller than the one for the right thumb.

These are surprisingly accurate revolvers. They don't have the gilt-edged precision of your true target revolver, such as the S&W K-22 or the Colt Officer's Model Match, but they'll keep pace with the smaller frame S&W .22/32 Kit Gun or Colt's rare lightweight .22 revolver in the Cobra series. A 2.5-inch group or better is par for the course at 25 yards, shooting off the bench. I've never put one in a Ransom Rest and don't know if the machine rest people ever even made an insert for the High Standard .22 revolver. However, I've learned as a rule of thumb that if five hand-held shots from the bench look and feel to the shooter as if they've gone off perfectly, measuring the best three will factor out human error sufficiently to get a very good approximation of what the same handgun will do from the Ransom for all five shots. By that standard, a Sentinel that hasn't been too battered over the years should be good for 1-to 1.5-inch potential accuracy. To achieve this, however, you want to experiment until you find the most compatible ammunition. Many technical tests in *The Accurate Rifle* and *Precision*

Shooting attest to this fact in match grade .22 rifles, and it's likewise true in recreational or target grade .22 rimfire handguns. Groups I shot with Remington .22 Long and Winchester .22 Long Rifle HP had stayed in the head of the International Practical Shooting Confederation target, but in disappointing four to five inch groups, when I shot my $75 Sentinel snubby. It was not until I switched to the Remington Thunderbolt that the five-shot group shrank to a magic inch and an eighth.

The Sentinel literally had a built-in grip adapter, to which Keith alluded in the first quote above. Interestingly, only Gaylord chose to fit a grip adapter to his Sentinels. Virtually every other specimen you see was left as is by its owner, testimony to a design that naturally fits the human hand.

Personal Perspective

My first revolver of my own, and my first brand new handgun, was a 4-inch aluminum frame Sentinel. I was 12 years old. When I was 11, my dad had given me a used

Above: The Sentinel series was always a good value, and has become extraordinarily so in recent years. Author bought this one for the tag price in 2003.

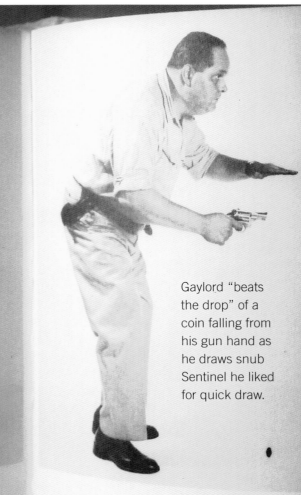

Gaylord "beats the drop" of a coin falling from his gun hand as he draws snub Sentinel he liked for quick draw.

Above: Sentinel at top left and Double-Nine he's drawing graced the cover of Gaylord's classic book. Publisher did not catch the fact that negative was reversed and showed the Sentinel backwards. Ditto the 3-inch S&W Model 36 Chief Special shown two guns down on the same cover.

Right: The High Standard .22s of the great Chic Gaylord, from his book *Handgunner's Guide*. This nickel 4-inch looked better than the flat gray frame of the basic model, and Gaylord added both trigger shoe and grip adapter. Note characteristic streamlined ramp of front sight, attached to barrel with Allen screw.

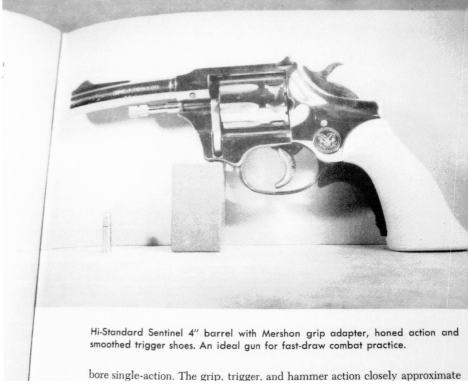

Hi-Standard Sentinel 4" barrel with Mershon grip adapter, honed action and smoothed trigger shoes. An ideal gun for fast-draw combat practice.

bore single-action. The grip, trigger, and hammer action closely approximate

Here he demonstrates an unusual speed shooting position with 4-inch Sentinel.

Above: In the then-popular Western motif, catches a dropped cowboy hat with the muzzle of his quick-drawn Double-Nine.

Ruger Standard Model .22 pistol in excellent condition. I cherished that gun, but it was just too heavy for a boy the size I was then to hold at the end of one arm for any length of time. In the 1950s, my dad figured, only sissies shot a one-hand gun with both hands. He never did meet Jeff Cooper...but I digress. Diagonally across the street from the shop Dad owned was a Western Auto store with a modest display of handguns. I hefted the Sentinel. At about 24 ounces, it was fully a third lighter than the all-steel Ruger auto, and I could hold it much steadier. The Ruger was traded in against the High Standard's $37.50 retail price.

What a difference! All of a sudden, the sights stayed on target and I could concentrate on carefully pressing the trigger back instead of on holding the gun up. The im-

provement in performance was dramatic. With the Ruger I had learned to be safe with a handgun, but with the Sentinel I learned to hit with one. In years to come, a Smith K-22 would teach me to shoot with more accuracy, and a Colt Woodsman Match Target would teach me to shoot competitively. On my twelfth Christmas, I got a 1911 Colt .45, and was growing fast enough that I grew right into it. Had I kept the Ruger for another year, I would have grown into that, too. But would a young boy's attention span have stayed enthusiastic until then? I'll never know. Suffice to say that with its light weight and its short, easy trigger reach, that High Standard Sentinel was the right handgun at the right time.

Needless to say, I'm a bit sentimental about the Sentinel. But a clear and objec-

Above: Hi-Standard made Sentinels for Sears, Roebuck under that company's J.C. Higgins brand, the Model 88. This unfired example was found at The Gun Connection in Rochester, Indiana. Note also the new condition Sears-branded holster for it. Sweeping curve of the grip and faintly "dragoonish" trigger guard treatment were unique to the gun they did for Sears.

tive look at handgun design history shows how much its then-radical design features influenced subsequent developments in double action revolvers, the Ruger line for example.

For today's serious shooter, these guns occupy another unique niche. The undeserved bad rap for being a cheap gun drove prices down further. My last three such guns – a 4-inch Sentinel Deluxe, a Double-Nine, and the snubby Sentinel mentioned at the beginning of this article – were bought at gun shops for $95, $90, and $75 respectively. (Expect the going price to be higher by the time you read this, of course.) Forty years ago, a Sentinel sold for $40, the same price as the top line H&R or Iver Johnson, which didn't perform nearly as well. The six-shot S&W Airweight Kit Gun, functionally identical to the nine-shot High Standard in performance, sold for exactly twice as much. The best price I've seen on a good used Kit Gun lately was $245, and the now-collectible Airweight would be significantly more than that. The High Standard Sentinel is a better bargain than ever now that it's confined to the used gun market.

I think it's the best buy in a quality handgun that you will find today, better even than the "deal of the (last) decade," the wave of mint condition police service revolvers that were traded in en masse for autoloaders. In fact, the pre-owned Sentinel may arguably be the consistently best buy available today in firearms, period. The fact that it embodies some fascinating and revolutionary elements of American handgun design is simply icing on the cake.

And for the arms historian, never forget that this is the gun that broke the logjam in double action revolver design. Colt and S&W lockwork had been fixed in time in the 1890s when, at last, something new called the Sentinel came out in the mid-1950s. It cured the paralysis in double action revolver design and showed other engineers that it might just be worthwhile revisiting this type of handgun with some fresh blueprint paper. Before the Sentinel was discontinued, Colt would have its Mark III series, Ruger would be well along in the double action revolver market with their own new designs, and the radical Dan Wesson would be the toast of the gun magazines. Harry Seifried and his little High Standard Sentinel had started something good.

Notes

[1]Gaylord, Chic, *Handgunner's Guide*, New York City: Hastings House, 1960, p. 52.

[2]Keith, Elmer, *Sixguns*, New York City: Bonanza Books, 1955, pp. 80-81.

[3]Cary, Lucian, *Lucian Cary on Guns*, New York City: Fawcett Publications, 1959, p. 128.

[4]Cooper, Jeff, *The Complete Book of Modern Handgunning*, Englewood Cliffs, NJ: Prentice-Hall, 1961, p.47.

[5]Keith, *op.cit.* p. 81.

[6]*Ibid.*, p.81.

[7]Schwing, Ned, 2003 *Standard Catalog of Firearms*, Iola, WI: Krause Publications, 2002, p. 554.

The Luger Pistol

The Luger pistol is a truly iconic handgun, a classic recognized even by non-gun people. Along with the Colt "Peacemaker," the 1911 "Army automatic," and perhaps a handful of others, it played a huge role in the history of modern sidearms.

Pedigree

Unique in shape and function, the Luger pistol could not be ignored by gun experts. Elmer Keith commented positively on its balance, "feel," and pointing qualities. Confirmed Chic Gaylord, "the Luger Parabellum semi-automatic pistol of World War I fame…can be shot effectively by almost everyone without the need for changes or alterations." He considered the Luger among "three outstanding examples of guns whose grips are so

One of the all-time classic firearms, though over-rated by today's standards, the Luger constituted a great leap forward in handgun design and opened the door to semiautomatic pistols as we know them today.

Above: Sleek and unique, the Luger's distinctive looks captured the imagination of American shooters.

Left: Blast from the past: author firing Luger 9mm, 2004. The trigger hasn't gotten any better.

Left: Much more portable and ergonomic than the broomhandle Mauser, above, the Luger was the first truly practical auto pistol for all-the-time carry.

Below: Thumb-activated magazine release button was a Luger innovation that dominates auto pistol design even today.

cleverly designed that they seem to make any changes unnecessary."[1] He numbered the Colt Single Action Army and the High Standard Sentinel revolver among this select number along with the Luger.

Perhaps the most glowing praise for the Luger from a mid-century American handgun expert came from Henry M. Stebbins, whose long life encompassed most of the Luger's period of relative popularity in the United States. "A good gun if you understand it," he pronounced. "The best Lugers are splendid, regardless of whether or not an individual shooter likes the type; the poorest, assembled most likely from junk parts, are not safe to fire."[2]

Others among his peers thought less of the toggle-operated pistol. Revolver crusader Bob Nichols declared in 1950, "The centerfire automatic pistol fooled a lot of really good minds around the turn of the century. The Continentals, and especially the Germans, were completely misled by this exciting new pistol. The quick fire power of the centerfire automatic pistol, even in inept and un-skilled hands, curiously appeared unbeatable. Now, of course, we know better."[3]

For many, the dislike of the gun was rooted less in its representation of a twice-hated enemy, the Hun and then the Nazi, than it was in a matter of practicality. Upon his return from heavy combat in WWI, Herbert McBride explained why he much preferred the American 1911 despite extensive experience with the Luger. He opined, "That old .45 slug has more authority than any of the others, not excepting the 9 m/m Luger, and as for accuracy, there never was a Luger or Mauser made to even come within hailing distance of our Service Colt."[4] McBride said the only instant stop he saw a Luger deliver in his extensive experience was when it was used as a bludgeon. "It was all over in a second – the kid just swung the belt and

that holstered Luger made a circle and came down on top of the German's head with a 'womp'...And that is about the only time I can remember a 'slug' from a Luger having sufficient wallop to do a 'bang up' job of things."[5]

Without question, the Luger pistol has been obsolete since before WWII. The Germans themselves obviously thought so, since in 1938 they ostensibly replaced it with the double action Walther, though Luger production continued through the war. Yet it lingers, a gun of legend and mystique. Stebbins explained in 1961, "They are still popular, and for use as well as to round out a collection. For one thing, they have a romantic appeal. Some of us, including this one, think there is nothing very romantic about war, but there's the other side of Luger service, the wilderness these guns saw and continue to see."[6]

A Brief History

The story of the Luger pistol is long, rich, and well documented, from Fred Datig's authoritative text *The Luger Pistol: Its History and Development from 1893 to*

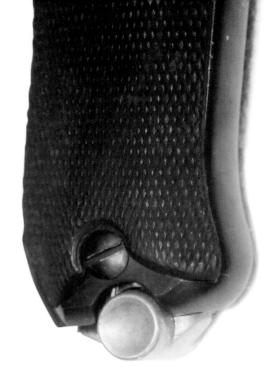

Left: Toggle-shaped magazine floorplate aided malfunction clearing and gave the gun a "balanced theme" look. Lug on lower back of grip-frame is for attaching shoulder stock.

Far Left: Square backed receiver configuration made the Luger less than ideal for concealed carry. Rectangular loop at rear of receiver is for a lanyard.

Above: Gun collector and dealer J Stuckey, a man with large hands, shows the Luger's relatively long trigger reach.

1945, through today's excellent resource on the Internet, www.lugerforum.com. Georg Luger transformed the ugly, ungainly 1893 pistol of Hugo Borchardt into the sleek, elegant, eternally modern shape that would bear Luger's name forever after. The gigantic mainspring housing that hung over the back of the Borchardt's frame was eliminated in favor of a simple leaf mainspring. Luger refined the Borchardt's signature toggle mechanism, and invested the new gun with ergonomics by steeply angling a grip frame that, on the 1893 pistol, had been reminiscent of a T-square. Forevermore, the Luger would be a classic example of human engineering in a handgun's grip to barrel angle, with brilliant gun designers of the future from William B. Ruger to Gaston Glock paying homage.

Both Borchardt and Luger worked for DWM, a subsidiary of a company owned by machine tool manufacturers Isidor and Ludwig Loewe (sometimes spelled Lowe). The design was pretty much complete by 1899, and guns had been manufactured by 1900. In 1901 the first military adoption of the Luger pistol was claimed by Switzerland. It was chambered for the 7.65mm Luger (.30 Luger) cartridge, a round developed by Georg Luger by shortening the 7.65X25 Borchardt round a couple of millimeters. A 93-grain .30 caliber projectile at plus/minus 1200 fps did not look promising as a manstopper, however, and to gain a more powerful round, Luger essentially expanded the bottlenecked 7.65mm casing to a very slightly tapered straight wall cartridge case, and the 9mm Luger (9mm Parabellum, 9X19) was born in 1902. It was destined to become the most popular military cartridge of the 20th century.

People speak of this gun as the "German Luger," but that does not tell the whole, cosmopolitan story. The Swiss adopted it years before the Germans, and eventually manufactured it under license in Bern. The Swiss Lugers are typically found with grip safeties and flat-front grip straps. Adopted by the German Navy in 1904 and the German Army in 1908 (hence its enduring alternate designation, the P.08), the Luger was manufactured there at many locations over the decades. It was even produced in small quantities in England. It was adopted by many countries. It is well known that Luger's firm, Loewe & Company, manufactured a very few .45 ACP Lugers for the US Army tests, but it comes as a surprise to most gun enthusiasts that .30 Lugers were briefly adopted by the United States.

According to firearms historian Harry M. Campbell, "The American Eagle – US Army Luger M1900 cal. 7.65mm – was issued mainly to cavalry units. After a short period it was withdrawn and sold as surplus. Now it's a collector's item."[7]

Campbell lists seven recognized makers: DWM (Deutsche Waffen und Munitionen), "Erfurt, Simson, Krieghoff and Mauser of Germany; Vickers Ltd. of England and Waffenfabrik Eidgenossische of Bern, Switzerland. Additionally, some few P-08 military specimens bear the toggle markings of the Spandau arsenal, probably having been reworked there."[8]

As the decades went on, Luger pistols logged service under the flags of Bulgaria, the Netherlands, Portugal, Brazil, Sweden, Persia, Austria, and even Russia, and I may have missed some. Long barrel Navy and Artillery models, often with snap-on rifle stocks and even handsome fore-ends, became famous for ease of shooting and would one day be among the flagships of the Luger-collectors' fleet. It was said that Kaiser Wilhelm, an avid outdoorsman, used a shoul-

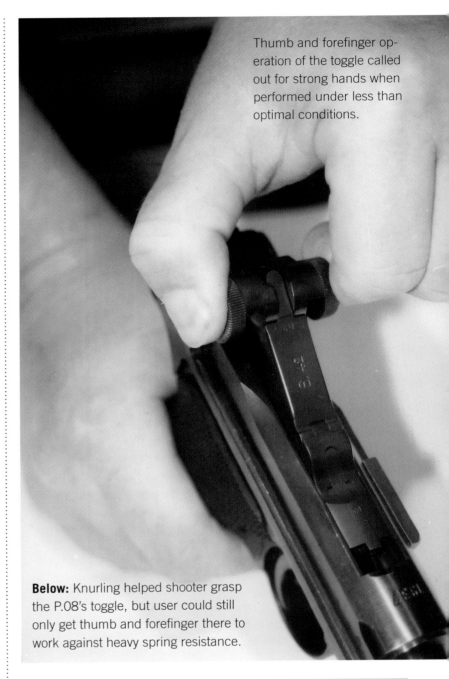

Thumb and forefinger operation of the toggle called out for strong hands when performed under less than optimal conditions.

Below: Knurling helped shooter grasp the P.08's toggle, but user could still only get thumb and forefinger there to work against heavy spring resistance.

Above: The toggle action's cycle disrupts the shooter's sight picture with every shot when firing a Luger.

der-stocked Luger as his primary hunting weapon because he had a withered arm.

Though intended for replacement by the Walther P-38 in that gun's eponymous year, Germany's military expansion so far outpaced its handgun manufacturing capability that the Luger remained in wide use by Hitler's forces throughout WWII. It is said to have been particularly prized by senior members of the officers' corps, who perceived the Luger as a "gentleman's gun" and the P-38 as a *volkspistole* for the cannon fodder in the ranks they commanded. The Luger was perhaps the most prized war souvenir among victorious Yanks returning from the European Theater.

"Reel life" and real life combined to make the Luger a colorful icon of adventure in the eyes of Americans. It was the stereotype weapon of Nazi spies in movies, and as standard as a monocle and a Heidelberg dueling scar for any actor playing a German officer. The director armed Lee Marvin with one when he played a mob killer in *The Big Heat*. Yet, John Steinbeck made a Luger the gun George uses to euthanize the tragic character Lennie in *Of Mice and Men*. Inexplicably, when Gary Cooper played the title role in *Sergeant York*, he wielded a Luger to drop an advancing line of German soldiers. My friend and fellow gun writer Duane Thomas makes an articulate argument that York may

"Baby Luger" .380 produced by Erma in the late 20th century did not catch on.

indeed have used a captured souvenir Luger to perform the feat of arms that earned him the Congressional Medal of Honor, but most historians insist that it was an Army-issue Colt 1911 .45 automatic that York fired when his P-17 Enfield ran too low on ammo to handle the whole enemy squad.

It would appear that during the immediate postwar years, unscrupulous individuals gathered remaining parts from occupied Germany and sloppily threw Lugers together to feed the demand for this most popular of war souvenirs. All experts of the period agreed that it was a matter of caveat emptor, and suggested that wise and wary buyers take their Lugers to a gunsmith to examine before shooting them, unless they were certain of the given specimen's pedigree.

The Luger's days were pretty much over after WWII. Now and then,

an entrepreneur with more love of guns than business sense would try to resurrect the beloved old pistol, but never with commercial success. The finest of these guns were virtually hand-made in the USA by John Martz. Only a few hundred were produced, and by all accounts their fine accuracy and superb craftsmanship make them worth the many thousands of dollars they command today. Particularly desirable are the .45 ACP versions, each built from a pair of conventional Lugers eccentrically split lengthwise and welded together to handle the fatter American cartridge.

Erma produced functional but uninspiring Luger copies. Perhaps the worst "Lugers" were the .22s made late in the 20th Century for Stoeger, which had once imported the finest genuine commercial Lugers into the United States. The Stoeger Luger .22s appeared to have been die-cast out of melted-down license plates or some-

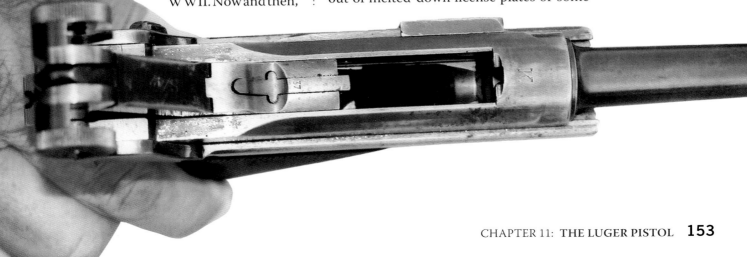

Prominent Luger collector Harry Beckwith demonstrates proper use of his favorite gun with shoulder stock.

Below: Luger was designed to let average size man get pad of finger on trigger, worked particularly well in large hands, and could be awkward for those with long fingers. Trigger pull was terribly mushy.

thing. At first glance, they looked like well-made toys, until you realized that they were actually crudely made .22 caliber handguns.

It is said that in the old days, some European marksmen – particularly the Swiss – gave good accounts of themselves in pistol matches with Lugers. Those days are long gone. Today, when people fire Lugers, it is as a curiosity, not a test of performance. But, for all that, the unique history of the Luger endures.

Shooting the Luger

Major McBride's damnation of the Luger's accuracy, quoted earlier, may have owed more to chauvenism than reality. Most who were experienced with the Luger found it to be quite accurate for its time. The famously good workmanship on the commercial models and the best military versions was part of that, but so was a barrel secured rigidly to the frame. In *The 100 Greatest Combat Pistols*, T.J. Mullin got a 1.5-inch group at 50 feet with a 7.65mm Swiss Luger he tested, and said of the long barreled 9mm Artillery Luger, "…the weapon does shoot quite adequately. At 300 yards, I found it easy to put the shots out fast and to engage 12-inch plates with it." He says of the Luger in general, "…it is a very accurate weapon."[9]

Another friend who was a most credible modern authority, the late Dave Arnold, echoes Mullin's sentiments. "Even though the Luger is not a target arm, I have shot a number that have produced impressive accuracy. This is especially so of the long-barrel versions."[10]

No gun expert shot Lugers more enthusiastically than Henry Stebbins. He describes the experience thus: "When they are up to normal they shoot accurately – and very flat, of course. With a two-hand hold and a good sit you can really lay them in from a Luger, if ever you have to. As you fire, the empties whirl madly out the top of the receiver, glinting in the sunlight, if there is any, and they land a fairly even two feet behind you, not all over the proverbial half-acre."[11]

The toggle action is part of the unique appearance of the Luger, and that much more unique a part of its operation. Slightly dished on early models, flatter and usually checkered on later specimens, the grasping surfaces of the toggle allowed limited purchase for the human hand. With a conventional auto pistol's slide, the entire support hand can take a firm grip to rack a cartridge into the chamber, clear a jam, or lock the gun open. With the Luger, there is room for little more than a thumb and a forefinger. Because the jack-knifing bolt does not seem to utilize energy as efficiently as a back-and-forth spring loaded slide, it is important to work the action smartly. This means that those with strong hands and fingers are those who will be most effective in operating the Luger pistol.

The Luger popularized the push-button magazine release situated for the right-handed shooter's thumb, behind the

trigger guard on the left of the frame. This remains the standard today, with only a handful of modern designs clinging to the butt-heel magazine release. One wonders if John Browning ever thanked Georg Luger for it when he made that feature a part of his most famous designs, the 1911 and the P-35.

If the Luger pistol exhibited such fine workmanship, was so accurate and pointed so superbly, what apart from its calibers turned off American shooters? I would guess that there were three primary factors. One, the least of them, was the trigger pull. Some described its trigger pull as creepy, but that understates the sensation of firing the Luger pistol. The pull on an unaltered Luger is mushy, spongy if you will, especially to the hand of someone accustomed to a good trigger pull on a proper handgun, or a target rifle or a good hunting rifle.

Particularly in the years after WWII, which seem to have been the height of recreational Luger shooting in the USA, there were some gunsmiths who because of popular demand learned to clean up Luger trigger pulls. None apparently were successful enough, or saw enough demand, to specialize in that – though

Above: Garishly emblazoned "Luger," this .22 imported long after the real deal's heyday totally lacked the quality of the original.

Far Left: Plastic grips and what looked like stamped metal characterized this "imitation Luger."

A huge problem with the Luger was that its manual safety worked in the wrong direction, and of course, was not readily accessible to left-handed users.

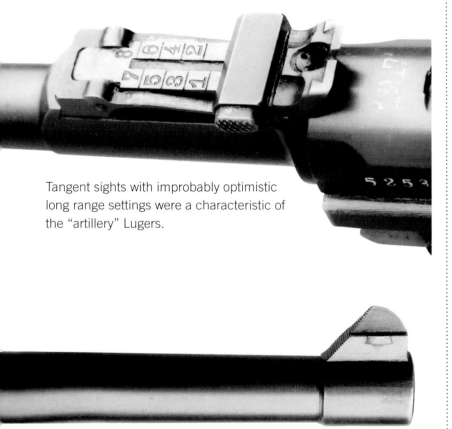

Tangent sights with improbably optimistic long range settings were a characteristic of the "artillery" Lugers.

Gracefully tapered barrels and distinctive front sights were part of the Luger's memorable "sculpture."

it is said that the masterfully crafted modern Lugers of John Martz had decent trigger pulls – and eventually, the tuning of the Luger became something of a lost art.

A second problem was condition of readiness. Americans had learned with the Colt Pocket Model of 1903 to carry a semi-automatic pistol with a round in the chamber and the safety on, and to swipe the safety off with a stroke of the thumb as they drew the gun. This tradition continued with the 1911. History tells us that soldiers cocked and locked it as soon as battle was imminent, despite regulations that demanded the chamber be kept empty, and we know that almost from the time they made the 1911 their unofficial standard pistol, the Texas Rangers carried it cocked and locked. The Luger's thumb safety, unfortunately, worked in the wrong direction. Up was "fire," and down was "safe." This can work on a modern double action auto – the Beretta 92F, the Ruger standard model, or the conventional Smith & Wesson, for instance – because their wing-type safeties are easily flipped upward into the fire position by the thumb. The flat little lever at the left rear of the Luger's receiver, on the other hand, required the shooter to either use his other hand – and hand that might not be available in time of crisis – or shift the pistol awkwardly out of firing position until the ball of the thumb's median joint could be brought to bear against the recalcitrant lever.

Mullin feels this egregious design alone disqualified the Luger from serious consideration as a fighting handgun to be carried ready-to-go. Many apparently felt the same before him.

Finally, and most seriously, there was the matter of reliability. The Luger simply did not earn the stand-up reputation of, say, the 1911 in this respect. Ask the experts:

Stebbins: "It has a bad reputation for jamming, which is strange for so popular a military pistol; still, it can do it. When your .45 Colt fails, you generally know why, if you live to find out. But I think that Lugers are a little less predictable, less understandable."[12]

Arnold: "Probably the greatest complaint against the Luger is questionable reliability. Even though it appears to have served the German troops well enough in the dirt and mud of the trenches, it has a reputation for poor feeding with some types of ammunition."[13]

Mullin: "Many people have reported over the years that Lugers are unreliable, but I have never encountered any problems with functioning. Most problems that people report are traceable to poor magazines or low-power ammunition. Assuming that you have a pistol with matching numbers, you should use ammunition that is rated to what we in the United States call +P power levels, as well as good magazines. There are a lot of mismatched clunkers about, which may well have functioning problems. The action is open at the time of firing, allowing mud to get into the action. At one time, people used to think this was a cause of malfunctions, but I do not believe so. The problem is the closely fitted parts, which are common in many German handguns. When they get mud in them, the parts lose their ability to move, and the Luger is full of such parts. The German solution at the time of the pistol's introduction was to use a totally enclosed holster. Such a rig is too slow for a combat handgun, but apparently was necessary in the mud of France to keep the weapons clean."[14]

Personal Experience

When I was a little boy, one of my favorite toys was a plastic Luger exactly to scale, and I couldn't wait to get old enough to shoot a real one. I did so in my early

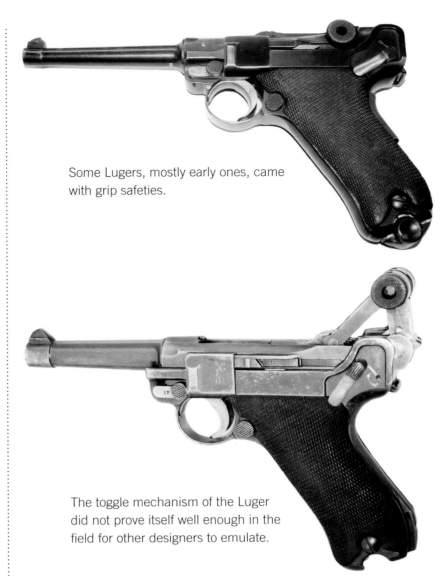

Some Lugers, mostly early ones, came with grip safeties.

The toggle mechanism of the Luger did not prove itself well enough in the field for other designers to emulate.

teens, and found it a huge disappointment. Lousy trigger; awkward-to-operate mechanism; impossible safety; and barleycorn front sight and V-notch rear which, along with the trigger pull, got in the way of the pistol's obviously good inherent accuracy. I spent a good part of my adulthood looking for a Luger that didn't just feel good when you held it, but "worked good" when the shooting started. I never did find one. And, yes, I saw a lot of them jam. I realized that Georg Luger hadn't put the toggle-like shape on the floorplate of the magazine just to visually balance the "look," top and bottom. I suspect he put it there to help the shooter claw the magazine out of a jammed pistol.

Above: Seen from above, the machining challenge presented by the Luger is evident.

For my personal shooting needs, I think Tim Mullin said it better than I could: "Although I think a Luger pistol is one of the worst semiautomatic pistols for military purposes, many people like the mystique that goes with them, and they are generally very accurate. If offered one, you should take it, get powerful ammo for it, and then try to swap it for something better as quickly as possible. Given its mystique, you are likely to find someone who will swap you a useful handgun for your Luger in no time."[15]

But that would be a cruel way to end an chapter about a pistol that was a milestone in handgun history. While the big, awkward Mauser had already proven that a semiautomatic pistol could not only work, but might have great advantages in battle, Georg Luger's pistol proved that the same could be accomplished in a compact and relatively ergonomic package that was easy to carry all the time. In that greater conceptual sense, it changed the face of the handgun world, and in lesser elements, its much-copied grip angle and more-copied magazine release design would prove the model for the future, more than a century later.

Therefore, let us close instead with the words of Harry M. Campbell: "For more than half a century the Luger was a controversial weapon; millions extolled its virtues while just as many condemned it. However, now that it has passed into history, most of us admire it for one reason or another. The Luger was something special in firearms. There will never be another gun like it."

Notes

[1]Gaylord, Chic, *Handgunner's Guide*, New York City: Hastings House, 1960, p. 18-19.

[2]Stebbins, Henry M., *Pistols: A Modern Encyclopedia*, Castle Books, 1961, p. 151.

[3]Nichols, Bob, *The Secrets of Double Action Shooting*, New York City: G. p. Putnam's Sons, 1950, p. 37.

[4]McBride, H. W., *A Rifleman Went to War*, 1935 (orig.) and 1987 (reprint), Mt. Ida, AR: Lancer Militaria, p. 184.

[5]*Ibid.* , p. 185.

[6]Stebbins, *op. cit.* p. 154.

[7]"The Famed Luger of Fact and Fantasy" by Harry M. Campbell, *Gun Digest*, 1972, p. 194.

[8]*Ibid.*, p. 197.

[9]Mullin, T.J., *The 100 Greatest Combat Pistols*, Boulder, CO: Paladin Press, 1994, Pp. 161, 162, 307.

[10]Arnold, David, *Classic Handguns of the 20th Century*, Iola, WI: Krause Publications, 2004, p. 21.

[11]Stebbins, *op. cit.*, p. 154.

[12]*Ibid.*, p. 154.

[13]Arnold, *op. cit.*, p. 21.

[14]Mullin, *op. cit.*, p. 158.

[15]*Ibid.*

[16]Campbell, *op. cit.*, p. 197.

The Ruger .22 Auto Pistol

I knew the late, great William B. Ruger, Sr., and was privileged to count him as a friend. One night at dinner at his home in Croydon, New Hampshire, I asked him which of all the many famous guns he designed was his personal favorite. He smiled indulgently and told me it was his first commercial design, the Standard Model .22 caliber semiautomatic pistol. It wasn't that it was his firstborn brainchild – he had patented other designs earlier – and it wasn't just that it was the product that kicked off his company and led to his huge success in his chosen field.

From the beginning, the name "Ruger" was synonymous with "value" in the firearms industry, and the Standard Model was the case in point, even from its first review. That was written by the great Julian S. Hatcher

Loved more than all its siblings by the patriarch who created it and the large family it shared, this modern classic became a great American favorite.

Right: The shape of the classic Ruger Standard Model .22. In silhouette, if not in function, it resembles a Luger, and the closeness of the names further confused some people.

Left: Heather O'Keefe, 15, won the National Junior Handgun Championships of 2002 – yes, against the boys – shooting her grandfather's well-worn Ruger Mark I with 6-7/8-inch tapered barrel.

Ruger .22s go modern: polymer 22/45 is shown with competition-stocked Clark Custom 10/22 rifle.

in the pages of the only gun magazine of the time, *The American Rifleman*, and it read in part: "Shaped like the Luger pistol, the gun looks good and handles splendidly. It hangs and balances just right, and points naturally, which is a great aid in quick shooting…One can readily see that the designer of this gun knows something about shooting as well as

The 22/45 has lightweight polymer frame, separate slide lock release of the Mark II series, 1911 grip angle, and optional adjustable sights.

designing…We like this new gun a lot and at the very moderate price of $37.50 it represents real value."[1]

Forever after, through the present day, the Ruger .22 auto pistol would be a mandatory inclusion in every gun magazine list of "best buy" firearms. It retained its $37.50 price tag for an incredibly long time, and remains an excellent buy even now. It has been in continuous production since 1949, and reached a production level of over a million guns sooner – 30 years – than any non-service handgun this writer can recall.

Pedigree

When a gun breaks the million mark in sales, one purchaser at a time, the public has voted with its wallet and the comments of the critics pale by comparison. This writer has noted that among shooters who designate themselves riflemen and own few handguns or only one, the Ruger .22 auto is the single most likely pistol to be found in their gun case. Appreciation of function, and of course that value thing, are probably the reasons why.

That said, though, the voices of the critics have been one reason so many shooters tried it and liked it, and reviews in the gun and hunting press were crucial to the pistol's initial success. The Ruger .22 pistol was all over the magazine covers in 1999, commemorating its 50th year of production, and not a word seemed to be negative. In the gun's seminal years, the firearms press was likewise enthusiastic.

Elmer Keith: "The Ruger gives one a pistol with the weight in the hand and less muzzle heaviness and it points more like the German Luger. Many fine shooters prefer this feel and balance to the muzzle-heavy makes of Colt and High Standard."[2]

Jeff Cooper: "The Ruger design permits front and rear sights to be fitted to the same rigid unit."[3] Cooper had sagely noted this factor, because most pistols of the period mounted the rear sight on a moving slide that *might* return into exactly the same relationship with the front sight after it cycled back into battery. This had also been noted from the beginning by Julian Hatcher: "One very desirable feature is that the front and rear sights are both on the same piece of metal, so that there is no chance of relative

The Ruger delivers match-winning accuracy, and is particularly popular with entry level competitors.

motion between them, as is the case when one sight is on the barrel and the other on the moveable breech block."[4]

A Brief History

To the enthusiast, the history of the Ruger .22 auto in all of its many subtle permutations over more than half a century is worthy of a book. The variations cover several pages in *Standard Catalog of Firearms.* For a mere segment in a magazine article, we must concentrate on the high points. At Bill Ruger's funeral, I watched R. L. "Larry" Wilson deliver the eulogy. There's a reason he was picked: he knew the man and what he created. The following is adapted from Larry's splendid and authoritative book, *Ruger & His Guns.*

1946-49: Bill Ruger's fertile brain conceives a semiautomatic pistol with tubular receiver and fixed barrel, with enclosed blowback bolt, chambered for the .22 Long Rifle cartridge.

1949: Ruger convinces his brilliant artist friend Alex Sturm to invest some of his inheritance in a gun manufacturing company. Sturm, Ruger & Company – and a handgun designated simply "Ruger .22 Pistol" – are born. Sturm's investment is $50,000. Sturm designs the phoenix-like eagle, which will thereafter be the company symbol. The first pistol has a tapered 4-3/4-inch barrel which will prove to be its most popular format,

Right: Described in detail in text, this method of holding down the follower button makes it easy to load a Ruger .22 magazine all the way up.

soon followed by a 6-7/8-inch barrel at about the same time Ruger introduces the Mark I target version with Micro adjustable sight.

1953: James Clark, Sr. wins the National Handgun

Championship shooting a Mark I he customized himself in the .22 stage, and the Ruger is established as a legitimate competition pistol for the serious shooter.

1982: The Mark II series is introduced, differing from its predecessor most noticeably by having a separate slide lock and release lever which causes the bolt to lock back on the last round. Prior to this, a million and a quarter Standard and Mark I Target models have been sold, which only lock back by manually holding the slide to the rear while the right thumb pushes the button-shaped manual safety lever up. By this point, according to Wilson, there have been at least 30 variations of Ruger .22 auto pistols produced.

1991: The "22/45" pistol is introduced, becoming the most significant design change in the history of the Ruger .22 caliber semiautomatic handgun. Designed by Jim McGarry around Bill Ruger's original concept, it features a lightweight polymer frame, the grip-to-barrel angle of a 1911 .45 auto instead of the Luger/Woodsman/High Standard angle of its predecessors, and also a push-button magazine release in the generally preferred position, behind the trigger guard on the left side of the frame.

The low-price, high-performance Ruger pistol proved to be a giant-killer. It crushed sales of Colt's classic Woodsman, and tolled the funeral bells of that beautifully made, but labor-intensive and therefore expensive, .22 auto pistol. It probably put more than one nail in the coffin of the original High Standard .22 autoloader as well. Bill Ruger told his biographer Larry Wilson, "Of course, Colt and High Standard knew we were around very early on, because I can tell you that within a year of offering our pistol, their sales had fallen off drastically."[5] Ironically, the first prototype of Bill's pistol not only had a Woodsman-shaped grip, it actually used a Colt Woodsman magazine.

At this writing, the Ruger .22 auto pistol exists in a variety of formats. Frames in polymer or steel. Mag releases in push-button or butt-catch style. Stubby barrels for hikers and campers, and humongously long barrels for target shooters. Super-light or super-heavy. This pistol lends itself particularly well to sound suppressors.

The modern legend continues.

Shooting the Ruger .22 Auto Pistol

Just for the hell of it, I took the nearest Ruger .22 to the range. This is an old Mark I with 5-inch bull barrel and factory sights and trigger – right out of the box. It's an old beater I keep around as a loaner and plinker. Four loads were on hand for testing from the 25-yard bench rest position, no machine rest being available. In addition to the overall measurement, the tightest three shots were also recorded. Experience has taught me that if all five shots felt clean to an experienced shooter, factoring out the worst two would remove enough human error to give a reasonable approximation of what the same gun/ammo combo would do for all five shots in a Ransom Rest. Charles Petty and I tested this hy-

Right: With conventional techniques, Ruger mags tend to catch on the butt-heel release like this. The solution, says author…

Below: … is to roll the pistol thusly with the dominant hand, using support hand thumb to push straight to the rear, as index finger-nail comes in from the side…

Bottom: … and effortlessly pulls the magazine free. Muzzle is always oriented to backstop.

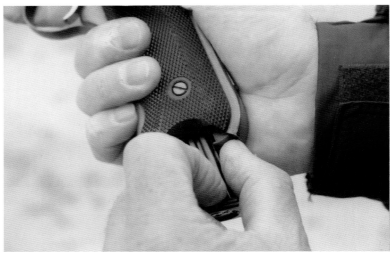

Top: Straight thumb position, favored by target shooters, works well for some with the Ruger .22…

Bottom: … but for a specimen with a heavier trigger pull, curling the thumb down gives a stronger hold that may better stabilize the pistol against the index finger's pressure.

pothesis in 2002 for American Handgunner magazine. The variation between the average bench rest group and the average "best three" from the five shots fired hand-held off the bench had less variance than that between the best and worst machine rest groups.

Bearing in mind that while this gun might have been cleaned sometime in the last 10 years, I couldn't remember when, I thought it did OK. The attached table shows that the pistol has ample accuracy for plinking and small game hunting within rational distances, depending on the sighting system. Put in a match trigger instead of a plinker's pull, slap on some optical sights, and you can see why

guys and gals win matches with these guns, particularly the more sophisticated new versions of today. When it puts five rounds of cheap plinker ammo into just over an inch at 25 yards, in the hands of an old shooter with the sun in his eyes while the gun is filthy, and shows promise of three-quarter inch inherent accuracy under those circumstances, you know you're dealing with a pistol that delivers the sort of precision that seasoned riflemen appreciate.

Every machine, including every firearm, has its idiosyncrasies. The Ruger .22 auto pistol is no exception. It is said that the most perfect battle plan never wholly survives its first contact with the enemy, and in the same sense, the most perfectly planned machine is not going to wholly survive its contact with a seven-figure count of end-users. Firearms are no exception.

Many find this pistol's magazine difficult to load all the way up to full 10 round capacity because the spring gets so tight as cartridges accumulate. Special tools have been made for it. The secret is this: hold the magazine with your pinky finger tucked under the floorplate. On the button side, place that hand's thumbnail and median thumb joint against the side of the magazine, with the tip of the thumb on the button. This aligns the skeleto-muscular support structure of the thumb in a way that gives you much more strength to easily push the follower down and hold it down to get those eight, ninth, and tenth cartridges into the stack.

Most Ruger .22s have the butt heel magazine release of the original standard model. The exception is the 22/45, which has a conventional side-mounted push button mag release built into its polymer frame. It's much easier to operate, and certainly faster, though the 22/45's magazines do not interchange with its all-steel sibling pistols. The Ruger butt catch is awkward because as the

Ruger .22 Auto Accuracy Test

Ruger Mark I, 5-inch bull barrel, .22 LR, hand-held bench rest, 25 yards

Load	Five-Shot Group (")	Best Three Shots (")
Eley Subsonic unplated solid	2-5/16	1-3/16
Remington solid "Golden" Hi-Speed	1-3/16	3/4
Remington HP "Golden Hi-Speed	1-7/8	11/16
Winchester Wildcat lead bullet Hi-Speed	1-1/8	7/8

Note: This particular pistol hasn't been detail-stripped, let alone customized, in the quarter-century or so since it came out of the factory box. It has had tens of thousands of rounds through it, yet still shows sub-one-inch 25-yard grouping potential. This tells you something about the enduring accuracy, as well as the enduring reliability, of a truly enduring American firearm: the Ruger .22 auto pistol. It perhaps reflects on the "personality" of the gun that it does its best with ordinary-priced American ammunition and not with expensive match grade loads from overseas.

A young lady contestant takes her Ruger .22 to the NRA Hunter Silhouette range, and finishes with a creditable score.

The Ruger design lends itself well to lawfully-owned sound suppressors.

magazine comes out, the top groove at the rear of its floorplate tends to snag on the release latch. Since the lower surface of the floorplate blocks your thumb's access to the catch, this typically necessitates re-inserting the magazine to start the withdrawal process over.

Let me share an easier way. With trigger finger safely on frame and muzzle safely downrange, rotate the gun 90 degrees so that its butt is presented to your support hand. The tips of the index finger and thumb of the support hand move right in together. The thumb forcibly pushes the release latch to the rear and holds it there. Now, the tip of the index finger comes in from the side instead of the front and effortlessly withdraws the magazine past the sticking point. You might wish to consider the extended magazine release for the Mark II pistols offered by Ranch Products.

Given its fairly heavy trigger pull, the Ruger pistol wants a firm hand at the controls. A four-pound pressure on a 36-ounce object will move the object if it is not stabilized: it's that simple. While on the range with my old Mark I, whose trigger weighs about five pounds, I did a simple test at 25 yards: light hold versus hard hold, with the same ammo. With the light grasp, the group measured just under an inch high by two and three-quarters inches wide, with the best three in an inch and a quarter. With a hard hold, the group was the

Longer barrels were added when the Ruger .22 became popular for two-handed shooting games like NRA Hunter Pistol.

same height but under an inch and a half wide (an inch and seven-eighths when measured diagonally, farthest shot to farthest shot) with the best three grouping in eleven-sixteenths of one inch. The ammo was inexpensive bulk-pack Remington high velocity hollow point.

Takedown is a sore point with many Ruger .22 owners. When I disassembled my first Standard Model at the age of 11, I couldn't get the damn thing back together. I got the hang of it after a while, but it never got easy. Confirms small arms authority Peter Kokalis, "If you don't follow the instructions explicitly – and a few hints are not found in the manual – reassembly of any Ruger .22 LR semiauto pistol can prove to be a nightmare."[6] Kokalis found as I did that to remove the barrel/receiver assembly from all but the polymer frame, it's sometimes helpful to have a soft mallet handy.

The out of the box trigger pull of the Ruger auto does not

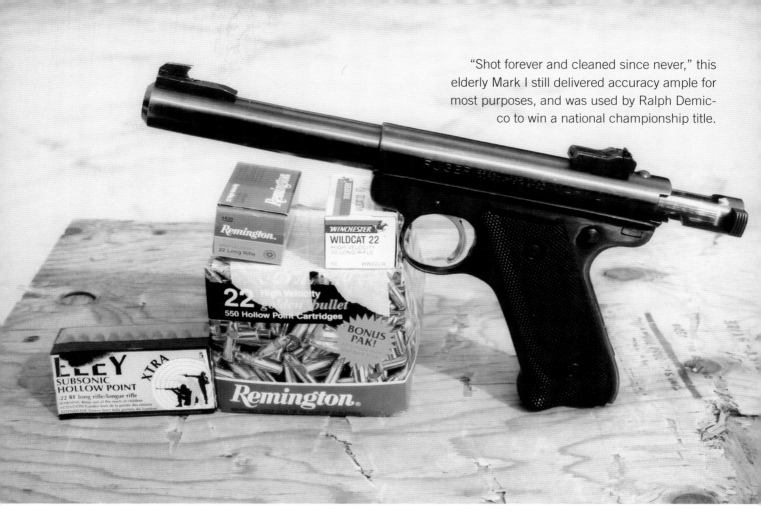

"Shot forever and cleaned since never," this elderly Mark I still delivered accuracy ample for most purposes, and was used by Ralph Demicco to win a national championship title.

compare to the best High Standards or the S&W Model 41, let alone such European exotics as the Pardini or the Hammerli. But a 'smith who knows what he's doing can get a damn good trigger pull out of one. To start with, lose the aluminum trigger that comes on the gun and install a steel one by Clark Custom, the past masters of the Ruger .22. Better yet, have Clark or Volquartsen install it for you. If you're a home gunsmith, the Clark steel triggers are only $20 apiece from Brownells, which can also sell you an adjustable position steel trigger from Marvel.

Personal Perspectives

No one can be 100% impartial and objective when discussing their first love, their first automobile, or their first gun. Consider that a filter through which to strain this chapter, because my first handgun of my very own, at age 11, was a Ruger Standard

For every Ruger .22 ever shot in a match, countless more have been used to plink targets like this Styrofoam coffee cup.

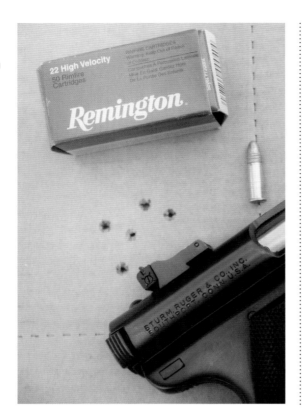

Ordinary Remington .22 LR Hi-Speed shot well in this old Mark I.

model .22 auto with the traditional 4-3/4-inch barrel. It was a rite of passage.

As Hatcher noted at the beginning, this was a 36-ounce pistol. Heavier than a .38 service revolver, and less than a quarter pound shy of the heft of a GI 1911 .45 automatic. In the late 1950s, handgunners shot with one hand only unless they were fortunate enough to hang out with Jeff Cooper and his crowd on the West Coast, and the Ruger Standard was just too heavy a pistol for me at that time. My dad traded it in on a much lighter High Standard Sentinel .22 revolver. The Ruger Standard taught me to shoot a handgun safely and maintain it competently; the Sentinel taught me to shoot one well. Later, a Smith & Wesson K-22 would teach me to shoot a handgun precisely, and a Colt Woodsman Match .22 auto would teach me to shoot one competitively.

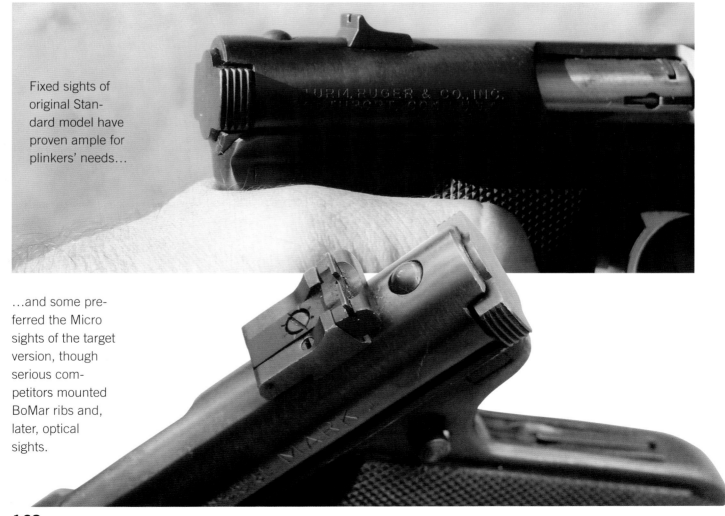

Fixed sights of original Standard model have proven ample for plinkers' needs…

…and some preferred the Micro sights of the target version, though serious competitors mounted BoMar ribs and, later, optical sights.

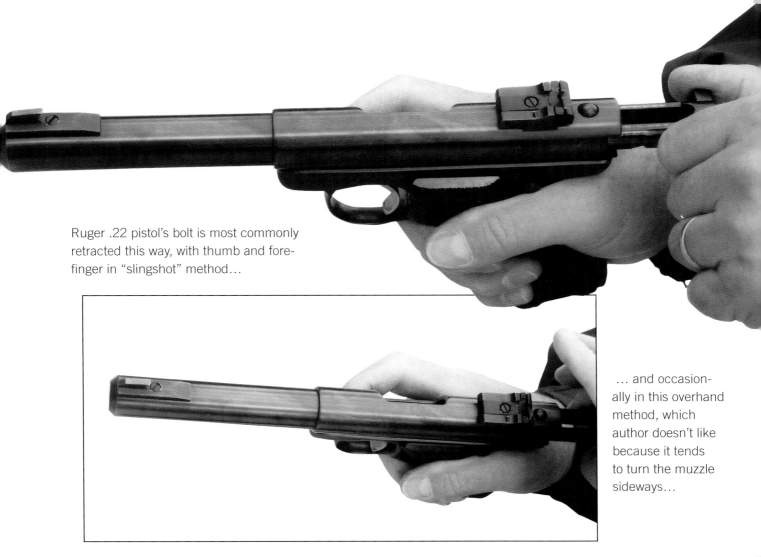

Ruger .22 pistol's bolt is most commonly retracted this way, with thumb and forefinger in "slingshot" method…

… and occasionally in this overhand method, which author doesn't like because it tends to turn the muzzle sideways…

Still, there was always a soft spot for that great Ruger pistol concept. I watched Don Mara, a highly decorated Marine just back from combat in Vietnam, win our state's bulls-eye championship multiple times with an ordinary Mark I he had worked on a little himself. I would go on to meet, and become friends with, Jim Clark himself, and pretty much sit at his feet as he told me why he appreciated the Ruger design so much. When Jim talked, it was well worth listening.

Over the years, I accumulated quite a few Ruger .22 autos. The one I used most was a Mark I bought new some 25 years ago. It has been a ruggedly reliable learner gun and loaner gun for friends ranging from new shooters to plinkers to beginning target shooters.

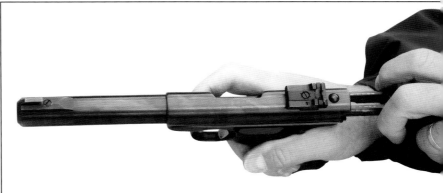

A few years ago, when the now-defunct National Junior Handgun Championships went .22 only, I couldn't help but notice that the Ruger was by far the most popular pistol on the line. It helped that in the sub-junior class (age 13 and younger) the boys and girls were allowed to shoot two-handed. The 22/45 variation has proven particularly

…or this "claw" or "pincer" method with index and middle fingers.

The Ruger Standard Model .22 Automatic in its most memorable format: a classic outdoorsman's handgun.

popular with juniors (ages 14-17) who have to shoot the one-third of the match that is NRA bulls-eye one-hand-only, but I saw 15-year-old Heather O'Keefe win the title with her grandfather's all-steel Mark I and her own all-steel concentration. The following year, Samantha Kemp won the title with a spanking new stainless Mark II her father had given her for the occasion.

At the same match, bulls-eye shooter Ralph Demicco outfitted his son Michael with a sweet High Standard target .22. When the dad brought his youngster there it was a last minute decision, and he didn't realize that there was a parent/child championship event that both shot side-by-side against Bianchi Cup falling steel plates. Ralph had brought just the one pistol for his son. Michael, of course, stayed with the High Standard he'd been practicing with. My old Ruger Mark I loaner came out of the trunk of my car and went into Ralph's hands…and a few minutes later, Ralph and Michael Demicco

had won the 2003 National Champion Parent/Child Team title.

It is, in the end, moments like those which define the reasons why Bill Ruger's first handgun design was his favorite, and why that pistol has become so endearing, so enduring, and so deservedly popular a piece of American firearms history.

Notes

[1] Dope Bag: ".22 Ruger Pistol," by Maj. Gen. J.S. Hatcher, Director, NRA Technical Service, *The American Rifleman*, November, 1949, P.43.

[2] Keith, Elmer, *Sixguns*, New York: Bonanza Books, 1955, P.60.

[3] Cooper, Jeff, *The Complete Book of Modern Handgunning*, Englewood Cliffs, NJ: Prentice-Hall, 1961, P.23.

[4] Hatcher, *op.cit.*

[5] Wilson, R.L., *Ruger & His Guns*, New York City: Simon & Schuster, 1996, P.29.

[6] Kokalis, Peter, *Weapon Tests and Evaluations: The Best of Soldier of Fortune*, Boulder, CO: Paladin Press, 2001, P.335.

The Ruger P-Series Semiautomatics

Comedian Rodney Dangerfield passed away in 2004. His trademark schtick had been, "I don't get no respect!" The line was a wry irony, since he died one of the most respected and beloved men in his field.

Ruger's semiautomatic service pistols are a little like that. They didn't make it to the JSSAP trials in time to be in serious contention for the new US military 9mm service pistol selection. Nor did they catch on like wildfire with law enforcement. In an old issue of *The Accurate Rifle*, a police instructor who favored Glocks was quoted as saying something like, "...and some police departments issue Rugers, if you can believe that." Jeez...glad he wasn't an elitist or anything.

The Rodney Dangerfield of service pistols "don't get no respect"... except from those experienced with it.

Right: Ruger's low priced P95 has proven itself utterly reliable, and hugely popular.

Left: The standard and DC variations of the P90 work well with gloves, as Capt. Ayoob demonstrates during a bitterly cold winter qualification.

Top: Firing the P90. Thumb is in position to verify off-safe (if standard model is carried on safe, which this DC variation can't be), and index finger can reach DA-mode trigger only with pad…

Bottom: …but when self-cocked into single action mode, metal frame Ruger allows more finger on the trigger.

Meanwhile, Ruger and their stockholders laugh all the way to the bank. The Ruger P-series may well be the most popular centerfire pistol manufactured in the United States. A number of the gun dealers I'm constantly interviewing for my column in *Shooting Industry* tell me it's their single biggest seller. Those who pull their noses down out of the air long enough to shoot Ruger pistols, know why.

Pedigree

Some years ago Clay Harvey wrote a slim book with a wide title, *Everything You Really Need to Know About Choosing A .45 Automatic for Self Defense.* Clay took his usual analytical approach, and added a neat little fillip: he approached a number of commercial shooting ranges that rented handguns and kept tabs on their round count and maintenance profiles. Thus, in addition to his own subjective commentary on ergonomics, and objective accuracy testing, he could add frequency of repair ratios and documented durability testing.

The result was that the Ruger P90 beat every other .45 then available. The SIG, the Glock, the S&W, and the Colt and all its clones of the period, which was the early 1990s. Beat 'em all. Harvey said the P90 Ruger "would be my first choice as an all-purpose defensive pistol," because of its "superior reliability, unprecedented precision, and the best double action trigger pull ever put in an autoloader. Its anticipated longevity and the fact that it enjoys a more than modest price advantage on any other stainless .45 auto is simply frosting."[1]

John Taffin is another modern authority who has given the Ruger autos the ultimate endorsement. Calling the company's latest P345 an "extreme makeover," this expert associated with classic revolvers, blue steel, and walnut confessed to adopting that polymer frame Ruger .45 auto as his by-the-bed home protection gun, with a Streamlight M6X white light and laser unit mounted on its integral frame rail. He respected its predecessor, the P90, as well. Said John of the latter gun, "It was big, it was not nearly as svelte as the 1911, and it was, well, sort of clunky. It was not a handgun deserving of ivory stocks and engraving, but it shot well, and it worked. Always. Instead of a classic handgun, it was a marvelous working tool. Col. Charles Askins even opinioned it was (the) best .45 Auto ever offered."[2]

Dave Spaulding is another of today's top experts. He and I served together on the firearms committee for ASLET, the American Society for Law Enforcement Training, and having seen him both teach and shoot, I can tell you he knows his stuff. Dave wrote recently, "In my part of the country, which is Ohio, many of those who desire to enter law enforcement must put themselves through the police academy...This process usually requires the cadet to purchase his own sidearm for training purposes. Since most of these students have limited knowledge of firearms, the primary reason that a particular handgun is purchased is price, thus, I see a large number of Ruger P90 series pistols come through the basic program. Ruger semiautomatic pistols are built like an Abrams tank. They are big, bulky, solidly built pistols that will outlast many higher priced pistols. The trigger action is quite smooth, and the vast majority of cadets who use these guns perform to a very high level while in the academy. The reason that many of these folks eventually sell the Ruger pistols is that they don't like their looks. One student told me, 'There is no pride in ownership. While the Ruger has served me well, it isn't very attractive. It's blocky and doesn't have the streamlined looks of the European guns.'"[3]

When Clyde Caceres was at Crimson Trace, he showed me his company's new LaserGrip for Ruger autos. "The demand has

Bob Cogan at his shop in Safety Harbor, Florida. He builds a great custom Ruger service pistol.

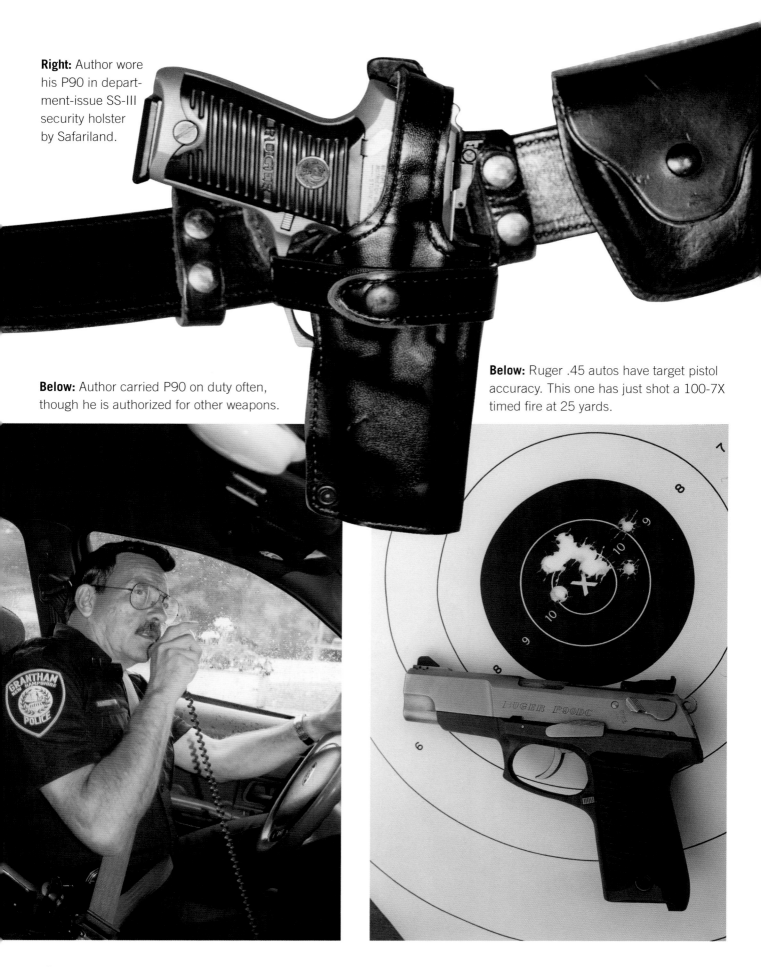

Right: Author wore his P90 in department-issue SS-III security holster by Safariland.

Below: Author carried P90 on duty often, though he is authorized for other weapons.

Below: Ruger .45 autos have target pistol accuracy. This one has just shot a 100-7X timed fire at 25 yards.

been huge," he told me. "I don't think most people in the industry realize just how many consumers have bought these guns." More proof that the Ruger P-series strikes a resonant chord among shooters in America. And elsewhere. A lot of these guns have gone overseas, purchased in volume by such entities as the Israeli air force. Thousands of 9mm Ruger P95s have been bought by the US government to arm indigenous friendly forces in Iraq and Afghanistan.

A Brief History

One day in the early 1980s, Bill Ruger, Sr. sat me in his office and swore me to secrecy and showed me the blueprints and a frame casting for what would be his first centerfire semiautomatic pistol. "A 9mm for Everyman," he said. The "wondernine" fad – high capacity, double action semiautomatic pistols chambered for 9mm Luger – was upon us. Bill's finger had always been on the pulse of Capitol Hill, so he knew that after thirty-some years of talking about it, the US government was finally going to bite

the small bullet and adopt a service pistol chambered for the NATO round. Police were adopting such guns in large numbers, and having roared past Colt to take a strong second place in the police revolver market (and biting on S&W's first place butt) Bill saw the new pistol fulfilling three roles. He wanted it to win the JSSAP (Joint Services Small Arms Project) tests; he wanted it to win police bids when cops switched from six-shot .38s and .357s to sixteen-shot 9mms; and he wanted an affordable, high quality pistol that would allow a responsible armed citizen to protect his home with the same technology the military used to protect the borders and the police used to enforce safe streets.

The gun was dubbed the P85. This began two Ruger service pistol traditions. The first was naming the gun for the year of its ostensible introduction. The second was coming in late by a year or two on that designation. Announced to great hoopla in 1985, the eponymous pistol didn't make it to gun dealers' shelves until 1987.

There had been tremendous pressure to finish the gun in time for the military tests.

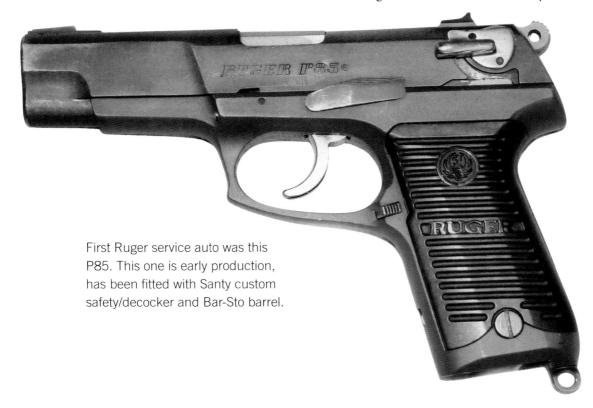

First Ruger service auto was this P85. This one is early production, has been fitted with Santy custom safety/decocker and Bar-Sto barrel.

Right: Built-up safety/decock lever by Nolan Santy on early P85 presaged later improved Ruger parts…

Below: …as seen on this later P89, with extremely ergonomic ambi decocking lever.

As a result, something happened that was extremely rare in the history of Sturm, Ruger Inc.: the gun was rushed, and was born with defects. Accuracy was mediocre at best, sometimes but not always making the generous gun magazine standard of four-inch groups at 25 yards, depending on the ammunition. The blued chrome molybdenum steel of the early P85s was not particularly rust resistant. Worse still, some of the early guns did not meet the long-established Ruger standard of reliability.

Before there was the Internet, cops had teletype. Word got out quickly to law enforcement agencies of tests in which the new Ruger 9mm had jammed. As Ruger engineers worked feverishly to fix the problems, with input from some of us outside the company, the US Government finalized the adoption of the Beretta 92 as the new M9 service pistol, and countless police departments bypassed the Ruger to adopt Beretta, HK, Glock, SIG, and Smith & Wesson 9mm autos. A single accidental discharge inspired Bill Ruger to lead his engineering team in a sweeping redesign of the P85 that also incorporated most of the fixes suggested by outside consultants. The result was an interim pistol, the P85 Mark II, with design changes finalized as the P89.

Meanwhile, the FBI had in the late 1980s announced its intention to adopt the 10mm Auto cartridge across the board as its new service round. Experts of the time predicted that this would be the new trend that would bury the 9mm fad. Bill, Sr. and his design team set about crafting a new heavy-duty, large bore P85 that would take this powerful round. The result was the P90. By the time production got into full swing in 1991, it had already become clear that the 10mm Auto had nose-dived in popularity, and instead, Ruger chambered the P90 for the .45 ACP. Built for the brutal 10mm Auto in full power (read: 200-grain bullet at 1200 feet per second), the P90 was literally over-engineered for the low-pressure .45 round. That meant it could handle +P .45 ammo in stride, and would have a theoretically almost limitless service life in .45 ACP. It was an instant success with the commercial market, as shooter after shooter discovered what Clay Harvey did: that it was a "best buy" gun based on its low price, its extraordinary durability, and its fine accuracy. One- to two-inch groups were standard at 25 yards, out of the box, with the best factory ammo.

Meanwhile, the .40 S&W cartridge emerged in 1990, a compromise between the 9mm and the .45. Ruger, like virtually every other auto pistol manufacturer, jumped on the bandwagon. At the same time, the company began offering newer, smaller, more streamlined models of the 9mm. The P91 was a .40 caliber service pistol. The P93 was a compact 9mm. The P94 was a compact offered in both 9mm and .40.

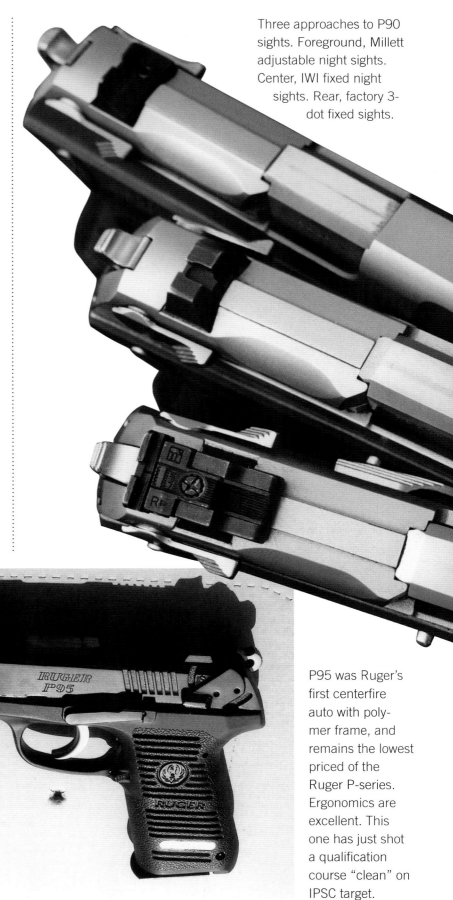

Three approaches to P90 sights. Foreground, Millett adjustable night sights. Center, IWI fixed night sights. Rear, factory 3-dot fixed sights.

P95 was Ruger's first centerfire auto with polymer frame, and remains the lowest priced of the Ruger P-series. Ergonomics are excellent. This one has just shot a qualification course "clean" on IPSC target.

Officer Glenn Jenkins finds his issue Ruger P90 as rugged and reliable as Chevy Tahoe patrol vehicle.

Left: Like its predecessor the P90, the P345 is an omnivorous .45 that cycles perfectly with loads from "mild to wild." Author finds it most accurate with 230-grain bullets.

Lower Left: Easy-operating safety and good trigger reach are features of latest in the series, Ruger P345.

Most were offered with a choice of three fire control systems. The standard, with no identifying model suffix, was traditional double action (that is, double action for only the first shot, and self-cocking thereafter), and fitted with a slide-mounted lever that acted as both decocker and manual safety. The DC suffix on a Ruger service pistol's model number indicated that the lever on the slide served as a decocker only. Most were also made available in DAO (double action only) format. In factory insider parlance, a "K" prefix such as KP90 or KP94DAO, meant the gun was stainless, and a simple "P" prefix meant a blue finish. In practice, however, shooters and gun magazines and gun dealers and cops all ignored the "K" and called the stainless guns "P90s," "P89s," etc. All of the above models had steel superstructures and internals with lightweight aluminum frames.

The P95, typically introduced the year after its designation, was a polymer frame 9mm. Intended to attack the Glock market, it didn't make deep inroads in the police sector

Raised loaded chamber indicator on top of slide, manual safety (shown in "on" position), and integral gun lock operating through right side safety lever, are features of P345.

Millett sights, Bob Cogan trigger job enhanced the shootability of author's personal P90DC.

Far Left: P95's accuracy at 25 yards will get its job done. It handles this +P+ ammo well, and attached SureFire light does not affect reliability or point of impact.

but was a definite hit among private citizens. Initially produced in DC and DAO formats only, it was offered in a safety/decocker format five years later. 1997 saw the .45 caliber version, the P97, which again was offered with decocker-only and DAO fire mechanisms.

Finally, in 2004, Ruger introduced its latest generation of service pistol, the P345. In a departure from previous nomenclature, "P345" apparently stands for "Pistol, 3rd model, caliber .45. It replaced the polymer frame P97, which had fit most hands much better than its all-metal predecessor, the P90, which remained in the catalog. Moreover, to better deal with the market in California and other states with increasingly stringent firearms safety design requirements, the P345 was the first Ruger auto to come with a magazine disconnector safety, a loaded chamber indicator, and an internal gun lock. The latter worked via the ambidextrous safety/decock lever. Its polymer frame even friendlier to short trigger fingers than the P97's, and with better traction to the hand, the P345 is indeed the fine pistol Spaulding says it is, and worthy of a connoisseur of fine revolvers like Taffin placing it at bedside.

Shooting the P-Series Rugers

By the time I got my first T&E P85, Bill Ruger and his team had already worked out the reliability problems. However, it was still sloppy in accuracy, and its vestigial thumb safety was difficult to operate. I bought my

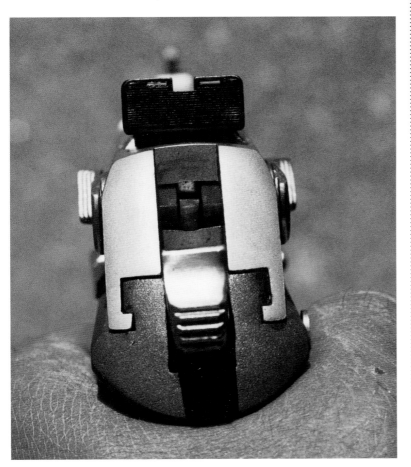

Shape of frame acts like a beavertail grip safety on a 1911, spreading and softening the P90's "kick."

test gun, and gave it to Nolan Santy, who smoothed the action and installed a properly-sized ambidextrous thumb safety he custom made. I then sent the gun to the late, great Irv Stone at Bar-Sto, who thereupon made the first Bar-Sto barrel for a Ruger service pistol. "I liked yours so much, I bought a P85 and made one for myself," Irv wrote me later.

Now, the damn thing would shoot! Two inches or better at 25 yards. I brought the gun up to Bill, Sr. and left it with him for a while. Much of what Santy and Stone had done to my gun was reflected in subsequent Rugers. The Ruger's slide-mounted safety lever went from almost unworkable to one of the two easiest in the industry, equaled or exceeded only by that of the Beretta 92F. The first P85s had delivered poor accuracy, but the new ones equaled or exceeded a Smith & Wesson 9mm.

I learned later from Irv's son Stony, who took over the business after his dad's death, that Irv Stone had flown to the Ruger plant to consult at length with Bill, Sr. Their business deal fell through, unfortunately, but the Stone legacy is clear in the superb barrels of the P90 and subsequent Ruger .45 autos. The P90 and P345 are literally match grade, delivering stunning groups at 25 and 50 yards. My first P345 put five rounds of 230-grain Federal HydraShok .45 JHP into 0.90 of one inch at 25 yards, and I've won pistol matches with my P90s.

As Clay Harvey noted, the double action pull on the P90 is extremely smooth, and that continued through the P95, P97, and P345 pistols. On the self-cocking models, the trigger re-set is reasonably short, and a sweet single action pull is more the rule than the exception. They remain hell for rugged. I deliberately drove over a P95 with a 4800-pound SUV, and it still worked fine.

The polymer frame P-Rugers fit the hand well. The metal-frame guns have a long trigger reach, at least for double action. The low-dropping angle of the trigger guard on most of them exacerbates this problem. The pre-polymer models tend to feel square in the hand. This, of course, is subjective; I know one cop who swears his issue P90 fits his hand better than any other handgun he has owned in his long career. On the other hand, the P90 fits my own hand about like a brick with a trigger. Many find that Hogue grips, or rubber grip-sleeves with added finger grooves, improve the feel. The polymer frame models, by contrast, fit most shooters extremely well as they come from the box.

If you choose to carry on-safe, the easy movement of the slide-mounted lever on all but the earliest P85s makes off-safing smooth and easy. Run the thumb upward on a 45-degree angle toward the ejection port to guarantee this part of the operation. Unlike SIGs and Berettas, a high thumb grasp doesn't seem to ride over and de-activate the slide lock lever.

Ruger service pistols kick softly. The broad back of the frame distributes recoil into the hand like a beavertail grip safety on a custom 1911 pistol. However, with a fairly high bore axis, the .45s will jump a bit like the SIG, which is to say a little more than the lower-barreled 1911 or Glock. (Remember that kick, the rearward impact into the hand, is a different recoil element from muzzle jump.) In TDA format, like most of their kind, they work particularly well in gloved hands.

These guns are omnivorous and reliable. Like Glocks or any other auto pistols, they need to be lubed occasionally or they'll jam. Take care of that, and they'll feed most anything. My P90s and my P345 will cycle everything from feeble softball target ammo

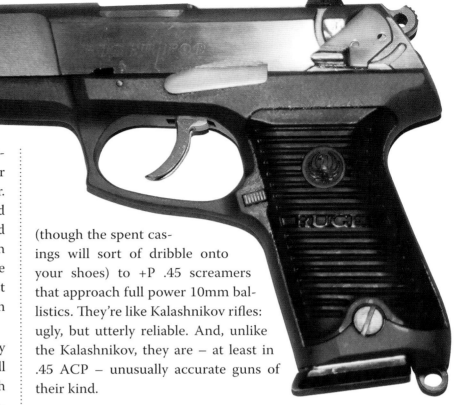

(though the spent casings will sort of dribble onto your shoes) to +P .45 screamers that approach full power 10mm ballistics. They're like Kalashnikov rifles: ugly, but utterly reliable. And, unlike the Kalashnikov, they are – at least in .45 ACP – unusually accurate guns of their kind.

Personal Experience

When the P85 came out, I tested it and approved it as optional for the police department I then served. Shortly thereafter, we adopted the Smith & Wesson .45 automatic as standard issue, and I didn't have to think about it much.

By 1993, however, I was working for another PD and the chief decided that all of us would carry the same gun. It was determined early that it would be a rust-resistant double action .45 auto. Glock had not yet worked out the magazine problems with its G21 .45 – though they would get it running fine later – and the choice narrowed to the SIG P220, the S&W 4506, and the Ruger P90. The Ruger actually beat the other two. It delivered the fine accuracy of the SIG, and flawlessly fed 200-grain JHP bullets, which the SIG didn't always do; it fed anything, like the S&W, but beat the Smith by about an inch in accuracy and

Author's P90, issued to him for more than 11 years, never failed him. He even won a state shoot with it.

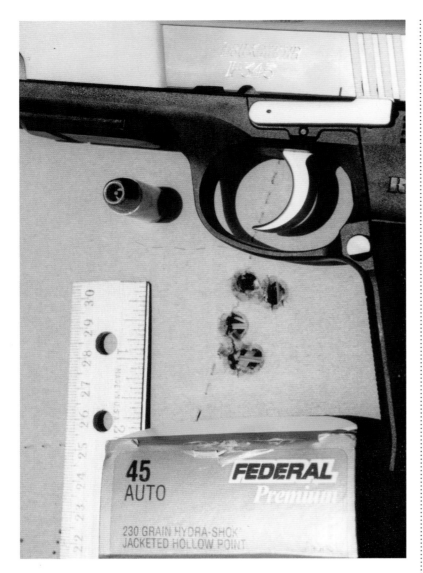

Measured center to center, these five rounds of Hydra-Shok, fired from bench rest 25 yards away, are just under an inch. Pistol is bone-stock Ruger P345.

In 2005, we adopted the P345 to replace the P90, and our troops like it even better.

The P90, I think, was Bill Ruger's apology for the flaws of the original P85. The year my department adopted that gun, I was shooting a match in Boston and my expensive, tricked-out 1911 comp gun broke down. I was wearing the issue pistol off-duty, so I drew it and finished the match with that Ruger...and won. In 2000, I won the state shoot for cops with my department issue P90 and fixed IWI night sights. It included a 50-yard stage, and the P90's inherent accuracy was a decided advantage there. Circa 2005, I was testing a $2600 "factory custom" 1911 in the same time frame as I tested the Ruger P345; both were 100% on reliability, but the $540 Ruger shot the tighter groups. A few years ago I had Bob Cogan at Accurate Plating and Weaponry tune up a P90 for me with Millett adjustable night sights; the thing shoots better than a Colt National Match, at a fraction of the price.

I'm authorized to carry other guns on duty, but for more than a decade I've worn the issue Ruger .45 to work more often than any other. It ain't fancy, and it's totally lacking in snob appeal, but it does the job better than many, many guns that cost far, far more. There's no higher compliment you can pay to a firearm than to carry it to protect your life, and the lives of those you swore an oath to protect. The Ruger pistol lives up to both the task and the oath.

was distinctly lighter. We adopted the Ruger P90 as our service pistol that year.

From 1993 to 2005, they stood up remarkably well, literally outliving their night sights. Ours had the semi-permanent lubricant bond of Sentry Solutions applied by an armorer (Rick Devoid, Tarnhelm Supply, 431 High St., Boscawen, NH 03303 www.tarnhelm.com), and the damn things just never jammed. Rugers are popular among police in our area; the largest city near us issues DAO Ruger .40s, the sheriff's department issues the Ruger 9mm, and two contiguous towns issue P90s like ours. We got some teasing from other cops with Smiths and SIGs and Glocks until our pistol teams beat theirs, issue duty gun to issue duty gun.

Notes

[1]Harvey, Clay, *Everything You Really Need to Know about choosing A .45 Automatic for Self Defense*, Hope Mills, NC: Hames Press, 1993, p. 87.

[2]"P345 Extreme Makeover" by John Taffin, *American Handgunner* magazine, Jan/Feb 2005, p. 60.

[3]"Ruger Model P345" by Dave Spaulding, *Handguns* magazine, Dec '04/Jan '05, p. 40.

Smith & Wesson's Military & Police Revolver

Quick, name a whole bunch of handguns that have been in production uninterrupted for over 100 years and are still in widespread service protecting innocent people in the United States and around the world!

Well, let's see...there's the Smith & Wesson Military & Police revolver...and there's...uh...um...well, there might be....

Oh, the hell with it.

At this writing, there's only one. The Colt 1911 came 12 years after the Smith & Wesson Hand Ejector Model of 1899, and the Colt revolvers that predated it never sustained the model name integrity or the direct conti-

A hundred and ten years after its introduction, the S&W M&P is still on patrol in New York and Chicago, and still protects countless American homes.

Right: Author's most unusual M&P, a 2-inch .357 chopped and channeled for deep concealment by master revolversmith Travis Strahan of Ringgold, GA. Grips by Strahan; finish is aftermarket hard chrome.

Left: Using +P 158-grain .38 Special ammo, is seen here winning the Midwest Regional IDPA Stock Service Revolver Championship with it a few months later.

Below: The beginning of the M&P, 1899: From Supica & Nahas' *Standard Catalog of Smith & Wesson*, the first model S&W .38 Hand Ejector.

Bottom: A pre-war, long action S&W M&P customized for Bob Nichols and depicted here in his classic book, *The Secrets of Double Action Shooting.*

nuity of manufacture. Even the Luger came too late, and the Colt Single Action Army "Peacemaker" was in and out of production. For sustained continuity of production, constant readiness to defend the righteous and the innocent, no handgun has stayed the course like the .38-frame Smith & Wesson revolver.

The Military & Police began in caliber .38 Long Colt but three years later would be chambered for the cartridge that defined it, the .38 Special. It would be produced in calibers from .22 rimfire to .41 Magnum. It would be a .38 Special first and foremost, a .357 Magnum as a distant second in popularity by the end of its first century of service,

but always it would be the Military & Police, and the most popular by far of all Smith & Wesson handguns. It was also the first of the hugely successful K-frame guns.

A Brief History

"There is no doubt," wrote S&W historian Roy Jinks, "that the most important development for Smith & Wesson was the Model K line of handguns for, within this line are some of Smith & Wesson's most famous revolvers. The fact of the matter is that the K-frame size handgun has been and continues to be so popular that its production exceeds the combined quantities of all other handguns ever produced by Smith & Wesson."[1]

Jim Supica and Richard Nahas, noted authorities on Smith & Wessons, write, "The introducton of the .38 HE (Hand Ejector) Military & Police marks the beginning of what would become the quintessential police handgun of the twentieth century and the workhorse of S&W production for many decades."[2] No one has debated with the authorities who've called it the "bread and butter" Smith & Wesson.

The First Model M&P of 1899 was chambered in .32/20 and .38 Long Colt. It lacked a front locking lug, and had the round butt found to this day on K-frames built for concealment. The Second Model of 1902 had the front locking lug for the ejector rod that would become a Smith & Wesson characteristic, but more important, it was the first handgun chambered for the .38 Special cartridge. Authorities Roy McHenry and Walter Roper explained, "Failure of the .38 Long Colt cartridge in the Philippines led Daniel B. Wesson to design a better one, and the result was the .38 Smith & Wesson Special. It had a powder weight of 21 grains compared with 18 in the regulation cartridge, and the bullet gained 8 grains for a total of 158 simply by filling in the hollow

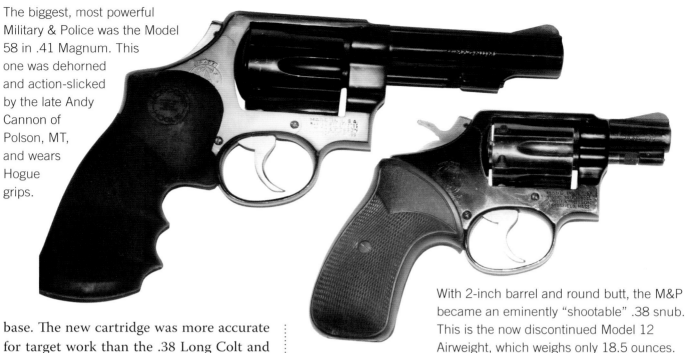

The biggest, most powerful Military & Police was the Model 58 in .41 Magnum. This one was dehorned and action-slicked by the late Andy Cannon of Polson, MT, and wears Hogue grips.

With 2-inch barrel and round butt, the M&P became an eminently "shootable" .38 snub. This is the now discontinued Model 12 Airweight, which weighs only 18.5 ounces. Grips are Pachmayr Compacs.

S&W's Combat Masterpiece (Model 15) is basically a Military & Police .38 Special with adjustable sights and trigger stop. Its inherent accuracy is essentially the same as that of the more basic Military and Police.

base. The new cartridge was more accurate for target work than the .38 Long Colt and was heavy enough for ordinary police work, but the War department had learned its lesson and refused to issue hand guns to soldiers of less than .45 caliber."[3]

The first change within the Second Model variation was addition of a square butt, the same profile now in use on service/target grade K-frames. The Third Model in 1905 was the first "five screw" Smith & Wesson, and in the Fourth Change within that series in 1915, the M&P got its first 2-inch barrel. Until then, the tubes had ranged from 4 to 6.5 inches.

This remained the format of the M&P through WWII. Production was now focused on the wartime M&P, the Victory Model. In its American incarnation, the Victory was a .38 Special, generally with a 4-inch barrel. In the British version, it was chambered for the UK's .38/200 cartridge, an analog to the US .38 S&W round, usually with 4 through 6 inch barrels, with the 5 inch being most common. The Victory Model was distinctive with its flat gray Parkerized finish and smooth, dark brown walnut stocks. S&W produced 568,204 Victory Models just for Great Britain (Jinks, p.163).

In 1942, M&P serial number 1,000,000 was manufactured. By the war's end, American police and civilians were hungry for guns. Though the war had begun with Colt perhaps more popular among cops than S&W, the postwar years saw a rapid domination of the police market by Smith & Wesson in general and the M&P in particular. By third quarter 1948, S&W had produced their second million M&Ps. That year saw the refinement of the new short action design. During the war, the hammer block had been redesigned after a sailor was killed when a

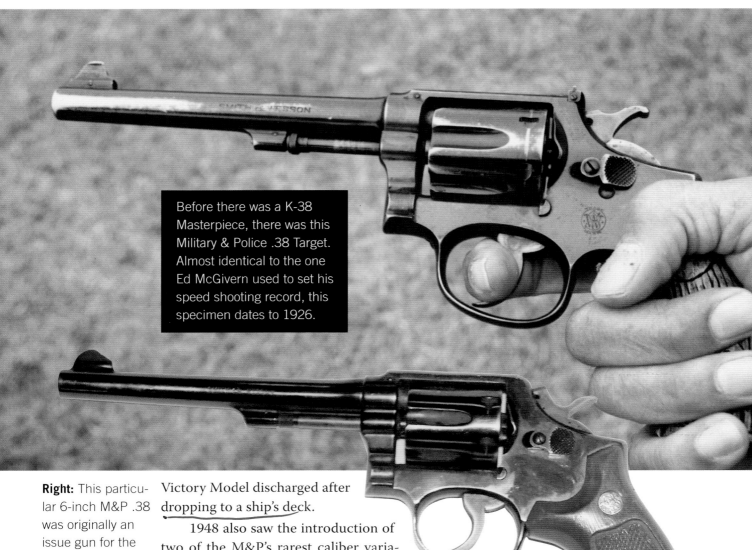

Before there was a K-38 Masterpiece, there was this Military & Police .38 Target. Almost identical to the one Ed McGivern used to set his speed shooting record, this specimen dates to 1926.

Right: This particular 6-inch M&P .38 was originally an issue gun for the Rhode Island State Police. World combat pistol champ Ray Chapman bought it thereafter, and the author subsequently traded it from Ray.

Victory Model discharged after dropping to a ship's deck.

1948 also saw the introduction of two of the M&P's rarest caliber variations. One was .32 S&W Long: "When production was completed, the firm had produced a total of 4,813 revolvers. Today, one of these revolvers would be a rare find for the Smith & Wesson collector," notes Jinks. The other *rara avis* was an M&P in .22 Long Rifle. Produced at the request of the US Postal Service, this sole rimfire M&P of the century was intended as a training gun for armed postal inspectors. It was produced off and on as a special order item for law enforcement agencies for some 30 years and was never cataloged. According to Jinks, one lot of 500 was released through public channels.

1952 saw the introduction of the M&P Airweight. This handy, accurate gun was an outgrowth of the Air Force's ill-fated Aircrewman revolver project that encompassed aluminum cylinders as well as frames. The relatively few surviving Aircrewman guns are prized collectors' items. For some years, the Airweights (and all the Aircrewmen) had the rectangular cylinder latch that had been introduced for the Chiefs Special.

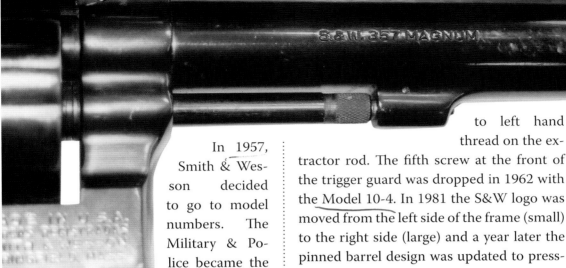

In 1957, Smith & Wesson decided to go to model numbers. The Military & Police became the Model 10, and the Model 12 in Airweight. Two years later S&W introduced their first "dash" model, connoting a hyphen between the model number and a suffix that indicated a variation. The 10-1 was a 4-inch heavy barrel M&P with 1/8-inch ramped sight. This raised the weight of the 4-inch .38 Special from 30.5 ounces to 34.0. It instantly became the national standard, and within a few years, NYPD officers who carried them were referring scornfully to the older models as "skinny barrel Smiths."

Most of the other "dash" variants involved minor changes like going from right to left hand thread on the extractor rod. The fifth screw at the front of the trigger guard was dropped in 1962 with the Model 10-4. In 1981 the S&W logo was moved from the left side of the frame (small) to the right side (large) and a year later the pinned barrel design was updated to press-fit (Model 10-8). An M&P that fired the 9X19 cartridge, using wire "rim-catchers" in the chambers, was produced for the European police market and was met with a collective yawn from stateside shooters.

More meaningful evolutions were occurring with the Military & Police. In summer 1964, S&W debuted the first of two M&Ps it ever made in other than K-frame configuration. It was the Model 58, a 4-inch, fixed sight service revolver built on the big N-frame and chambered for the .41 Magnum cartridge newly introduced by S&W and Remington. Unfortunately, the bulky revolver did not catch on with law enforcement, and the Model 58 was discontinued

Below: In the Fifties, the Model 10 heavy barrel configuration became the defining shape of the .38 service revolver for the rest of the century…

Above: …and for all of the M&P .357s that would follow.

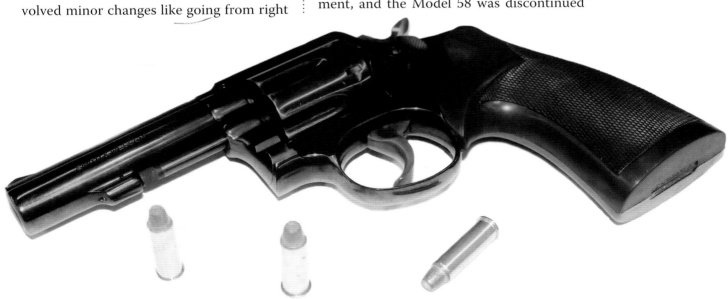

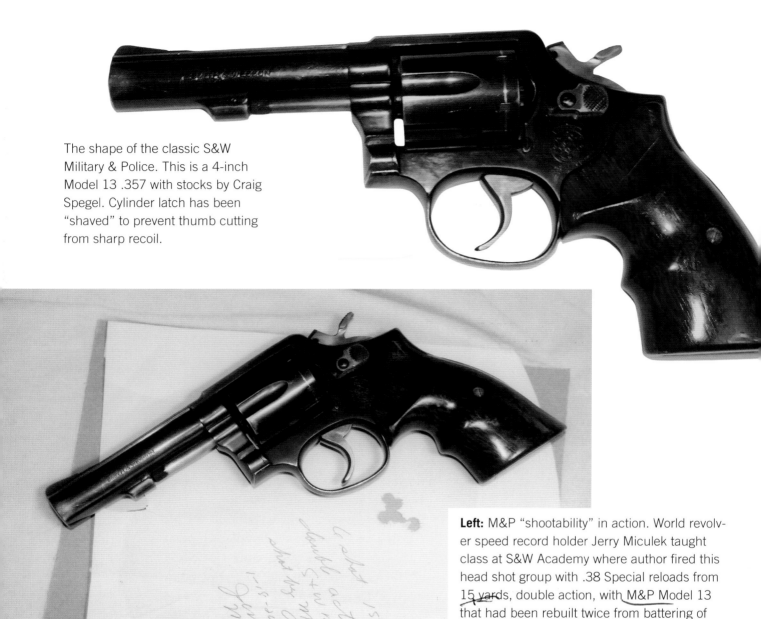

The shape of the classic S&W Military & Police. This is a 4-inch Model 13 .357 with stocks by Craig Spegel. Cylinder latch has been "shaved" to prevent thumb cutting from sharp recoil.

Left: M&P "shootability" in action. World revolver speed record holder Jerry Miculek taught class at S&W Academy where author fired this head shot group with .38 Special reloads from 15 yards, double action, with M&P Model 13 that had been rebuilt twice from battering of constant diet of 125-grain Magnum ammo. The Military & Police has every bit of the inherent accuracy of the more expensive target models.

in 1978. Two years later, the firm manufactured 3,000 Model 520 revolvers listed as Military & Police models (Supica/Nahan, p.138). These were N-frame .357 Magnums with fixed sights and shrouded ejectors, built to spec for New York State Police, which decided at the last minute to go with adjustable sight S&Ws. The 520s were sold through regular distributors and never catalogued.

Other variants were more successful, however.

M&Ps: The New Breed

In the late Sixties and early Seventies, the buzz term among cops was "the new breed." The phrase certainly applied to S&W's new generation of Military & Police service revolvers.

First came the Model 64. It was the second stainless steel handgun ever, following the Model 60 Chiefs Special. For the first two years it was made with the tapered 4-inch barrel. The Model 64-1 ushered in a much more popular version, with the now-paradigm 4-inch heavy barrel.

By 1974, S&W had quietly been producing special Model 10s in .357 Magnum for the New York State Police. They had worked out well, and in '74 the company jumped in and announced the M&P .357 for the public as the Model 13 (chrome-molybdenum steel construction) and Model 65 (stainless). Their first customer for the latter was the Oklahoma State Patrol, whose first .357 K-frames were marked "64-1" (Jinks, pp.167-8).

All these .38 Special models remain in the S&W catalog to this day. One of the most popular variants in all four models was the 3-inch heavy barrel originally developed for the FBI. K-frame .357 Magnums were discontinued a few years ago due to documented longevity problems with the hot 125-grain Magnum defense/duty round.

Target Variations

From its first year of production in 1899, the M&P has been available with adjustable sights for those who required especially precise accuracy and shot placement. Until the Forties, these guns were known simply as the M&P Target. By the post-war years, they had been redefined as the Masterpiece series in calibers .22, .32 Long, and .38 Special. (There had not been a "Military & Police Target .22" as such. That gun was known at its beginning as the "Outdoorsman.") The K-22 and K-38 went on to great popularity, still offered today with improved full-lug barrels and, in the case of the K-22, a 10-shot cylinder. The K-32 never caught on, despite an attempt to

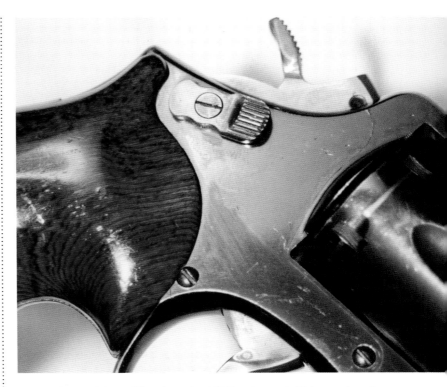

Above: Potential modifications for M&Ps abound. This one has been fitted with a left-handed thumb safety by Frank Murabito, seen here "on-safe"…

Below: …and here, "off-safe." Conversion is still being done by Rick Devoid at www.tarnhelm.com, who can also do a right-handed version employing the cylinder latch.

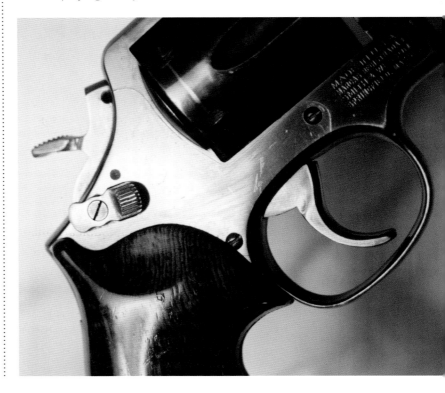

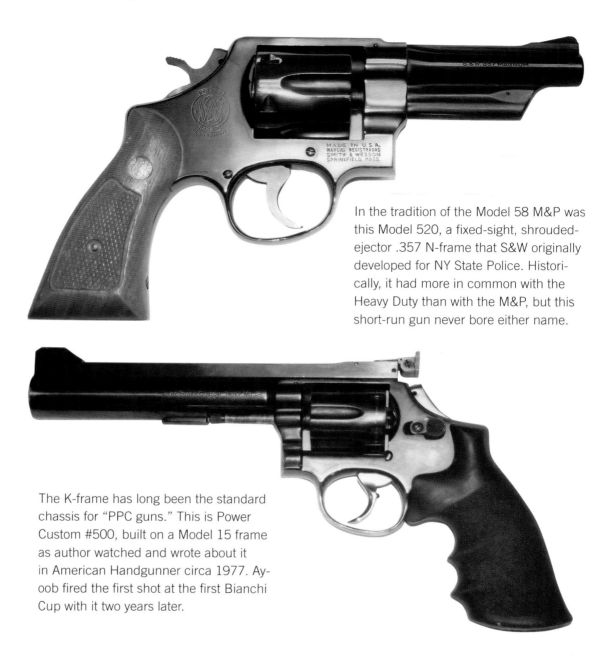

In the tradition of the Model 58 M&P was this Model 520, a fixed-sight, shrouded-ejector .357 N-frame that S&W originally developed for NY State Police. Historically, it had more in common with the Heavy Duty than with the M&P, but this short-run gun never bore either name.

The K-frame has long been the standard chassis for "PPC guns." This is Power Custom #500, built on a Model 15 frame as author watched and wrote about it in American Handgunner circa 1977. Ayoob fired the first shot at the first Bianchi Cup with it two years later.

revitalize it a few years ago in .32 Magnum chambering, and remains something of a collector's item.

A 4-inch version of the K-38, the Combat Masterpiece, was introduced in 1949 and became a highly successful item that defined the "target grade service revolver." It would be better known to some as the Model 15 in blue or nickel, and the Model 67 in stainless.

1955 saw the introduction of another modern classic, the Bill Jordan-inspired .357 Combat Magnum. Known as the Model 19 when made of chrome-moly and the Model 66 in stainless, the .357 Combat Magnum was another revolver that left a big footprint, and is discussed elsewhere in this book.

The Centenarian M&P

These guns have served the nation's police in every state and most cities. From London to Hong Kong they've been issue weapons for the constabulary. For most of the last half of the 20th century, the Royal

This well-worn Model 15 police trade-in still groups in an inch at 25 yards with ordinary, generic 158-grain round nose lead ammo. The target version of the M&P, it's no more inherently accurate than the fixed sight version, author believes.

Canadian Mounted Police carried Model 10s with 5 to 5-1/2-inch barrels in their trademark rigs consisting of lanyard and flap holster. (RCMP is also the FBI of Canada, and their investigators carried 2-inch Model 10s). Only in the late part of the century did the Mounties switch to S&W DAO 9mm auto pistols.

To this day, you'll see a lot of Model 10s and 64s in the holsters of New York City and Chicago police officers, and until recently there were FBI agents who still carried their issue 3-inch heavy barrel Model 13s. The gun to beat at the National Police Shooting Championships is still the customized S&W Military & Police .38 Special.

S&W still produces these solid-value guns at "bread and butter" prices. For the last few years, however, they've sported two-piece barrels and the internal lock

An M&P "transition gun." Frame is marked with model number 10-6, but gun is chambered for .357 Magnum and barrel so marked. It was an uncatalogued, special-order forerunner to the Model 13. From the J Stuckey collection.

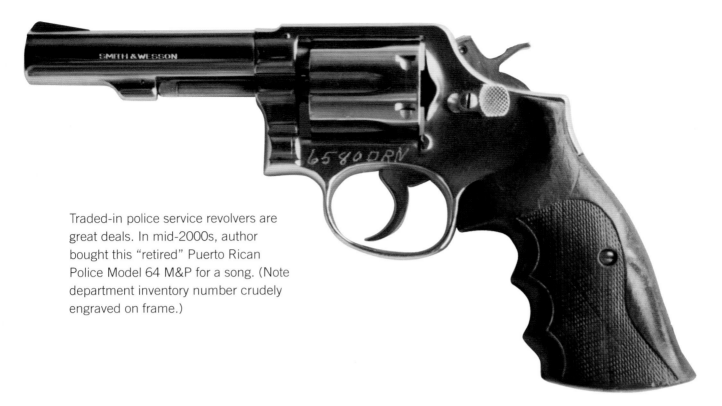

Traded-in police service revolvers are great deals. In mid-2000s, author bought this "retired" Puerto Rican Police Model 64 M&P for a song. (Note department inventory number crudely engraved on frame.)

mechanism that has so antagonized Smith & Wesson connoisseurs.

There's another "value angle." American police have traded in several hundred thousand service revolvers, a lion's share of which are M&Ps, so they could get their high-speed, low-drag semiautomatics. A great many of these guns were expertly maintained by factory-trained department armorers.

If you go with a used M&P, know how to check the gun for wear. The hot 125-grain Magnums most cops were using for training and qualification as well as duty with the .357 revolvers were hell on K-frame guns. When in doubt, buy a Model 10 or 64 .38 Special. Even with +P ammo, the K-frame would absorb a large volume of training fire without "shooting loose." These police trade-ins are some of the best buys on the used firearm market today.

Shooting the M&P

From the very beginning, when they put the adjustable sights on it they called it the "Target Model" and it performed just fine in the arena. This tells you something. The Model 10, built on the same machinery with the same steel guts as the K-38, shares the fancier revolver's inherent accuracy. Once you've got the M&P's fixed sights where you want them, the gun will keep up with the target revolvers as far as groups.

In Canada, Photios Giannakis won many trophies in PPC shooting, pitting his trade-in RCMP 5" Model 10 against the tricked-out heavy barrel target revolvers of the others. For most of the 1970s, NH state champion Richard Brown almost drove the other cops to madness, beating their Pythons and Combat Magnums in 4-inch service revolver matches with his WWII-vintage Victory Model, which his police department had purchased through Civil Defense for – are you ready for this? – three dollars in the late 1960s.

The famously accurate K-38 is little more than a Military & Police with adjustable sights. The actions are basically inter-

A machine rest, such as this Caldwell HAMMR unit, will show the startling accuracy of the K-frame Smith & Wesson revolver.

changeable. The Smith & Wesson M&P set the "gold standard" for smoothness in double action revolver trigger strokes.

And none of this has changed.

The M&P In The New Millennium

What works, works. Constants, by definition, do not change. The Smith & Wesson Military & Police has done the job for well over 100 years. The only complaint about it was that, in its .38 Special incarnation, it might not be sufficiently powerful. The 1972 development of the 158-grain lead .38 Special +P hollowpoint round, a cartridge that by all accounts equals GI .45 hardball for "stopping power," changed that. Two years later, the introduction of the Models 13 and 65 that could fire the devastating 125-grain .357 Magnum hollownose ended that point of debate forever.

Those who still rely on the M&P have reason to be confident. They possess the knowledge that their sidearm has spent a successful century defending the innocent from evil.

Supica and Nahas may have put the Military and Police best in its place in the first edition of their *Standard Catalog of Smith & Wesson*. They wrote, "The basic design of this gun has been continuously improved over nearly a century, and in its current variations such as the Models 10, 19, and 66, is still considered by many expert authorities to be the finest personal defense or police handgun available."

Notes

[1]Jinks, Roy, *History of Smith & Wesson Revised Tenth Anniversary Edition*, North Hollywood, CA: Beinfeld Publishing, 1977, p. 159.

[2]Supica, Jim, and Nahas, Richard, *Standard Catalog of Smith & Wesson*, Iola, WI: Krause Publications, 1996, p. 91.

[3]McHenry, Roy, and Roper, Walter, "Smith & Wesson Hand Guns," Prescott, AZ: Wolfe Publishing, 1945/1994, p. 88.

Smith & Wesson's K-22

Q uality. Accuracy. Fine handling. One handgun that had 'em all was the classic Smith & Wesson K-22, whose manufacturer did not call it "the Masterpiece" for nothing.

Pedigree

Those who appreciate the qualities of a fine rifle tend to love the S&W K-22. The 20th century probably did not produce a more famous rifleman than Jack O'Connor. Asked once to draw up a list of the guns he'd keep if he could have but 10 firearms, O'Connor put a single handgun on that list: his K-22.

Graceful and accurate, the K-22 set the standard as a "gentleman's handgun" in the world of the sportsman, and even found use in the rough and tumble world of training cops and soldiers.

For most of its existence, this was the shape of the Smith & Wesson K-22.

Left: The K-22 is generally found to have a wonderful double action trigger pull.

Men who won fame with both rifle and the handgun have likewise been unstinting in their praise of this revolver. Ernie Lind, the last of the great old-fashioned trick shooters with rifle, shotgun and handgun, favored the K-22. Charlie Askins once wrote, "I had small love for the Smith & Wesson."[1] Even so, he praised the K-22 highly and criticized it not at all in one of his first books, a pre-WWII guide to handgun shooting.

In his classic *Sixguns*, Elmer Keith said, "...Major D. B. Wesson brought out the first K-22 on the .38 Special M&P (Military & Police) frame with encased cartridge heads and 6 inch barrel with a weight of 35 ounces. Early this became a very popular target arm and he sent the writer one of the first ones. It proved much easier and steadier to hold than the old Bekeart model .22/32 or the various S&W and Colt single shot pistols. It soon became a more or less standard target arm and was brought out to handle High Speed ammunition. . .They are now made in .22 L.R., .32 S&W Long and in .38 Special with ribbed barrels, the rib of various widths, so that matched sets can be offered the target shooter having the same weight for all three calibers. These are as fine target arms as human ingenu-

Most sportsmen have tended to use the K-22 in single action.

ity and modern manufacturing methods have been able to produce to date. They will all three group in 1-1/2 inches at 50 yards, which is very fine revolver accuracy...."[2]

Jeff Cooper, likewise a connoisseur of both rifle and shotgun who influenced the designs of both, said of the K-22: "It is a very fine gun, and, if you wish to go target shooting with a .22 revolver, this is the way to go."[3]

While the above were recognized experts on both long guns and short ones, the K-22 was just as much appreciated by the pure pistoleros. One such was Chic Gaylord, one of the dominant handgun experts of the 1950s, who at the close of that decade wrote, "The K-.22 Combat Masterpiece and the K-.22 give yeoman service as fun guns."[4]

Writing in *Shooting Times*, Mike Venturino did an article on the legendary Ed McGivern which included a photo of a pre-war K-22 captioned, "McGivern favored double action revolvers; he seemed to prefer .38 Specials, but this S&W K-22 is one of several that he owned."[5] This is confirmed in McGivern's own famous book, *Fast and Fancy Revolver Shooting*. In those pages, McGivern is shown demonstrating two-hand hold, use of the support hand for thumb-cocking, and the sitting position with his early K-22.[6]

The cumulative praise and endorsement of the K-22 was grounded in the gun's proven quality and functionality. Slowly evolving over almost three- quarters of a century, this classic is a mature design that has proven itself in multiple environments.

The Model 17 often left the factory with target stocks, and wide target hammer and trigger.

A Brief History

The year was 1931. S&W's Military & Police centerfire revolver had been available as an adjustable sight target model literally since the year of its introduction, 1899, but had not been produced in .22 rimfire. The rationale of the early 20th century seemed to be that light calibers belonged in light guns. S&W's .22 target revolver had been the .22/32, the latter number designating its frame size, since 1908 when San Francisco firearms distributor Phil Bekeart had ordered a thousand of them and proven that they would sell.

The "Bekeart Model," as collectors have called it since, was not deemed suitable for the new generation of high-speed .22 Long Rifle ammunition that Remington had pioneered circa 1930. Also, because the little .22/32 target revolver only weighed about 23 ounces and had a tiny trigger guard, a demand was perceived for a "man-size" .22 revolver. S&W's official historian Roy links would explain later, "As early as 1927, Smith & Wesson began receiving suggestions from competitive shooters to develop a .22 caliber revolver with the same balance as the .38 M&P Target model. The factory began development of a new .22 caliber revolver that same year and, upon investigating various facets of the market, they found that a revolver of this kind was also in heavy demand by the sportsmen of the United States."[7]

Major Douglas Wesson, then head honcho at S&W, decided the time had come. A .22 on a .38 frame was offered up, its chambers counterbored to enclose the heads of the rimfire cartridges and dispose of concerns with the hot new ammo. It had a 6-inch barrel and was fitted with the same adjustable rear sight and high

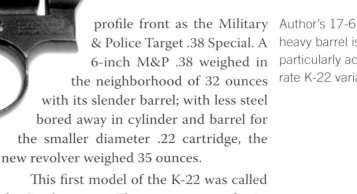

profile front as the Military & Police Target .38 Special. A 6-inch M&P .38 weighed in the neighborhood of 32 ounces with its slender barrel; with less steel bored away in cylinder and barrel for the smaller diameter .22 cartridge, the new revolver weighed 35 ounces.

Author's 17-6 heavy barrel is a particularly accurate K-22 variation.

This first model of the K-22 was called the Outdoorsman. The name was prophetic. Though it had been geared largely for serious target shooters, the Colt Woodsman .22

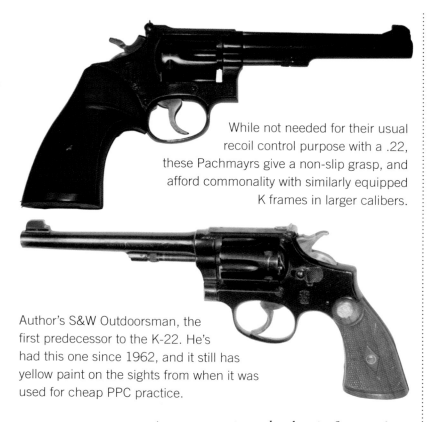

While not needed for their usual recoil control purpose with a .22, these Pachmayrs give a non-slip grasp, and afford commonality with similarly equipped K frames in larger calibers.

Author's S&W Outdoorsman, the first predecessor to the K-22. He's had this one since 1962, and it still has yellow paint on the sights from when it was used for cheap PPC practice.

Below: Original S&W Outdoorsman, seen from the right.

auto was soon to make the rimfire revolver obsolete for the bulls-eye game. Where the new ".22 on a .38 frame" shone was in the field, its precise accuracy making it a natural for small game hunting. The glassy smoothness and crisp, light single action pull of the Smith & Wesson action made it easy to shoot well enough to deliver its high inherent accuracy. Hunters and trappers took it to their hearts and their holsters instantly, and a number of the new revolvers did indeed find their way to the competitive shooting ranges.

Cops liked them too. The action and grip were identical to those of the Military & Police service revolver. Everything was the same except the recoil and the report, and the ammo was a lot cheaper. Numerous departments bought K-22s as training guns.

The first K-22 left the factory in late January of 1931. Though this first model was an instant success, the Outdoorsman was replaced nine years to the month later by the second model, the Masterpiece. The first gun's tiny rear sight, which needed a jeweler's screwdriver to adjust, was replaced by a bigger, sturdier micrometer sight. S&W's new "short action" was featured, complete with adjustable internal trigger stop. "Magna" stocks, whose walnut swept up to the high horn at the top rear edge of the grip frame, were installed. These had been created to better distribute the recoil of the large frame .38/44 and .357 Magnum revolvers to the web of the shooter's hand. Obviously, these

stocks were not needed for that purpose in a .22, but they were undeniably more streamlined and would be the distinctive "shape of Smith & Wesson" for decades to come.

WWII interrupted K-22 production, with only 1,067 Masterpiece and 17,117 Outdoorsman revolvers having been produced.[8] When production resumed in the postwar years, with Carl Hellstrom now at the helm of Smith & Wesson, the company's premium .22 entered a third incarnation. This was the K-22 Masterpiece, companion gun of the K-32 and K-38 Masterpieces as described by Elmer Keith above.

For half a century, this would be the configuration of the Smith & Wesson K-22. The barrel was now less tapered, and ribbed. Weight was up to 38-1/2 ounces. It was the gun that many of today's generation of handgun experts cut their teeth on. Ken

Hackathorn, for example, tells me his first handgun was a K-22.

In 1949, S&W supplemented the Masterpiece series of 6-inch target revolvers with a 4-inch set sporting ramped front sights. They called it the Combat Masterpiece line. The .38 Special version was an instant success with cops, quickly becoming standard issue for LAPD, LA County Sheriffs, and numerous other agencies. It was much less popular in .22. By now, the market saw the K-22 as a 6-inch gun, and while the 4-inch version was the second most popular barrel length in the caliber, it was a distant second. (Jeff Cooper noted dryly that calling a .22 caliber handgun a "Combat Masterpiece" was "the exaggeration of the season.")

Minor changes in the K-22 series would take place over the succeeding years, most of them generic streamlining spread through-

Above: The K-22 revolver will of course function with a very broad range of .22 ammo. It has also been produced in .22 Magnum rimfire and .17 Hornady Rimfire Magnum.

The older classic style K-22 has the best balance for one-handed firing, most shooters find…

Above: …but for two-handed shooting, the heavier barrel of later models may hang steadier. This little pig was not safe from Model 17-6 and Blazer plinking ammo at 50 yards.

out the S&W revolver line. In 1957, when the company went to numeric designations for their different models, the K-38 became the Model 14, the K-32 the Model 16, and the K-22 the Model 17. (The Combat Masterpieces were designated Model 15 in .38 and Model 18 in .22; no .32s were made in that format since a very small production run circa 1949. long before model numbers were issued.) An 8-3/8-inch barrel would be offered. A handful were made with nickel finishes instead of the traditional blue, and a very small number of 5-inch barrel K-22s (and K-38s) would be produced.[9] The K-22 was offered in .22 Magnum in 1959 as the Model 48 with 4-, 6-, or 8-3/8-inch barrel.

Construction went from five- screw, to four-screw, to three. Many specimens left the factory with optional wide serrated target trigger, and/or broad beavertail hammer spur, and/or oversize target-style stocks In the 1990s, S&W's traditional walnut stocks gave way to black "rubber" aftermarket grips by Uncle Mike's and Hogue.

The configuration above is the K-22 most of us know and love. But, by the late 1980s, S&W had enjoyed huge success with the underlugged barrel of their L-frame .357 and was going that route with just about everything else in the line. That design treatment was given to the K-22, now designated Model 17-6, in 1989. This brought the weight of a 6-inch K-22 up to 42 ounces unloaded. A year later, this heavy barrel K-22 would be offered in stainless as the Model 617. Circa 1991, a very few K-22s were supposedly produced in stainless with the traditional barrel configuration. I've never seen one, but they'll definitely be collectors' items.[10]

With 1964 hunting license and an old K-22, a teen-age hunter was ready for squirrel season.

There were those who had always felt that a .38-size cylinder for a six- shot .22 left a lot of room for more chambers. When Jerry Miculek of Team Smith & Wesson was shooting for the company at shows, it occurred to him that a 10-shot revolver could do tricks that a six-shot revolver couldn't, and he prevailed on the engineers to put a couple of 10-shot K-22s together. The gun magazines got hold of it, and the rest was history. Ten-shot K-22s in the heavy barrel configuration, in blue and stainless, debuted in 1996. For some reason, S&W used an aluminum cylinder for these guns. This strange concept on a heavy barrel gun did not sit well with shooters, who stayed away in droves. An all-steel 10-shot cylinder replaced it a year later, and remains available. Still, most new K-22s that I see on the gun shop shelves are still the six-shot variation.

In early 2003, S&W introduced the stainless version in the third caliber it has ever been chambered for: .17 Hornady Rimfire Magnum. Recoil is mild and the gun shoots flat. I wonder if they'll call it a "K-l7" someday.

Below: This late model K-22 is chambered in .22 Magnum.

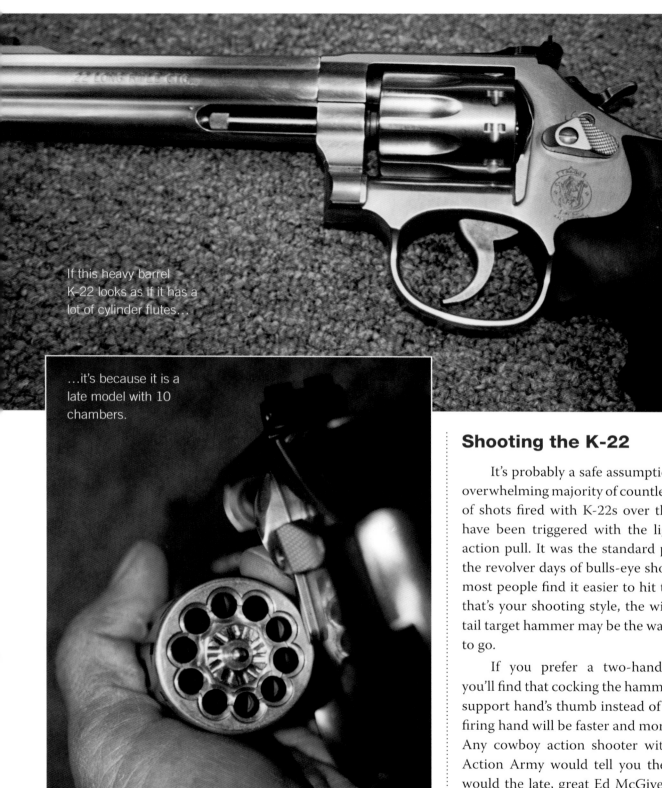

If this heavy barrel K-22 looks as if it has a lot of cylinder flutes…

…it's because it is a late model with 10 chambers.

Shooting the K-22

It's probably a safe assumption that the overwhelming majority of countless millions of shots fired with K-22s over the decades have been triggered with the light single-action pull. It was the standard protocol in the revolver days of bulls-eye shooting, and most people find it easier to hit that way. If that's your shooting style, the wide beaver-tail target hammer may be the way you want to go.

If you prefer a two-handed stance, you'll find that cocking the hammer with the support hand's thumb instead of that of the firing hand will be faster and more effective. Any cowboy action shooter with a Single Action Army would tell you the same. So would the late, great Ed McGivern; in fact, he did tell us all so in that part of *Fast and Fancy Revolver Shooting* where he used a K-22 to demonstrate.

Many forget that the K-22 incorporates the very same double action trigger stroke that made Smith & Wesson the standard by which such revolvers are judged. It was rare for target shooters to fire that way in the sixgun's glory days of bulls-eye shooting, though the practice was by no means unknown. Such pioneers as Bob Nichols in the '40s and '50s and Paul Weston in the '50s and '60s won bulls-eye matches firing double action back then. For the combat training function in which the K-22 is the understudy gun for the .38 or .357 service revolver, of course, it would be unclear on the concept to shoot any way but double action.

For DA shooting, you want a different configuration of trigger. The wide, serrated target trigger was meant to distribute a very short and light single action trigger press and make it feel even easier. For the long, heavy double action stroke, that wide trigger will have your finger pulling the gun laterally as you try for a straight-back pressure. A smooth surfaced trigger, fairly narrow, is the all but unanimous choice of the double

action revolver masters. Only the aforementioned Jerry Miculek seems to like a serrated trigger for fast double action work, and he still wants it narrow.

Stocks? K-22s have left the factory with everything from Circassian walnut to plain-Jane rubber. In aftermarket grips, you'll find K-22s adorned with Tiffany silver, antique ivory, and exotic hardwood on the one end, and the most pedestrian "imitation rubber' on the other. The grips may be gracefully slim for small hands, or flower pot-size with wide-flaring thumb rests and finger grooves. No revolver has been offered a wider variety of aftermarket stocks than the K frame Smith & Wesson.

In the time of glass sights for handguns, mounts are readily available for the K-Smith. I have a Tasco Pro Point on my Model 18 .22. I put it there originally to make it an understudy gun for my Bianchi Cup revolver of the time, an Andy Cannon custom S&W Model 686 with identical scope. I kept it set up that way after I discovered what a won-

Left: For most of its existence, K-22 has been a six-shot revolver.

derfully easy gun it was to train new shooters with. By putting the red dot on the target, allowing both to be seen on the same focal plane, it was much easier for the student to concentrate on steady hold and clean trigger press. The K-22's function as a "starter handgun" may prove to be eternal.

From the beginning, S&W advertised these guns as being capable of 1.5-inch groups at 50 yards. While I don't doubt that some examples are every bit that accurate (1 had one that shot consistently well under an inch at 25 yards) it might be optimistic to expect that lofty degree of accuracy from every K-22 that was ever shipped from Springfield, Massachusetts. Nonetheless, they are uniformly very accurate indeed. From the

Author's "Coast Guard" fixed sight K-22s, dating to 1935, two of 14 known to exist of approximately 25 manufactured.

first Outdoorsman to the latest heavy barrel Model 617, the K-22 can shoot better than we can, and that's one reason it's a classic.

Personal Perspective

I got my first K-22 in the spring of 1962. I was 13. My dad's friend Walter Huckins, the vice president of a local bank, was supervising some in-house renovations when he heard a scream from a female employee who was moving some files. She had discovered a revolver in a forgotten file drawer she had unlocked. It was a pristine Smith & Wesson K-22 Outdoorsman, fortunately unloaded.

Mr. Huckins looked into the matter. He discovered that prior to WWII, a spate of bank robberies in the area had caused the management to purchase a quantity of S&W M&P .38s for the tellers, along with the Outdoorsman as a training gun. By the 1950s, the .38s had been disposed of, and the now-forgotten .22 had been relegated to a locked file drawer. His boss told him to get rid of the gun; he didn't care how, just get rid of it. Well, Mr. Huckins knew that his friend's kid was into handguns big time, and....

To make a long story short, I practiced with that revolver daily for a while. Other handguns had made me a safe pistol shooter; this one taught me to be a good shot.

It would take any length of .22 cartridge from BB and CB caps to Shorts, Longs, and Long Rifles. 1 would come home from junior high school each day and head to the cellar. There I would fire 30 shots — ten each slow, timed, and rapid — with Revelation brand .22 Shorts that cost 29 cents per box of 50 at the Western Auto outlet across the street from my dad's jewelry store. The pristine old K-22 had the tiny square rear notch and little square gold insert front sight common to the First Model, but I also had young eyes. Other handguns had taught me to shoot; this one taught me to shoot accurately. You have my

undying thanks, Walter B. Huckins, wherever you are.

Time went on. As a young cop, I got into PPC shooting. Even reloaded .38 wadcutters were expensive on what I was making then, so I used the old Outdoorsman as an understudy gun. Its tiny sights didn't show up well against the black B-27 silhouette, so (Heresy!) I painted them with yellow enamel. It was a sloppy job, and it's still there. The old beast wore a lot of different stocks over the years, but I saved the original Circassian walnut and have them back in place now. My current "using" K-22 is a blue 6-inch heavy barrel Model 17-6 with plain black Patridge sights. It has had an exquisite action job, and its trigger narrowed and polished for DA work, by Rick Devoid, Tarnhelm Supply, 431 High St., Boscawen, NH 03303, www.tarnhelm.com.

A couple of K-22 variants recently joined my collection. I was driving through the Midwest and stopped to visit a gun shop I'd bought from by mail but never seen in person. In their used gun case were what appeared to be a couple of pre-WWII Military & Police .38s...but they were tagged "K-22." I asked to see them. Sure enough, the serial numbers on barrels and cylinders matched those on the frame (S&W numbered redundantly back then). They obviously weren't fakes. I had two guns I'd never heard of: fixed sight, pre-war, K-frame S&W .22s. The Model 45, a K-frame .22 Military & Police usually found with 4-inch tapered barrel, was rare enough, but I had not encountered a pre-war

variation. I bought 'em both. After they were shipped to me, I went to the brain trust of S&W collectors and authorities that is www.smith-wessonforum.com.

I learned there that in 1935, the US Coast Guard special-ordered 25 6-inch barrel revolvers with fixed sights in caliber .22 Long Rifle. They were shipped to a Coast Guard base in Maryland which, history shows, was involved at the time in a lot of marksmanship training for local police. I learned that only 12 of those 25 were known to exist. Well, it was now up to fourteen.

These guns had obviously been shot a lot, but were still in pristine shape inside. I took them to the range...and, yes, they still held a group, too. I'm honored to be the current caretaker for these rare specimens of a fine gunmaker's art.

Above: Seeing ".22 Long Rifle" on a six-inch fixed sight S&W revolver barrel seems incongruous.

Below: Something you don't see every day – the counterbored chambers of a K-22 cylinder, with the fixed sights of a service revolver. One of the "Coast Guard" K-22s of 1935.

The K-22 won't be obsolete any time soon. The bulls-eye folks have recently introduced the Harry Reeves Memorial Match, fired entirely with iron-sighted revolvers. I'm told that two National Match Courses, one each with .22 and centerfire, make up the event. A National Match bulls-eye course starts with 10 shots in as many minutes slow fire at 50 yards. The next 10 are in strings of five in 20 seconds, timed fire at 25 yards, and the last 10 rapid fire, which is two strings of five shots in 10 seconds at the 25 yard line. I hope this will do something to revitalize the lost art of bulls-eye revolver shooting.

All manner of revolvers will be pulled out of mothballs for the centerfire stages. I bet you'll see a lot of Colts: the .38 Officer's Model that once ruled centerfire bulls-eye, and the Python, and even the old heavy frame Shooting Master that Charlie Askins favored. Of course, you'll see S&Ws: K-38s, maybe even some K-32s, and .357s of all shapes and sizes from K frame to L frame to N.

But I'll bet dollars to doughnuts that the most popular .22 revolver by far that you'll see at the Harry Reeves Matches will be the Smith & Wesson K-22.

Below: This "Coast Guard" K-22 still shoots well after three-quarters of a century.

Notes

[1]Askins, Charles Jr., *Unrepentant Sinner*, San Antonio: Tejano Publications, 1985, p. 75.

[2]Keith, Elmer, Sixguns, New York: Bonanza Books, 1955 and 1961, p. 41.

[3]Cooper, Jeff, *Cooper on Handguns*, Los Angeles: Petersen Publishing, 1974, p. 170.

[4]Gaylord, Chic, "Handgunner's Guide," New York: Hastings House, 1960 p. 51.

[5]"Ed McGivern: Fast and Fancy Shootist," by Mike Venturino, *Shooting Times* magazine, March 1996, p. 43.

[6]McGivern, Ed, *Fast and Fancy Revolver Shooting*, Chicago: Wilcox & Follett, 1957, p. 457.

[7]Jinks, Roy, *History of Smith & Wesson*, North Hollywood: Beinfeld, 1977, p. 171.

[8]*Ibid*, pp. 172-173.

[9]Supica, Jim, and Nahas, Richard, *Standard Catalog of Smith & Wesson*, Iola, WI: Krause, 1996, p. 114.

[10]Supica, Jim, and Nahas, Richard, *Standard Catalog of Smith & Wesson*, Second Edition, Iola, WI: Krause, 2001, p. 195.

Smith & Wesson's Chiefs Special & Family

I n 1907, Colt extended the cylinder and frame of their Police Positive revolver, chambered it for the .38 Special cartridge, and called it the Police Positive Special. Twenty years later, they shortened its barrel to two inches, called the result the Detective Special, and created for themselves the nation's best-selling concealed carry revolver for the next 23 years.

By 1950, their arch-competitor Smith & Wesson was finally ready to do something about that. A project begun the year before at the command of then-CEO Carl Hellstrom came to fruition in October. Their .32-size revolver frame, known as the I-frame, would be stretched as Colt had done

With a simple idea, Smith & Wesson created the most popular concealed carry handgun of the second half of the 20th Century.

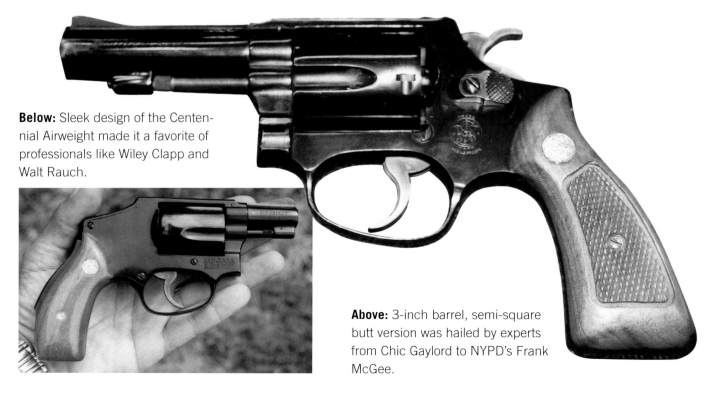

Below: Sleek design of the Centennial Airweight made it a favorite of professionals like Wiley Clapp and Walt Rauch.

Above: 3-inch barrel, semi-square butt version was hailed by experts from Chic Gaylord to NYPD's Frank McGee.

Above: One of the first Chiefs Specials to leave the factory. Now called the "baby Chiefs" by collectors because of its dimensions, it was an instant hit. Note square cylinder latch.

Below: High sideplate screw, half-coin shaped front sight, and tiny trigger guard distinguish first day's Chiefs Special production.

more than 40 years earlier to allow for the .38 Special cartridge. Known as the J-frame, this new gun would still be slightly smaller than the Colt counterpart and would hold only five rounds instead of the Detective Special's six. However, it would have a shorter butt for better concealment, would ride a little lower in the hand thanks to its narrower cylinder, and would weigh two ounces less. (To add to its cachet as the smallest .38 Special on the market, its nominally 2-inch barrel would actually measure only 1-7/8 inches, a practice that would continue to the present.) Lucian Cary, gun editor of the popular men's magazine *True*, got wind of it and

snagged a pre-production factory photo which he published that year with the caption, "Smith & Wesson Model J (temporary name)."[1]

In October of 1950, the new five-shot .38 Special snub-nose was ready for its debut. S&W introduced it in Colorado Springs at the annual conference of IACP, the International Association of Chiefs of Police. Somewhere in the marketing department, a light bulb went on. The "Model J (temporary name)" was ready for its permanent monicker.

Et voila!: the Chiefs Special.

Pedigree

The new gun was an immediate hit, even though a lot of folks got the name wrong. To this day you'll read "Chief Special" or "Chief's Special" (I've probably been guilty of both), but official S&W historian Roy Jinks assures us that the proper name is "Chiefs Special." Whatever they called it, contemporary experts loved it...and, far more important, so did rank and file cops and armed citizens.

Charles Askins, Jr. wrote in 1953, "This gun is the ultimate in extra light belly models in the .38 Special cartridge. Suitable for gunners with small hands."[2]

This was no small praise from a man who made his preference for Colts over S&Ws quite clear. Another unabashed Colt man surprised his following when Chic Gaylord wrote, "The Smith & Wesson Chief Special with the three-inch barrel is the best and most effective carry gun available 'as is' from the factory. It is nearly as effective as the regular .38 Special Service revolvers."[3] The 3-inch barrel had gone into production on December 6, 1950, according to Jinks.[4]

Elmer Keith liked these little guns, too, apparently figuring they were at least sized correctly for what he considered to be a piddling little cartridge, the .38 Special. Here was a man who appreciated a strong handgun, and after noting that he put 500 rounds of .38/44 ammo, the +P of its day, through one of them, he wrote in *Sixguns by Keith*: "One thing that adds greatly to the strength of these…little undercover arms is the fact they are five-shot, hence the bolt cut or stop in the cylinder comes between the charge holes, not over the center of them as is true of all six-shot arms. Another feature enabling them to handle such powerful ammunition is the fact that almost no barrel projects back through the frame, barely enough to take for measurement is all that protrudes. Very little barrel to bell or crack is left unsupported by the frame."[5]

Jeff Cooper confessed in *Cooper on Handguns* that he used a Chiefs Special

Well-worn Model 36, 2-inch barrel/semi-square butt, with Herrett's stocks. Steel J-frames stand up to some heavy abuse!

with hot handloads for concealment under a business suit, in lieu of his trademark Colt .45 auto. He also gave one to his lovely wife Janelle as a primary carry piece. Dwight Eisenhower owned one, received during his presidency from the National Sheriffs Association. Richard Nixon owned one that was presented to him, if I'm not mistaken, by the NRA. Bill Jordan carried a Chiefs Special Airweight with de-horned hammer in his hip pocket for backup. Such modern experts as Mike Boyle, Wiley Clapp, John Farnam, Ken Hackathorn, Frank James, Ed Lovette, Evan Marshall, Walt Rauch, Ed Sanow, Dave Spaulding, Jim Wilson, and many more are known to carry some variation of the Chiefs

Below: …and looked like this when the gun was cocked. This specimen is an all-steel stainless Model 649.

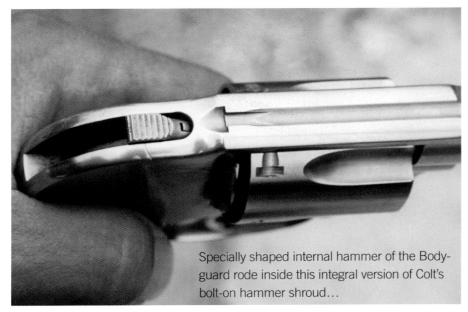

Specially shaped internal hammer of the Bodyguard rode inside this integral version of Colt's bolt-on hammer shroud…

Above: One downside of these guns is that they hold only five rounds, so when those are done it's good to have more at hand. From right, HKS J-frame speedloader, Bianchi six-shell belt loop set, and Bianchi Speed Strip, which fits nicely in watch pocket of jeans or business card pocket of blazer or suitcoat.

Special or one of its sister guns, the Bodyguard and Centennial, if only as backup.

The "Chief" and its improved versions quickly took over the market that Colt snubby had so long ruled, eventually driving the latter to extinction with its crushing sales superiority. Today, the J-frames in any given year will be the first or second place sales leaders for Smith & Wesson.

A Brief History

The "newer, smaller" .38 Special from S&W didn't hurt Colt as much as you might expect at first, because in the same year it was introduced, Colt debuted the first aluminum frame revolver, the Cobra. The Colt Detective Special tipped the scale at 21 ounces, while the likewise all-steel S&W Chief's Special weighed 19 ounces; the Colt Cobra was down to 15 ounces. Not about to have so promising an ace as the Chiefs Special trumped, S&W countered in 1952 with the Airweight version. Though advertised at 12.5 ounces, this may have been optimistic; most that I've put on a scale have been an ounce or two over that. Still, with its shorter round butt, it was unquestionably lighter than a Cobra. (What I think happened with the weight disparity was this: the Smith Airweights came out of the same USAF "Aircrewman" gun project for superlight snub .38s as the Colt Cobra. S&W's first entries in the commercial market had the same aluminum cylinders as the Aircrewman guns, which the armed services determined weren't strong enough. The first ones probably did weigh 12.5 ounces with aluminum cylinders. S&W soon went to steel cylinders for all their Airweights, but did not change the weight statistics as quickly in the various gun catalogs.)

The Colt/S&W race went on. People who actually shot these little guns found the Colt was more controllable than the Smith, in part because the short-

Small size, light weight give J-frames more carry options. Eagle-gripped Model 442 hides comfortably in DeSantis ankle holster, left, or Safariland pocket holster, right.

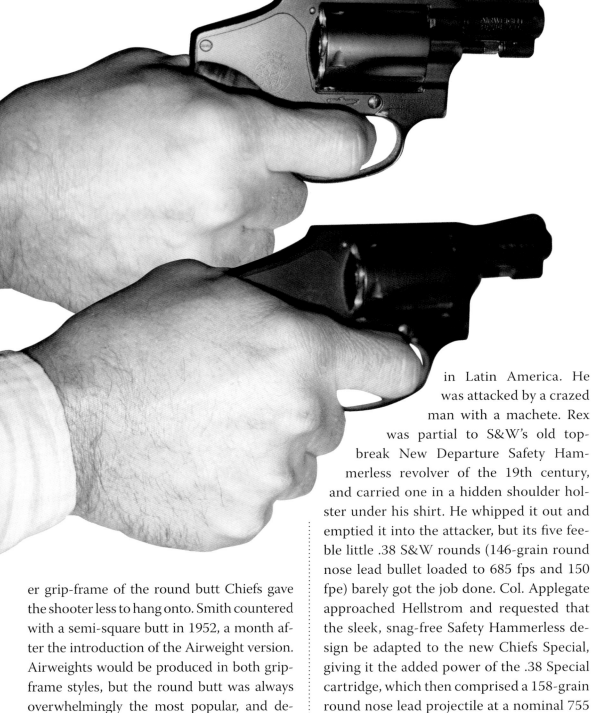

Top: Here's the Centennial's key shooting advantage. Sure, it can be held like this, the way you'd have to hold a Chiefs Special…

Bottom: …but you can also hold it like this, with the hand all the way up on that "hammerless" grip-frame. Notice how much lower the bore axis is vis-à-vis the wrist. The improvement in control and reduction in muzzle jump has to be felt to be appreciated.

in Latin America. He was attacked by a crazed man with a machete. Rex was partial to S&W's old top-break New Departure Safety Hammerless revolver of the 19th century, and carried one in a hidden shoulder holster under his shirt. He whipped it out and emptied it into the attacker, but its five feeble little .38 S&W rounds (146-grain round nose lead bullet loaded to 685 fps and 150 fpe) barely got the job done. Col. Applegate approached Hellstrom and requested that the sleek, snag-free Safety Hammerless design be adapted to the new Chiefs Special, giving it the added power of the .38 Special cartridge, which then comprised a 158-grain round nose lead projectile at a nominal 755 fps generating 200 foot pounds of energy. That request was granted, and for the 1953 model year, the catalogue announced the appropriately named Centennial. Actually coming off the production line in 1952, the S&W's hundredth year in business, they logically named this new gun the Centennial. It was a solid-frame Chiefs Special but

er grip-frame of the round butt Chiefs gave the shooter less to hang onto. Smith countered with a semi-square butt in 1952, a month after the introduction of the Airweight version. Airweights would be produced in both grip-frame styles, but the round butt was always overwhelmingly the most popular, and decades later, S&W would drop the semi-square butt configuration entirely. Meanwhile, in 1955, Colt had tried to counter the sales advantage of the Chief's short, round butt by introducing the Agent, a Cobra with a truncated grip-frame.

During this period, famed gun guru Rex Applegate was involved in an incident

Top: Late production Model 42. Note that S&W had by then returned to traditional style cylinder latch.

Bottom: Here's a very early Centennial Airweight, later designated Model 42. Note grip safety, and rectangular latch that J-frames had through most of the 50s and 60s.

with the concealed hammer New Departure treatment, right down to a grip safety on the backstrap. The guns came with a hole drilled through the frame and the internal part of the safety, and an appropriately sized pin to lock the grip safety out of commission if one chose.

Colt didn't try to gear up to produce a hammerless. Instead, they came out with what they called a hammer shroud. This attachment bolted onto the their small frame guns, shielding all but the very tip of the hammer spur. This made the Colt as snag-free as the Centennial, but allowed the exposed hammer tip to be drawn back to sin-

gle action if the shooter chose. This feature caught on.

S&W countered with the Bodyguard, a Chiefs Special with a built-in hammer shroud. The Bodyguard's hammer was re-shaped, presenting a "cocking button" at the top of the shroud. It not only looked better than a similarly configured Colt, whose bolt-on shroud was obviously an afterthought; it was also more comfortable to shoot. The bottom edge of a Colt hammer shroud could painfully pinch the web of a shooter's hand; not so the smooth, integral shroud of the Bodyguard. S&W sales again shot up past Colt's.

Time went on. At the request of Frank McGee, who took over the NYPD Firearms & Tactics Unit in 1970, S&W made a heavy, untapered 3-inch barrel Chiefs that was so popular it eventually replaced the original tapered 3-inch tube in the catalog. Frank also took steps to make sure that all Chiefs bought for the city's then-30,000 cops (most of whom carried .38 snubs for off duty and backup) were semi-square butt models, and the 2-inch Chief in that configuration became the unofficial standard of some 70% of the NYPD. (New York cops bought their own guns. Buying through the city, they could get the city's choice cheap. They could buy their own round-butt Chiefs, but would have to pay full retail.) Interestingly, the semi-square butt configuration was never applied to the Bodyguard or the Centennial.

Some gun historians think the Chiefs Special's greatest leap forward was its incarnation in 1965 as the world's first stainless steel handgun, the Smith & Wesson Model 60. It immediately commanded scalper's prices because of a huge demand from troops going to humid Vietnam, and of course, from cops, and was thereafter a perennial best seller in the S&W lineup.

In the old days, folks shot double action revolvers mostly in single action mode to get the easier trigger pull; the long, heavy, double action shot was seen as an emergency mode only. Sales of the double action only Centennial languished, and it was dropped from the catalog around 1974. However, it was about then that reality-based training was getting a foothold in both law enforcement and the firearms world, and people were realizing that all their shooting with a defensive revolver should be in the "emergency mode" of its intended purpose. Almost as soon as it was discontinued, the Centennials became much sought cult favorites among serious pistol packers, who haunted gun shows looking for them. In the late 1980s, Wiley Clapp sang the praises of the old Centennial in gun magazine articles and instigated a storm of reader mail to Smith & Wesson demanding its return. Steve Melvin was the CEO at Smith then; I knew him, and I can tell you he was an innovative man with a sharply tuned ear for what end users wanted. At a

focus group of gunwriters S&W hosted in 1988, all of us agreed with Wiley that reintroducing the Centennial would be a good thing, and this came about by 1990 with the Model 640. The grip safety that most of us considered to be useless was gone, and new metallurgy had made the gun ready at last for the factory to certify for .38 Special +P+ ammunition.

For most of their history, these fixed-sight J-frames were chambered for .38 Special. In the 1990s, more experimentation occurred. The .32 H&R Magnum was offered in the Chief and the Centennial, not selling well enough to remain in the catalog for very long. The lighter-kicking .32 Mag never got a chance to make its bones as a man-stopper and therefore never generated

Top: Original Model 640 all-steel .38, still produced on special order for NYPD off duty use. It had very controllable recoil and shot well, but the smooth "splinter" stocks were poorly suited to combat shooting.

Bottom: LadySmith version of the Model 642 Airweight. The 642 is probably the most popular J-frame in production at this writing.

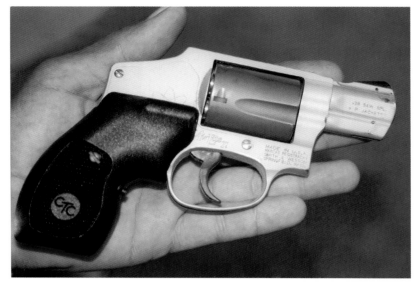

much demand in the self-defense or police market. One expert who loves the six-shot Centennial .32 Mag in its Model 332 Titanium-frame (11 ounce) variation is Charlie Petty, who appreciates the mild recoil even more than the sixth shot the .32 allowed in the J-frame, and Charlie thinks it's all about shot placement anyway.

Being stronger because of the shape of its frame, the Centennial got first crack at being "the high powered J-frame." Jac Weller wrote of having seen and shot a .357 Magnum Centennial produced experimentally back in the '50s, which S&W decided not to manufacture because they felt its recoil would be intolerable. Well, that had been a time when it was common for people to buy a Smith .44 Magnum, fire six shots, and sell the very slightly used revolver and a box of 44 .44 rounds back to the gun shop. By the '90s, American shooters had learned how to handle recoil, and S&W thought they were ready for a J-frame .357 Magnum.

Rendered first as a Centennial, the Model 640-1, the .357 was soon offered in Bodyguard and original Chiefs Special formats as well, all in stainless steel construction in the 25-ounce weight range. Then came the turn of the 21st century, and with the passing of the Cold War, the industry enjoyed a sudden availability of Scandium from once-Soviet mines. Suddenly we had the Centennial Model 340 PD, a snub-nose .357 Magnum weighing about 11 ounces. The term "handgun re-

Top: Model 342 Ti, thanks to titanium construction, weighs under 11 ounces unloaded. Recoil is so violent that factory recommends only jacketed bullets, since lead bullets will pull loose from recoil of +P cartridges firing in other chambers. Note weight-saving barrel treatment: thin steel inside ultra-light housing.

Bottom: One of the author's favorite J-frames, a 442 Airweight tuned by Ted Yost when he ran the Gunsite Gunsmithy, whose logo is applied. Stocks are "secret service" by Eagle.

Right: Short ejector rod due to front lug and 1 7/8" barrel limits ejection stroke.

coil" had a new definition. A Chiefs Special variation with conventional hammer spur followed.

Today, the J-frames (particularly the once-unloved Centennials) tend to be Smith & Wesson's best-selling revolver product line each year

Shooting the Chiefs Special and Its Relatives

For true defensive shooting, which with a revolver means rapid double action fire, the Bodyguard is more "shootable" than the Chiefs Special, and the Centennial more shootable than the Bodyguard. The reason has to do with recoil control and the shape of the guns.

Roy Jinks told the truth when he wrote, "The Chiefs Special is an extremely small re-

volver and, when fired, it becomes difficult for a large-handed person to control."[6] Truth to tell, it's no pussycat for small-handed folks, either. Almost from the beginning, people who actually shot them realized that the J-frame .38s weren't very controllable with the thin "splinter" grips that came from the factory. This got worse in the '60s when Super Vel ushered in the era of even more violent +P and +P+ ammo, but +P worked so much better "on the street" than the old stuff that almost all of us went to it. (Current production S&W J-frames are rated for +P+ in steel, Titanium, and Scandium construction, and +P with aluminum frames). The Chiefs and Centennial alike have been made in .32 Magnum, and the Centennial alone has been produced in 9mm Luger with moon clips (Model 940) and .356 TSW (Performance Center only), neither of which remains in production.

The 9mm with +P/+P+ ammo, and the .356, were prone to jamming because these

Top: For much of the latter 20th century, a J-frame was the traditional backup to 4-inch service revolver for countless officers. Top, 4-inch Model 15, below, snub Model 36.

Far Left: Today's shooter has broad choices. Top, Kahr PM9 holds 7 rounds of 9mm Luger, while J-frame below holds 5 rounds of .38 or in some models .357. Both can come in under a pound unloaded.

Crimson Trace La-serGrip has been a Godsend for many J-frame shooters.

Below: The old "FBI" load (author is partial to Rem-ington for its softer, better expanding bullets) tended to open up even when fired from snubbies, because there was no tough copper jacket to peel back. Do not use in lighter than Airweight guns, however.

high-pressure rounds would cause primer flowback into the firing pin hole, bringing cylinder rotation to a halt. By the time S&W had figured out that a differently-sized hole in the firing pin bushing would solve the problem, shooter interest in the 9mm J-frames had virtually disappeared. However, that feature would make possible reliable function in the .357 Magnum J-frames that followed.

But, back to the matter of recoil. Serious shooters quickly learned that the J-frame .38 Special needed a grip adapter at an absolute minimum. Even this was not enough to keep +P recoil from rolling the revolver back in the hand, to the point where the web of the hand could block the Chiefs Special's hammer spur. Bobbing off the spur prevented that, as well as making the Chief more snag-free.

However, the Bodyguard didn't need that. The point at the backstrap where the integral hammer shroud rose up would catch the web of the hand and stop the gun's movement. That was why, back in the '80s when the Centennial was "out of print," I called the Bodyguard "the thinking man's Chiefs Special" in the pages of *Guns* magazine.

However, the subsequent reintroduction of the Centennial made it "the thinking man's Bodyguard." The reason is illustrated in the accompanying photos. You can't comfortably hold a Bodyguard with your hand any higher on it than on a Chief. However, the high "horn" on the backstrap of the "hammerless" style lets you get the web of the hand all the way up to the edge. This proportionally lowers the bore axis of the gun vis-à-vis your wrist. The gun now has less leverage for the muzzle to rise. However hard the gun comes back into your hand, it comes straight back. However much the kick hurts, the muzzle doesn't rise. I can shoot and hit faster with .357 Magnum rounds out of that vicious little Scandium Centennial than I can with .38 Specials out of a Chiefs Special, because the Centennial styling of the 340 PD with a high-hand hold can't move in my fist as even a .38 Chief can. This is why, today, my Bodyguard and Chiefs Special Smiths usually live in my safes, and a Centennial lightweight with .38 Special +P ammo lives in my trouser pocket.

Since I'm still a cop and have to shoot a few 50-round qualifications a year with duty loads through anything I carry for backup, the Airweight .38 is my personal compromise of weight/power/controllability. The .357, even in all steel, is just too brutal for that kind of continued pounding. My friend Wiley Clapp

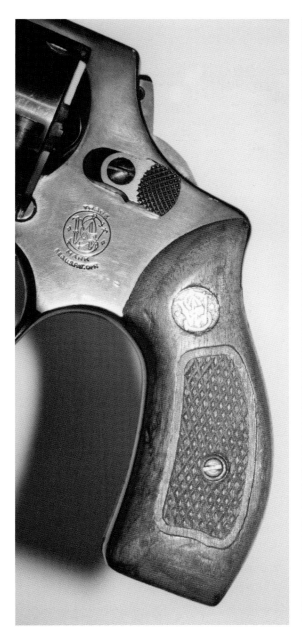

Left: This old Model 36 has round butt frame, by far the most popular; '70s-period square cylinder latch; and bobbed hammer spur…

Right: …while this 36 has earlier rectangular latch, conventional hammer spur, and semi-square butt used heavily by NYPD, which gave better shooting characteristics…

Bottom: …and this one has square latch, spur, and Pachmayr Professional grips. The latter compromise concealability, but wonderfully improve shooting characteristics.

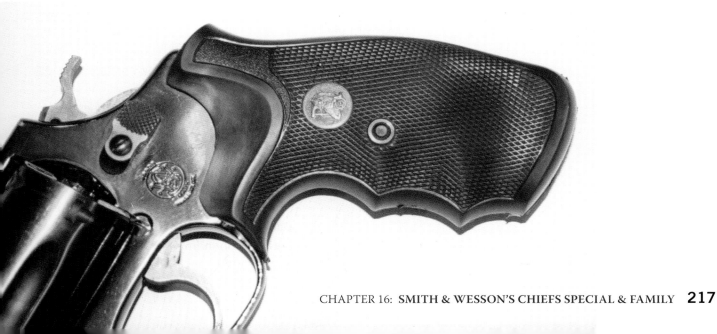

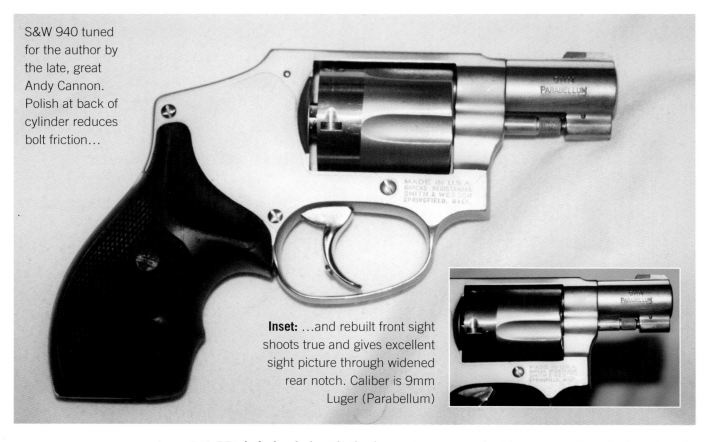

S&W 940 tuned for the author by the late, great Andy Cannon. Polish at back of cylinder reduces bolt friction…

Inset: …and rebuilt front sight shoots true and gives excellent sight picture through widened rear notch. Caliber is 9mm Luger (Parabellum)

carries a 340 PD daily loaded with the brutally-recoiling old Black Talon 180-grain .357 load…but he has bigger, stronger hands than mine, and being retired from police work, he doesn't have to go through those grueling qualifications with it anymore.

Stocks? Bigger is easier to shoot but harder to conceal. The optimum balance is something that fills the palm without bulging the clothes, and which fills in behind the trigger guard without extending the butt length. Craig Spegel's Boot Grips became the defining style: I have them on a couple of my guns. Uncle Mike's copied them with Spegel's permission in their Boot Grips, and Eagle Grips did so apparently without it in their "secret service" model. A functionally similar configuration is seen in the standard model of Crimson Trace's LaserGrip, which projects a red dot onto the target and solves another long-standing problem of the Chiefs Special and family: the tiny sights that are hard to see under stress or in the dark.

Ammo? For the recoil sensitive, the best-performing standard pressure .38 Special round was always the Nyclad 125-grain "Chiefs Special Load" from Federal, which was out of production for a long time but recently returned to the Federal production line by popular demand. The 158-grain all lead +P semiwadcutter hollow point has a great track record in the street out of 2-inch guns, but it has a recoil so nasty that in the super-light

Below: 2003 brought this 50th Anniversary Centennial Airweight.

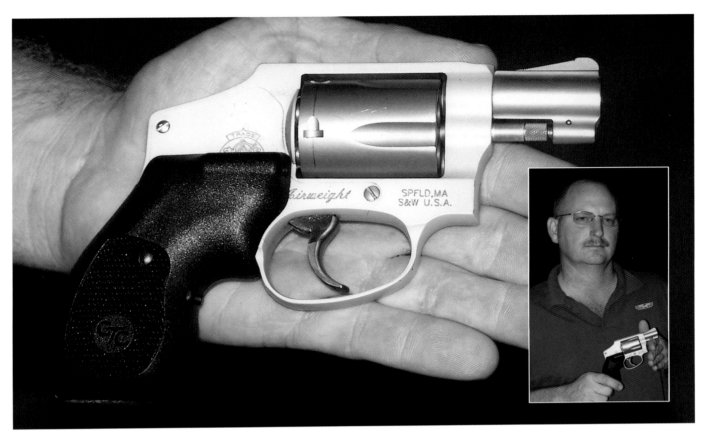

Above: A totally out of the box S&W Model 642 with Crimson Trace LaserGrips.

Inset: In 2005, shooters from all over the nation convened at Andy Stanford's Snubby Summit to train with guns like these. Winner of the match at the end was IDPA 5-Gun Master Jon Strayer, who used this gun.

Scandium and Titanium models, momentum pulls the bullets forward out of case mouths enough to block cylinder rotation and jam the guns. CCI brought out a 135-grain Gold Dot +P .38 Special expressly for these guns, designed to give optimum mushrooming at short barrel velocities and with case mouths tight into deep cannelures to prevent bullet loosening problems. Designed by a team led by Speer engineer Ernest Durham at the request of the NYPD, this round has now been well proven by collective street experience to do its job.

Personal Experience

Got my first J-frame, a Bodyguard Airweight, in my mid-teens to carry in my dad's jewelry store when it was too hot for the Colt .45 auto I normally kept under a jacket. (Traded a flat-top, 3-digit serial number Ruger Blackhawk .44 for it, and still shudder at that memory.) Got a semi-square butt 2-

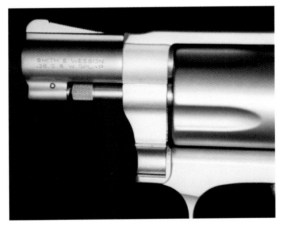

inch Model 36 from my dad to go with my concealed carry permit on my 21st birthday, and used it the first time I had to pull a gun on criminals on a public street, a couple of years before I pinned on a badge. Used it for backup as a young cop. Replaced it with a Detective Special, later with a nickel Bodyguard Airweight, and still later with the Airweight Centennial for off duty backup, still using it for backup in uniform on "light days" when not packing a Ruger SP101 .357 or Glock 27 for that purpose.

Left: Recent J-frame production modifications include sights like these, on a Model 637, which are easier to see.

Below: One of the author's civilian students daily carries this matched pair of S&W Model 940 9mm revolvers, both solid stainless with "boot grips."

Above Left: The three J-frame structure choices. Top, Chiefs Special (with current teardrop style cylinder latch) has conventional hammer. Center, the Centennial is externally "hammerless." Bottom, the Bodyguard has built in hammer shroud. All three here wear Uncle Mike's boot grips.

I gave a Cogan Custom 3-inch heavy barrel Chief to my youngest daughter when she was 10. She went through an LFI-I class with it at 11, still owns it, and considers it one of her favorite guns along with the Novak Custom 9mm Browning Hi-Power and the 1911 .45 autos she prefers to shoot. My older daughter was horrified to learn, when she moved to California with her husband, that she couldn't bring her high capacity pistol magazines because she wasn't "grandfathered" under state law. She took instead two California-legal S&Ws: a Model 3913 compact 9mm auto, and a 3-inch Model 60 Chiefs Special with LaserGrips.

Just one more of seven figures' worth of American families who have trusted the Smith & Wesson Chief Special and its descendants for protection for more than half a century....

Notes

[1] Cary, Lucian, *Lucian Cary on Guns*, Greenwich, CT: Fawcett Publications, 1950, p. 123.

[2] Askins, Lt. Col. Charles, *The Pistol Shooter's Book: A Modern Encyclopedia*, Harrisburg, PA: Stackpole, 1953, p. 20.

[3] Gaylord, Chic, *Handgunner's Guide*, New York City: Hastings House, 1960, p. 30.

[4] Jinks, Roy G., *History of Smith & Wesson*, North Hollywood, CA: Beinfeld Publishing, 1977, p. 225.

[5] Keith, Elmer, *Sixguns by Keith*, New York City: Bonanza Books, 1955, pp. 45-46.

[6] Jinks, *op. cit.*, p. 224.

Smith & Wesson's .357 Combat Magnum

O ne of Smith & Wesson's most aptly named guns, the .357 Combat Magnum, was introduced in the second great wave of revolvers in its caliber. The first, of course, had been 1935, the year S&W introduced its revolutionary large frame .357 Magnum. In the six short years that had followed before World War II put a stop to handgun production for domestic needs, Smith had enjoyed a virtual monopoly on what was then called, with some justification, "the world's most powerful handgun." Only Colt had produced competitive guns in the caliber, but none had remote-

Conceptualized by a top police gun expert, the "police officer's dream" was the prestige service revolver for much of the latter Twentieth Century.

Left: The Model 19 was a milestone in police revolver design. Bill Jordan called it "the answer to a peace officer's dream."

Left: 3-inch barrels were among the rarest, but most useful, on Combat Magnums. This M66 wears Meprolight night sight insert at front.

Right: Jon Strayer sights in a 4-inch 19. These are target grade revolvers.

ly approached the S&W in popularity. The Single Action Army revolver was seen as an anachronism; the double action Colt New Service had fixed sights that couldn't take advantage of the ".38 wadcutter through full Magnum" versatility of the .357 chambering, and the adjustable sight double action Shooting Master left the Hartford factory in pitifully small quantities. After the War's end, S&W's big flagship revolver was the only .357 Magnum on the market for almost a decade; Colt had not revived any of theirs.

That second wave came roughly 20 years after the .357 Magnum's introduction, during an approximately 18-month period in 1953-55. Five new revolvers from three makers hit the market almost simultaneously. Together they redefined the .357 Magnum's use, sometimes offering more compactness and in four out of five cases offering more economy. Colt fielded the service

grade "357," later to be dubbed the Trooper, and the deluxe Python; Ruger put forth its first centerfire handgun, the Peacemaker-style Blackhawk; and S&W introduced its economy grade Highway Patrolman and its revolutionary Combat Magnum, the most compact double action .357 yet offered to the market. Together, they vaulted the .357 Magnum to the forefront of cenerfire sporting handgun popularity.

Pedigree

This ".357 Magnum on a .38 frame" was the trademark gun of Bill Jordan, the legendary Border Patrolman and modern gunfighter who conceptualized it, about whom more later. The Combat Magnum was also a favorite of Charles "Skeeter" Skelton during his police career, and of another Texas lawman who filled his niche after Skelton's death, Jim Wilson. The great Marine Corps shooting champion Bill McMillan was partial to the Combat Mag in his second career as a police firearms instructor. Elden Carl, one of the original Combat Masters to whom Jeff Cooper dedicated his classic book *Cooper on Handguns*, had a pair of them made up with nickel-plated barrels on blue frames.

The greatest tribute to the Combat Magnum's function, however, came from the hundreds of thousands of end users who bought them, including underpaid cops who paid out of their own pockets to upgrade their defensive chances on the street. Countless police departments adopted the Combat Magnum, including the Border Patrol and the Secret Service at the Federal end. The popular "Street Survival" seminars in the '80s encouraged officers to purchase the snub-nose version as the ultimate off-duty revolver. The stainless version was the first issue handgun of the Navy SEALs.

However, not every expert swore by the Combat Magnum. In 1960, defensive handgun authority and fast draw champion Chic Gaylord wrote, "The current trend toward reducing the weight and barrel length of magnums seems to me ill-advised. A light gun of heavy caliber has far too much recoil

Top: Stainless Model 66 became the most desired and backordered service revolver of its time, but also the most mechanically troubled. This one, nicknamed "Fluffy the Pet Revolver," is one of the author's longtime companions.

Left: The "velocity war" between the three big ammomakers with the 125-grain Magnum led to serious problems with the stainless Model 66.

Combat Magnums are reasonably durable with +P .38 Special (below), but author advises that they be shot sparingly with hot 125 grain Magnums (above).

Development of "PPC guns" like Walt Sherman custom S&W Model 10, top, with BoMar sight rib and 1-inch diameter Douglas barrel pushed stock configuration Model 19, below, out of Open class and into Distinguished and Service Revolver competition classes, where it still won often.

Right: 1961 handgun catalog shows S&W's three .357s of the period. From top, original deluxe heavy frame at $120, economy grade big frame Highway Patrolman at $85, and .38-frame Combat Magnum at $110. Latter was 9.5 ounces lighter.

for accuracy. Smith & Wesson's Combat Magnum is the outstanding example of this trend."[1]

But Gaylord's was the minority voice. This first gun with the portability of a .38 but the power of a Magnum held enormous appeal. By 1976, combat shooting authority James D. Mason would be able to say honestly, "(The) Combat Magnum revolver is the most popular and effective gun of its type used by combat marksmen," and call it "ideal for sport or duty use."[2]

A Brief History

S&W's official historian, Roy Jinks, describes the genesis of the Combat Magnum: "The line of K [frame] Magnums began at Camp Perry, Ohio. In the summer of 1954, Mr. Hellstrom asked the prominent U.S. Border Patrol shooter, Bill Jordan, what he considered to be an ideal law enforcement officer's handgun. Bill Jordan stated that in his opinion the gun should be built on a K frame, having a heavy 4-inch barrel with an extractor shroud similar to those used on the large-frame .357 Magnum, target grips, target sights, and the .357 Magnum caliber. Mr. Hellstrom made many mental notes and returned to Smith & Wesson to discuss the feasibility of these ideas with his engineers...Tests were carried out on medium-frame guns throughout 1954 and into 1955 as Smith & Wesson tested various steels and different heat treatment processes. On November 15, 1955, the first production medium-framed Magnum was completed...."[3]

Hellstrom had more than Jordan's vision driving the Combat Magnum project. It was the hottest period of the long-running sales war between his company and Colt. S&W had finally wrested first place in police revolver sales from the older firm. Colt had just announced the first compact Magnum, the "357," built on the Official Police-size "I" frame. Essentially a .41 frame, this Colt was distinctly smaller than the big N-frame S&W .357 Magnum. If he could make the caliber work in the "K" frame, Hellstrom would have the smallest .357 on the market and a huge product niche advantage over Colt.

Commercial success was instantaneous. The Border Patrol adopted the gun that one of their own had literally conceived. So did many other police departments. Jordan received "serial number one" – actually serial number K260001, according to Jinks.[4] This particular revolver wound up in the Rex Applegate collection. After Rex died, his collection was auctioned off by Amoskeag, and I don't know where this historic .357 is now.

The standard gun had a 4-inch barrel, and this was always the most popular length. A 6-inch was offered in 1963, and a round-butt 2-1/2-inch in 1968. The former became

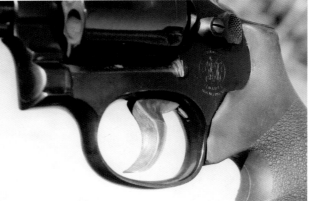

Four K-frame trigger configuration options. Wide serrated target trigger was great for single action bulls-eye, poor for double action combat...

...semi-wide, smooth "Ranger trigger" was favored by S&W Academy back in the day...

...narrow, serrated trigger would become the favorite of double action ace Jerry Miculek...

... and author prefers custom narrow, highly polished and smoothed trigger for double action work.

Know call the fastest draw of any living man.

Inset: Massad Ayoob discusses the .41 Magnum load with Bill Jordan, who helped develop it. Jordan proved as fast with his smile as a gun.

Above: The author at age 25 with Bill Jordan, the father of the Combat Magnum. Photo from an old issue of *Guns* magazine.

popular with police pistol teams and a few individuals, including the legendary supercop from the New Orleans area, Bob Lindsey, who fired his in the gunfight with the rooftop Howard Johnson's sniper. The short barrel became hugely popular among detectives, off duty cops, and armed citizens. I've seen only one specimen over the years with an 8-3/8-inch barrel. Charles "Skeeter" Skelton had at least one Combat Magnum made up special at the factory in his favorite barrel length, 5 inches. Uncatalogued small production runs of Combat Magnums would also be made with 3-inch barrels, their muzzles almost flush with the ejector shrouds. These were cherished among the cognoscenti because they offered a full-length ejector rod stroke, unlike the truncated ejector rod of the 2-inch snubby.

When model numbers were instituted in 1957, the Combat Magnum became the Model 19. When a stainless version entered the catalog in 1971, it was dubbed the Model 66. The 66 was so popular among police, it was back-ordered for years. Secret Service and several other Federal agencies adopted the 66, as did countless state, municipal, and county police departments. Interestingly, FBI never did adopt the Combat Magnum as an issue gun for the rank and file, although they acquired a quantity of special-run round butt 4-inch Model 19s from the Office of Naval Intelligence and made them the first issue handguns for their newly formed SWAT teams. However, both 19s and 66s were enormously popular among the Bureau's rank and file as "privately owned, agency approved" duty weapons. When the FBI went .357, it chose the fixed sight, blued steel S&W Model 13 with 3-inch barrel as standard issue.

The .357 Combat Mag was cloned in two other calibers. The ill-fated Model 53 (1961-74) in .22 Jet was a Model 19 in everything but chambering and hammer nose configuration. The Model 68, never catalogued, was a special production run of 4-inch and 6-inch Model 66s chambered for .38 Special at the behest of the California Highway Patrol. Some also found their way into the LAPD.

As time went on, all the S&W production economies that made purists gnash their teeth affected the Combat Magnum line. When some longer standing guns went from five-screw design to four-screw to three, the Combat Mags were not impacted. Notes firearms historian Ned Schwing of the Model 19, "It was the first revolver to be introduced as a three-screw model."[5]

Some production economies hurt only the feelings of the "Smith-ophiles," and not the performance of the gun. Changing from labor-intensive recessed chambers to conventional flat-faced cylinders may actually have improved performance. Unlike rimfire revolvers, centerfire sixguns have no real need for the case heads to be enclosed, and those expensively machined countersunk niches actually create extra ledges where dirt and debris can built up, preventing full cartridge insertion and interfering with reliability.

When pinned barrels were dropped, enthusiasts all but wept. Here, at least in the Combat Magnum, there was potential for performance degradation: there were stories in the field of barrels beginning to unscrew when powerful Magnum loads were fired intensively. (S&W apologists whined, "But Colt has been putting their barrels in forever without pins!" Colt fans replied smugly, "Yes, which is why they've learned to do it right.") Soon S&W had learned to do it right too, and the unpinned barrels ceased to be a meaningful issue.

Unfortunately, a much darker chapter in this gun's history was about to open. Combat Magnum fans were about to discover that they had a mechanical worry on their hands which was far more ominous than pinned versus unpinned barrels.

Serious shooters had noted that the buffeting of Magnum recoil on the .38-frame Model 19 would take its toll, hammering the gun out of time. There was the very occasional split forcing cone. From the beginning, Bill Jordan advised that his brainchild was a gun that should be carried with Magnum ammo and shot with it occasionally, but that most shooting with it should be with .38 Special

ammo. However, in the '70s and '80s, several new trends converged upon the Combat Magnum in general and the stainless Model 66 in particular.

Remington had introduced a 125-grain semi-jacketed hollow point .357 load traveling at a hot 1400 feet per second. It soon proved to be a devastating man-stopper, gouging a wide wound about 10 inches deep in human flesh. Departments like the Kentucky State Police, the Indianapolis Police Department, and many more found this to be the optimum duty load. Indeed, it made the .357 round viable for urban policing for the first time, since the old load had too long and narrow a penetration path and was seen as a danger to the public. 125-grain rounds mushroomed and stayed safely in felons' bodies. Federal jumped in with an even hotter 125-grain, at 1450 fps, and soon Remington and Winchester had kept pace.

While the .357 Magnum cartridge had debuted in 1935 loaded by Winchester with a 158-grain lead semi-wadcutter bullet at similar velocity, it was found to lead barrels badly and to be a bit much even for the original heavy frame revolver. The industry had backed off to about 1200 foot-seconds for 158-grain .357 ammunition, and this had worked fine in moderate doses in the Model 19, which was fabricated of chrome-molybdenum steel and

Below: "Back in the day," the S&W Model 66 was the prestige holster gun among many officers. This one rides in a Bianchi B27 breakfront security holster.

Above: The Combat Magnum was as accurate as a K-38, and hugely popular in PPC competition before the coming of the bull-barrel specialty guns.

exhaustively tested in the research described earlier by Jinks. However, it appears that no such testing was done when S&W made the same gun in stainless.

The 125-grain load upped the ante on pressure. The K-frame Smith & Wesson had been introduced in 1899, with 19th-century metallurgy, to handle a black powder .38 cartridge at some 15,000 psi (pounds per square inch) pressure. Round nose lead 158-grain .38 Special ammo with smokeless powder went maybe 17,000 psi. +P .38 Special would run probably no more than 23,000 psi, and the hottest +P+ at no more than 28,000. By contrast, the SAAMI standard for .357 Mag-

num was in the low 30,000 psi range, and at least one lot of 125-grain/1450 fps stuff had tested out to over 40,000 psi.

There was only so much that mid-20th century metallurgy could do, and it was a testament to S&W research and engineering that the Model 19 held up as well as it did. The Model 66, however, was something else entirely. Stainless steels expand more than traditional chrome molybdenum ordnance steel alloys like 4140 or 4130 when exposed to great heat. Before, Magnum rounds of lower pressure fired at a reasonable pace had caused few problems in chrome-moly 19s. But now we had the high-pressure

125-grain loads, and they were being fired much more heavily and much faster in police training. It was during this period that a Federal court judgment in the case of *Popow v. Margate* mandated more job-related law enforcement firearms training, and that was the death knell of the old practice of training with light .38 Special ammo but carrying hot Magnum loads on the street. Now, progressive departments shot all Magnum ammo in training, and they shot it fast and furious, and they were using stainless .38-frame guns to do it with.

The original Model 66 just couldn't take it. The gas ring at the front of the cylinder would expand and push forward from the heat, locking up the cylinder and making the gun non-functional. Sometimes it would happen within the first six shots. This, of course, turned "the answer to a peace officer's dream" into a "peace officer's nightmare." In addition, forcing cones (the portion of the barrel which extrudes through the frame toward the cylinder) cracked epidemically under this stress, much more often than did those of Model 19s.

S&W raced for fixes. The first was to move the gas ring from the cylinder itself to the cylinder yoke. This reduced swelling caused by heat, but on the yoke the gas ring no longer functioned to protect the inner axis of the cylinder from powder debris. This tended to build up under the ejector star, pushing it back and jamming the gun by a different means. The next fix was to return the gas ring to the cylinder, but swage it into place instead of merely press-fitting it as before.

Meanwhile, there were other

confluences of evil stars. The time of Bangor Punta's ownership of S&W had come, and with it a more than doubling of production on existing machinery with existing employees, but little capital investment in new equipment and additional skilled workers. Quality control plummeted all across the product line, including the Combat Magnums.

Ruger in 1969 had introduced their Security-Six revolver, a .357 that was compact enough to fit a Combat Magnum holster and about the same weight, but much sturdier. It would digest all the Magnum ammo you could feed it. Ruger soared past Colt and was fast challenging S&W's primacy of the service revolver market as the latter's flagship, the Model 66, foundered in the waves of poor quality control and jamming guns. In desperation, S&W introduced their L-frame revolvers in 1980, the Model 586 in chrome-moly and the Model 686 in stainless. Cloned shamelessly from the Colt Python with .41-caliber frame, which had never had a prob-

2-1/2-inch Combat Magnum was once a "must have" off duty gun, and was issued to Secret Service. This Model 66 wears Meprolight night sight and Hogue Bantam grips.

In outward appearance differing only in shrouded ejector rod and 1/10-inch longer cylinder, the Model 19 .357 Combat Magnum (top) was very similar to the Model 15 .38 Special Combat Masterpiece (below).

lem with the 125-grain Magnum loads, the L-frame soon became the choice of those who wanted Smith & Wesson .357s.

Some hard-core shooters who liked the Combat Magnum size package and the 66's less rust-prone characteristics bought blue Model 19s and had them hard-chromed.

By the time S&W got the Model 66 pretty well up and running for reliability, it was a distant third behind the L-frames and the heavy-duty Ruger GP-100, which had replaced the Security-Six and was on track to overcome even the L-frames and dominate the police revolver market. But soon it was

all a moot point. The wave of police adoption of semiautomatic pistols in the '80s became a tsunami in the '90s, and all service revolvers soon became quaint anachronisms in law enforcement.

The reign of the Combat Magnum, once the paradigm service handgun of America's police, had come to an end. Today, the .357 Combat Magnum, and indeed all of the Smith & Wesson K-frame .357s, are long since discontinued. S&W's Performance Center has built a goodly number of customized defensive revolvers in short Combat Magnum formats, and I for one would like to see them offer a finely-blued Model 19 as a Bill Jordan Commemorative. It would go nicely with the firm's recent and successful marketing theme of re-issuing old Classics.

Shooting the Combat Magnum

Follow the advice of the man who conceptualized the gun: do most of your practice with .38 Specials. Those who had the greatest success with the Model 19s and 66s used it with .38 +P (such as Chicago coppers and FBI agents who bought their own Combat Magnums), or .38 +P+ "Treasury Loads" (as issued along with Model 66s to ATF, Secret Service, Sky Marshals, and many more before the coming of the autos).

The Combat Magnum always delivered target accuracy. Before custom heavy barrel guns took over PPC revolver shooting, the 6-inch Model 19 won national championships in the hands of aces like Tom Gaines and Jerry Jackson of the Border Patrol. It was essentially a K-38 with a slightly heavier barrel thanks to the ejector shroud.

The sharp recoil of the Combat Mag was all that Gaylord warned about, but modern shooting techniques make the gun manageable even with Magnum loads. The target stocks originally furnished with these guns won't do for that, being geared for bulls-eye match shooting with mid-range .38 wadcutters. With Mag loads in most hands, a wedge effect tends to roll the gun back into the web of hand until the hammer spur is blocked. "Rubber" grips with finger grooves give the best stability in rapid fire with .357 rounds. Retrofit the new style cylinder latch, or round off or shave down the old one; the standard square latch had a tendency to lacerate the thumb in Magnum recoil while firing right-handed. Other than that, recommended modifications are "conventional wisdom K-frame": narrow, smooth triggers, for example, should enhance your control in double action shooting.

The K-frame .357 offers one great advantage in high speed shooting: its bore axis is lower to the wrist than a larger frame revolver, which gives the shooter more leverage against muzzle jump. It may feel like it's kicking more, but the recoil is straight back into your hand, and the muzzle stays on target for maximum rapid fire accuracy. In recent IDPA (International Defensive Pistol Association) championships, Brent Purucker won the stock service revolver class in one national match with .38 Special in a Model 19, and Dave Elderton won a regional using full Magnum loads in a Model 66, both with 4-inch barrels, the maximum length IDPA now allows.

Personal Experience

In the 1970s I was the one who broke the story on the jamming Model 66s, in the pages of the police journals *Sentinel* and *Trooper*, and in the "Industry Insider" column I wrote at the time for *American Handgunner*. Shortly thereafter, my then chief of police went against the recommendations of his firearms training staff and bought 66s for standard issue. I had to send half of them back to the factory. All brand new, some came to us already out of time. Barrel/cylinder gap is ideally about .006 inch. Out of the box, these ranged from zero (the cylinder grated on the forcing cone, and we wondered how the factory had ever test-fired it) to .013 inch, which seemed almost enough to spit through without touching the metal. They were constantly going back and forth to Smith & Wesson for repair. Personally, I felt the way Ralph Nader would have felt if he'd been issued a Corvair to drive, and I carried a Colt .45 automatic instead. When a subsequent chief insisted

In a more than tacit admission that the K-frame could not stand up to the continued pounding of the hottest .357 loads, S&W replaced it with this L-frame 7-shot Magnum with obvious styling homage to the Model 66. Two-piece barrel and "not quite the same" looks did not resonate with Combat Magnum fans.

that we all carry the Model 66, I went out and paid the then-going price, a scalper's rate, for a used first-generation 66 and took it to revolversmith Andy Cannon. He gave it a superb action job, and heli-arc welded the gas ring into the cylinder permanently, as I wish the factory had done on all of them. I carried that gun until I left the department in 1980; my last act there was to inspect the new Ruger Service-Six .357s we had purchased to replace the Model 66 Smith & Wessons.

Upon leaving, I had planned immediately to get rid of my *bete noir*, that detested 66. Inventor Joe Smith offered to do one of his Magna-Trigger conversions if I had a K-frame to spare. Did I ever! My Model 66 came back as the one "smart gun" that ever actually worked. The front of the frame is cut away to take a module that blocks the rebound slide internally with a little metal flag. There's a piece of powerful cobalt samarium magnet on the bottom of the "flagpole." The legitimate owner wears a magnetic ring on the middle finger, and when his or her hand closes over the stocks in firing grasp, reverse polarity spins the internal block and clears the gun to shoot. I found that the damn thing worked. My oldest was then three, and the Magna-Triggered 66 became my bedside gun. I taught with it often in the early days of Lethal Force Institute. I called it "Fluffy, the pet revolver," because it would only bark for its owner. When Joe Smith passed on, Rick Devoid (Tarn-

helm Supply, 603-796-2551 or www.tarnhelm.com) took over the MagnaTrigger conversions and still offers them.

That MagnaTriggered Model 66 remains in my gun safe today, for when my grandchildren visit. It is one of countless Smith & Wesson .357 Combat Magnums that once protected the public in the holsters of the police, and still serve as defensive weapons in countless American homes. It survived its troubles to hold its place in firearms history as a truly classic modern revolver.

Notes

[1]Gaylord, Chic, *Handgunner's Guide*, New York City: Hastings House, 1960, p .40.

[2]Mason, James D., *Combat Handgun Shooting*, Springfield, IL: Charles C. Thomas, 1976, p. 17.

[3]Jinks, Roy G., *History of Smith & Wesson*, North Hollywood, CA: Beinfeld Publishing, 1977, pp. 180-182.

[4]*Ibid.*, p. 182.

[5]Schwing, Ned, 2004 *Standard Catalog of Firearms*, Iola, WI: Krause Publications, 2003, p. 1022.

Smith & Wesson's Classic Model 27

In 1935, Smith & Wesson and Winchester announced a new revolver and a new cartridge simultaneously. Both would bear the same name. The cartridge would go on to become one of the most popular in the history of handgunning. The revolver would also be a milestone. More than 20 years later, it would get a mundane new name: "Model 27." But until then, it would be known simply as the "Smith & Wesson .357 Magnum."

To many purists, this model would forever be *the* Smith & Wesson .357 Magnum.

The very first .357 Magnum is still first in the hearts and minds of many advocates of that caliber. This milestone revolver continues to morph into the future.

Right: Gorgeous finish, "neutral balance," and built-in accuracy made the Model 27 a long-lasting classic.

Right: With today's iterations of the 27, you can put eight rounds downrange before reloading.

Pedigree

From its beginning, the revolver we now call the Model 27 (if only to distinguish it from its long list of descendants and stable-mates in the same caliber) was welcomed and then almost universally endorsed by gun experts. The ones of its time, and the ones that followed.

The great Elmer Keith, of course, cheered its creation: he was a part of that, as

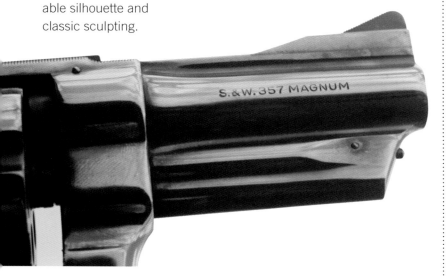

The 3-1/2-inch barrel Model 27 rivals the Colt Python for recognizable silhouette and classic sculpting.

we shall see in a bit. Charles Askins, Jr., carried one with a 4-inch barrel for a good part of his career on the United States Border Patrol. "This is the most sturdy revolver in the world," Askins wrote. "As a service weapon it is tops! A very great deal of care goes into the production of each weapon; they are in fact custom made."[1]

The most enthusiastic ambassador of the new gun and cartridge was a member of S&W's ruling family, Douglas Wesson, who had worked on the .357 Magnum project. Wrote Keith, "Major Wesson hunted big game and killed elk, antelope, moose and one grizzly with his 8-3/8 inch .357 Magnum."[2]

Later experts shared the appreciation. One was Henry M. Stebbins, who in 1961 noted that shooters were only then becoming adjusted to its power level. "When it came out in 1935 it was terrific enough to frighten some of us a bit by its noise and recoil," he admitted. "Since then it has done much to educate us as to the amount of such ruction that we can stand and still do

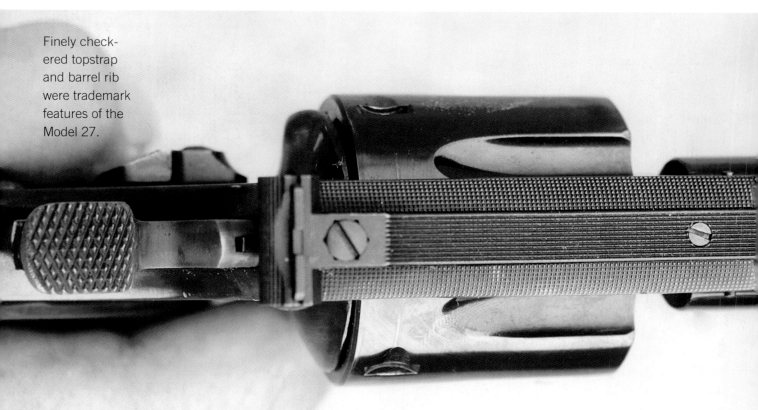

Finely checkered topstrap and barrel rib were trademark features of the Model 27.

effective shooting...what used to seem a ferocious gun is accepted in handgun society today, with almost everyone agreeing that it has its points."[3]

But more experts than those who wrote for gun magazines learned to appreciate the big Smith .357. George S. Patton bought one before he went overseas in WWII, embellishing it with his trademark ivory stocks bearing his inlaid initials. When he gave away one of his matched Colt Single Action Army revolvers to a Hollywood star, he augmented the remaining .45 with the Magnum, which he called his "killing gun." Patton's weapon had a 3-1/2-inch barrel. So, legend has it, did the very first .357 Magnum to leave the factory, which was presented to FBI director J. Edgar Hoover, though some who study the history of S&W insist it had an 8-3/4-inch barrel. Many agents bought identical revolvers for themselves, with the 3-1/2-inch barrel, or the 4-inch that Askins

preferred. Among those with the 4-inch .357s was Walter Walsh, the legendary FBI agent, fast draw ace, and pistol champion. One day in Maine in 1937, Walsh shot it out with the notorious Brady gang. Armed with a Colt .45 automatic in one hand and his Smith & Wesson .357 Magnum in the other – and with a .45 slug through his own chest, collapsing a lung – Walsh used the .357 to kill gang leader Al Brady. Ed McGivern, the famed six-gun wizard of the period, often used one in his demonstrations, and repeatedly shot man-size targets with it at distances out to 600 yards.

Meanwhile, S&W's archrival Colt quickly chambered three of their classic revolvers for the .357 Magnum cartridge: the Single Action Army, the massive New Service, and the "targetized" version of the latter revolver, the Shooting Master. Smith & Wesson, however, was inextricably associated with the new cartridge and dominated

Above: The first revolver to be dubbed "Model 627" was this 1989 version with heavy 5-inch barrel, unfluted cylinder, and round butt.

Right: A solid fistful of steel, the original Smith & Wesson .357 Magnum delivered memorable performance to go with its unmistakable look.

Below: Eight-shot cylinder and integral gunlock (keyway visible above cylinder latch) distinguish the Model 327 (shown) and current production Model 627.

sales in that caliber for twenty years. None of those Colt .357s resumed production after WWII. In 1954 and '55, for the first time, a wide choice of new models became available to those interested in the caliber. Colt introduced their deluxe

Python, even pricier than the S&W, in '55. A year or so before, Colt had brought out their "357," on the same theme as their service Trooper .38 whose name this adjustable sight Magnum would soon share. It was a slightly smaller, more "holster-friendly" gun, and much less expensive. In 1955, Bill Ruger brought out a highly improved single action on the Peacemaker theme, also budget priced: the Blackhawk .357. S&W countered in those years with a one-two punch.

One blow was the Highway

Patrolman. This was the regular large frame .357 Magnum with choice of 4- or 6-inch barrel, but with no checkering (except on the hammer) or other frills, and with a gray sand-blasted finish. It competed directly with the Colt Trooper for market and price point. The other punch was the smallest .357 Magnum yet, the Combat Magnum inspired by Border Patrolman Bill Jordan. This K-frame gun was, by Jordan's own admission, designed to be "carried mostly with .357 ammo and shot mostly with .38 Special."

Approximately a decade later, Super Vel introduced expanding bullet hollow point ammunition commercially, quickly followed by the larger ammo makers. This allowed the .357 Magnum's potential power to be harnessed for anti-personnel work, creating a shorter, wider wound channel that did massive damage inside the narrow confines of an erect biped's torso. It allowed the .357 to get past the widely held stigma that it was not suitable for defense or police use, since it would blast through a human body and kill whatever innocent bystander might be on the other side. Suddenly, long after its introduction, the .357 Magnum cartridge was becoming truly popular in American law enforcement. When Remington introduced a 125-grain hollow point at 1400 foot-seconds veloc- ity and Federal countered with one at 1450 foot-seconds, word quickly got around of the awe-

some wounds it inflicted, only about 10 inches deep but enormously wide, and the .357's popularity increased in police circles.

The police guns, by then, were .38-frame Combat Magnums and .41-framed guns like the Colts, Ruger's Security-Six and then GP100, and S&W's own L-frame, which was an intermediate size between the Combat Magnum and the original 1935 Magnum. Large for its purpose by late 20th century standards, the N-frame .357 Smith was discontinued, first in its economy Highway Patrolman variation, and finally, in 1994, in its original form.

By then, it had made a host of friends among discriminating shooters of yet another generation. Such

Above: The recessed chambers of the original S&W .357 may seem an affectation today, but display the intricate machining that characterized this top-line revolver.

Left: The latest incarnation of the .357 Magnum of Col. Wesson, Phil Sharpe, and Elmer Keith is this Model 327 Performance Center TRR8. Tru-Glo red dot optical sight is locked to rail on topstrap, and InSight M6X combined white light and laser sight is attached to shroud of its two-piece barrel.

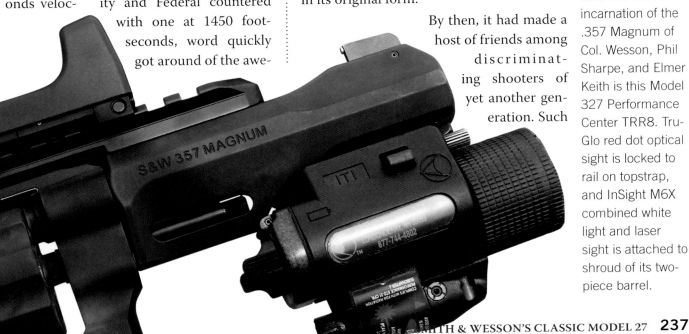

Above: Today's 27-series N-frames give you eight rounds of .357 Magnum, and they've been chambered for a like number of .38 Super rounds.

Right: This 27 delivers the accuracy at 25 yards that made the S&W .357 Magnum famous for precision "shootability."

late 20th century experts as Skeeter Skelton, John Taffin, Frank James, Walt Rauch and Chuck Taylor all had good things to say about the original S&W .357. Jerry Miculek, the top dog of modern speed revolver shooters, blasted his way to fame initially with the 8-3/8-inch barrel Model 27, because no smaller frame would handle the violent 200-grain handloads he developed to set speed records in bowling pin matches. Upon its discontinuation, the big Smith, now known as the Model 27 series, became an instant "cult favorite" among revolver enthusiasts, and prices of existing samples soared.

A Brief History

Phil Sharpe, Elmer Keith, and other experts of the time were involved in the development of the .357 Magnum. The

Left: One of the author's 4-inch 27-2 revolvers mates nicely in the field with light Marlin carbine chambered for same .357 Magnum round. 27 has action job and trigger stop from S&W Performance Center.

country was in a depression, and 1935 was not a commercially ideal time for Smith & Wesson to introduce its most expensive revolver ever. As Askins had noted, the guns were virtually hand built, and luxuriously finished, each fitted with an adjustable rear sight and the shooter's choice of front blade. The company kept records on the individuals who ordered these bespoke revolvers, and a great chapter of handgun history thus opened: the era of the Registered Magnum. Explained Dave Arnold, "Each revolver was registered to its new owner and was accompanied by a certificate bearing the customer's name. In addition, the registration number on the certificate, which had the suffix 'Reg', was stamped on the crane recess of the frame. The revolver had a bright blue finish in keeping with its fine fit and finish."[4]

The Great Depression notwithstanding, demand for these guns greatly exceeded S&W's expectations, and soon the custom/registration thing became unwieldy. Production ceased in late 1941 as the United States went onto a war footing. After the war, as S&W eased back into production of guns in demand by consumers, the .357 Magnum did not make its reappearance until 1948. It was upgraded with heavier duty sights, and with the short action modification that accompanied all of the company's postwar double action revolvers.

In 1957, Smith & Wesson gave numeric designations to all its handgun models. The original .357 Magnum became the Model 27 and its plain-Jane economy version, the Highway Patrolman, was designated

Below: Top, the exotic eight-shot Model 327 TRR8; below, the more classic six-shot Model 27-2 with "target hammer and trigger."

An original Registered Magnum from the Chuck McDonald collection. The iconic 5-inch barrel…

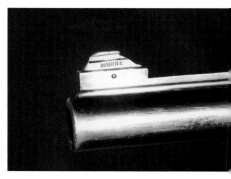

mounts a Marble bead front sight… which is also meticulously grooved on each side… which mates perfectly with the tiny U-notch popular in pre-war days, of the rear sight. Note complexity of checkering on top strap, and full, fine checkering on top of hammer.

Model 28. Various dash-suffixes appended the Model 27 name as the gun underwent such production economies as going from five-screw to four-screw frames, and then to three-screw, changes in ejector rods, and other minor updates. Against increasing competition – lighter guns, smaller ones, and of course, cheaper ones – Model 27 sales dwindled. In the late 1980s, S&W produced a stainless version, the Model 627, which featured stainless construction, a 5-inch heavy underlugged barrel, and a non-fluted cylinder. It did not look like a Model 27, and it did not sell well. By 1994, the Model 27 had disappeared from the Smith & Wesson catalog. It had been long since pre-deceased by the Model 28.

The concept of an N-frame .357 would not resurface again until the 21st century, and then in a very 21st century context. The new (and currently available) Model 327 series uses Scandium in place of steel to bring down weight. Strongly encouraged by Miculek, the factory discovered that modern metallurgy allowed the large .44-frame cylinder to be bored with eight .357 Magnum chambers instead of the original six. It has been produced in formats ranging from a snub-nose with truncated grip frame to a huge, optically sighted competition gun complete with Picatinny accessory rail under its sculpted medium-heavy barrel. Though it has not caught on as a defensive weapon, the latter model shows promise in bowling pin shooting and for ICORE (International Congress of Revolver Enthusiasts) matches.

Barrel Length Factor

Over the years, the Model 27 series has been produced in a great variety of barrel lengths. There are few handguns whose fans are so split as to ideal barrel length. During the Registered Magnum years, the ordering customer could specify whatever barrel length he or she desired.

Noted Arnold, "The .357 Magnum revolver was first made in two main barrel lengths – 3-1/2 and 8-3/4 inches."[5] The guns that Douglas Wesson used on his spectacular big game hunts may well have been the latter length, and not 8-3/8 inches as Keith wrote. The reduction from 8-3/4 to 8-3/8 inches as maximum length came about after Smith & Wesson discovered that their longest barrel exceeded the maximum length allowed in competition at the time. To

achieve the maximum allowed sight radius, 10 inches, the barrel had to be shortened to the 8-3/8 inches dimension.

Soon the company was making 4-, 5-, 6-, and 6-1/2-inch barrels among their standard offerings. I have heard of, but not handled, 7-1/2-inch versions.

Each had its adherents, because in this gun, the balance and overall esthetics changed significantly with barrel length. So, of course, did its ballistics. The .357 Magnum cartridge in most of its loadings dropped velocity dramatically as barrel length shortened.

The great double action revolver expert of the mid-20th century, Bob Nichols, appeared to favor the 3-1/2-inch barrel. However, he also said of this gun, "The .357 Magnum is a lot of gun for any man to hold; and it's too much gun for the average man."[6]

J. Edgar Hoover's Smith & Wesson .357 Magnum (now lost to history, and be-

Below: The most famous Registered Magnum this side of J. Edgar Hoover's: The one bought and carried by General George S. Patton, seen here at the Patton museum. Note S&W's proprietary grip adapter of the pre-war years, a duplicate of which is now available through the Smith & Wesson Collectors Association.

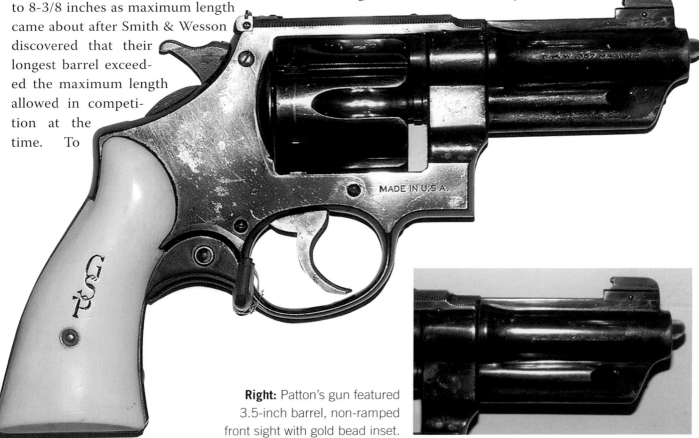

Right: Patton's gun featured 3.5-inch barrel, non-ramped front sight with gold bead inset.

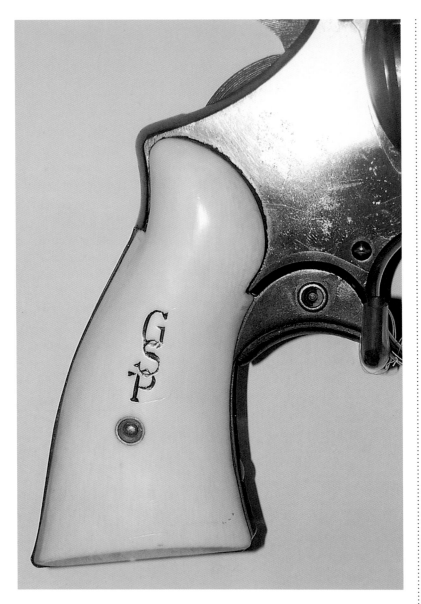

Patton's S&W .357 Magnum was unlikely to be confused with anyone else's. He called it his "killing gun."

famous Maine gunfight.

The 5-inch barrel was perceived by many as having the best balance, in both the visual and the tactile sense, of any of the slender barrels ever fitted to this large-frame, heavy-cylindered revolver. Skeeter Skelton was particularly fond of the 5-inch and influenced so much demand among his loyal readers that Smith & Wesson reportedly produced a short run of 5-inch Model 27s to satisfy the clamor.

The 6-inch and 6-1/2-inch barrels were ideally in proportion to the .44-size frame, in the eyes of some other enthusiasts. Many of the police departments that adopted these original .357 Magnums during their heyday seem to have gone to one or the other of these lengths, the New Hampshire State Police for example.

The 8-3/8-inch barrel was unique to this gun until the coming of the Smith & Wesson .44 Magnum in the mid-1950s. Ed McGivern seems to have used this length more than any other. Chic Gaylord, an influential gun expert in the '50s and '60s, wrote: "One of the finest sidearms to take along on a hunt is Smith & Wesson's .357 Magnum with the eight-and-three-eighths-inch barrel. It shoots as straight as a rifle and packs a lot of authority."[9]

Accuracy

I took a cherry (as-new, apparently unfired) Model 27-2 to the range and set up some NRA bulls-eye targets scaled for the 25-yard distance I was using. With me were three classic loads by three justly famous manufacturers, in as many different bullet weights.

First was the mild .38 Special 148-grain mid-range Match wadcutter load by Federal, which has been called the Gold Standard for accuracy in handgun ammunition. I used an MTM rest and, because

lieved to have been passed on to a relative of Hoover's heir Clyde Tolson) may have had a 3-1/2-inch barrel. Certainly General Patton's did. Writes modern authority John Taffin, an enthusiast who owns them in virtually all barrel lengths, "...we have the short-barreled 3-1/2-inch .357 Magnum that is absolutely the most business-like looking sixgun ever made available. Dirty Harry did not originate 'Make my day!', the 3-1/2-inch .357 Smith & Wesson Magnum did!"[7]

Charles Askins' original .357 Magnum had a 4-inch barrel. So did the specimen Walter Walsh used to kill Al Brady in that

for the ultra-powerful S & W .357 Magnum cartridge, its accuracy and effectiveness with all the .38 Specials (Mid-Range, Regular and High-Speeds) is actually amazing, and make it the greatest all-purpose hand arm ever developed.
*Registered U. S. Patent Office

SUPER UNDERCOVER SERVICE GUN

The S & W ".357" Magnum* with short 3½" barrel, and Baughman Quick-Draw Sight on King Plain Ramp. Favorite shoulder-holster gun with leading Federal and State peace officers.

Left: As a little boy, author "imprinted" on this picture of the 3.5-inch Magnum in his dad's 1948 edition of Stoeger Shooters Bible…

this specimen of the Model 27 had the wide target trigger and beavertail hammer intended for single action shooting, I fired it that way. Recoiling with a gentle bump at each shot, the pristine pinned and recessed Model 27-2 put five rounds in 1.15 inches. Curiously, four of the five bullet holes exhibited slight yawing of the projectiles. The best three shots in the group, a measurement that generally factors out enough human error to give me a

good idea what the gun could have done for all five shots from a machine rest, was 0.60 inch. All measurements were done to the nearest 0.05 inch.

The most famous "manstopper" in the history of the .357 Magnum cartridge

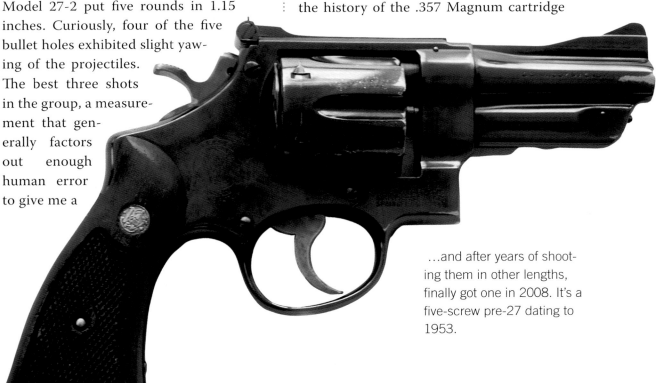

…and after years of shooting them in other lengths, finally got one in 2008. It's a five-screw pre-27 dating to 1953.

5-screw pre-27 is "barbecue ready" in custom Galco holster and matching dress gun belt.

is unquestionably the 125-grain semi-jacketed hollow point. I used Winchester. The uniform group measured 1.25 inches for all five, and 0.70 inch for the best three hits.

158s grain was the original weight of the .357 Magnum bullet, and is still very popular. Black Hills ammo, using Remington's 158-grain scallop-jacketed hollow point was my choice here. The 27-2 sent the quintet of 158-grain Magnums into 1.70 inches (measured center to center between the farthest bullet holes, like all groups here). The three tightest hits were 0.80 inch apart.

This is par for the course with a Model 27, and I've seen some that would put five consecutive shots under an inch at this distance with loads they liked best. Almost from the beginning, the big Smith & Wesson .357 proved itself accurate enough for bullseye shooting, and in the 1970s in the early days of IHMSA (the International Handgun Metallic Silhouette Association), the 8-3/8-inch barrel version was often the winning gun on the firing line. In IHMSA, remember, we're talking about knocking down steel rams at 200 paces, using iron sights.

The tradition continues. In mid-2006, I tested the Smith & Wesson 327 tactical model, introduced at the SHOT Show a few months earlier, flashlight rail and TruGlo red dot sight and all. Two of the loads I used were from the same lots as those

I had accuracy tested in the 27-2. The .38 Special Federal Match wadcutters put five keg-shaped 148-grain slugs into 1.65 inches, with the best three in 1.20 inches. With the Black Hills .357 Magnum loads, all five shots were in four fifths of an inch, and within that 0.80 inch five-shot group the best three shots clustered exactly half an inch apart, center to center.

Smith & Wesson built the original large frame .357 Magnum to be accurate. More than 70 years later, their new ones apparently still are.

Shooting the Model 27

Today's N-frame .357 cylinders hold eight rounds, but the original contained only six narrow chambers. With that little metal cut away, the cylinder was heavy. This had some interesting ramifications as to the gun's handling and shooting characteristics.

It was, of course, heavy, so much so that Gaylord, famous as a holster maker, called the 3-1/2-inch Model 27 one of "the top heavy trio," the other two being the 2-inch barrel versions of the S&W Model 10 and the .41-frame Colt Marshal. The Model 27 weighed about 44-1/2 ounces in the short form, and 48 ounces or so with its longest barrel.

That heavy six-round cylinder with its thick walls between chambers made the N-frame Smith a favorite for handloaders who experimented near the edge of red-line .357 Magnum loads. But it also made for a very fast, sure double action pull. Charles "Skeeter" Skelton noted that he particularly liked the feel of a Model 27 in fast double action shooting because the heavier cylinder seemed to gain momentum more quickly from the beginning of the trigger pull, making the end of the pull feel proportionally lighter with less resistance, because the

cylinder hand required less mechanical effort to raise for cylinder rotation.

The deep frame gave a high bore axis. Over the years, I and others discovered that the Model 27's muzzle actually jumped a little more than that of the much lighter Combat Magnum, whose barrel was lower and therefore much closer to the axis of the wrist. However, the weight of the N-frame absorbed more of the rearward kick of the recoil, making it a more comfortable gun to shoot, especially for long strings of fire. (The aforementioned Jerry Miculek began his spectacular competition career with an 8-3/8-inch S&W K-38. He told me he switched to the big N-frame Model 27 with the same long barrel, because his heavy "bowling pin loads" were killing his K-frames.)

The recessed chambers, which began in 1935 and continued late into the epoch of the Model 27, were prized by revolver aficionados. The reason was the exquisite machining that went into them. They served no actual purpose, according to most firearms engineers and experts, other than creating an illusion of more steel support for a high-powered cartridge. In field use, they actually had a downside. Particles of unburned powder could find their way there as spent casings were ejected, creating a buildup that could prevent full insertion of the next cartridge. This could potentially lock up the gun.

Personal Experience

I was in my mid-teens when my dad bought me an 8-3/8-inch Model 27, and I remain eternally grateful. I took it hunting, and shot matches with it ranging from deer targets at 50 yards at the local turkey shoots, to bulls-eye matches, where it served as my Centerfire handgun. (In .45, most of the time, I used a similar Smith

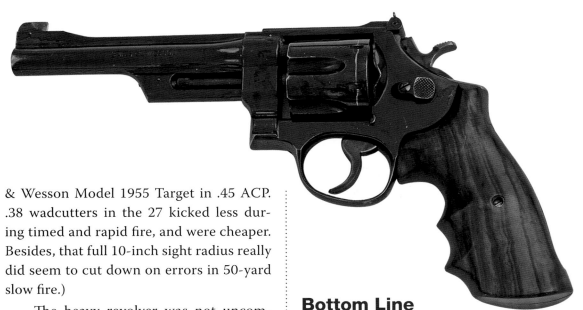

Author won his first state championship ("police combat") in 1973 with this Model 27-1, re-barreled to 6 inches and now wearing Eagle Grips.

& Wesson Model 1955 Target in .45 ACP. .38 wadcutters in the 27 kicked less during timed and rapid fire, and were cheaper. Besides, that full 10-inch sight radius really did seem to cut down on errors in 50-yard slow fire.)

The heavy revolver was not uncomfortable in its slim, simple Lawrence holster. I did find it unwieldy on one occasion. I was 16, finishing a fruitless deer hunt near dusk. The revolver was on the car seat behind me, about to be unloaded before I drove home, when I saw a fox standing in the road. Recalling that they were legal to shoot, I swung up the big Magnum – and the 8-3/8-inch barrel clanged against the wind wing on the driver's window of the '55 Pontiac I was driving. The fox scampered cheerfully away...and I found myself wishing for a shorter Model 27.

That came in my early twenties. I was a young cop who had just gotten into PPC shooting, and needed a 6-inch .38 I didn't have. Borrowing a good friend's 6-inch Python for the interim, I left my Model 27 with gunsmith Nolan Santy to have its 8-3/8-inch barrel replaced with a 6-incher. The slick old six-shooter worked out great, and at the age of 25 I won my first New Hampshire State Law Enforcement Pistol Championship with it. I own it to this day, still a fine example of the gunmaker's art.

What I always wanted, and could never justify purchasing until a recent self-indulgent moment, was a 3-1/2-inch Model 27. I agree with Taffin: there's just something classic in that gun's look.

Bottom Line

From the muzzle of whatever length barrel the user chooses, across the checkered topstrap, to the precisely grooved backstrap, this highly polished deluxe handgun is a significant piece of firearms history. In hard performance and subjective mystique, as an icon of American workmanship for the collector or a functional firearm for the outdoorsman or the defender of the innocent, the Smith & Wesson Model 27 .357 Magnum will always hold a special and distinguished place in the firearms world.

Notes

[1]Askins, Charles, *The Pistol Shooter's Book: A Modern Encyclopedia*, Harrisburg, PA: The Stackpole Company, 1953, p. 23.

[2]Keith, Elmer, *Sixguns by Keith*, New York City: Bonanza Books, 1955, p. 42.

[3]Stebbins, Henry M., *Pistols: A Modern Encyclopedia*, Harrisburg, PA: The Stackpole Company, 1961, p. 80.

[4]Arnold, David W., *Classic Handguns of the 20th Century*, Iola, WI: Krause Publications, 2004, p. 61.

[5]Arnold, *ibid*.

[6]Nichols, Bob, *The Secrets of Double-Action Shooting*, New York City: G. Putnam's Sons, 1950, p. 12.

[7]Taffin, John, *Big Bore Sixguns*, Iola, WI: Krause Publications, 1997, p. 55.

[8]Gaylord, Chic, *Handgunner's Guide*, New York City: Hastings House, 1960, P. 56.

Smith & Wesson's Highway Patrolman

The mid-1950s were a rich time for fans of the .357 Magnum revolver. 1953 saw the announcement of the Colt "357." The following year Smith & Wesson countered with the heavy duty Highway Patrolman. 1955 brought the Ruger Blackhawk .357 in its original flat-top format, S&W's compact .357 Combat Magnum, and Colt's then radical Python in the same caliber. Each of these was, in its way, a milestone gun.

This chapter focuses on the Highway Patrolman. While each of the handguns just mentioned begat its own small genre within the small world of handgunning, the Highway Patrolman begat a larger one: the stripped-

To some, the Highway Patrolman/Model 28 is but a subchapter in the history of its much more famous older sibling, the original S&W .357 Magnum. However, it established an entire modern genre of firearms: the stripped down, low-price, maximum "value vis-à-vis quality" working gun.

Below: Low cost and inherent ruggedness made this model a favorite for customizing. This one has had action tune, with Trijicon night sights and Hogue Monogrips added.

Right: Brad Lewis, an excellent gunsmith and superior pistol shot, squeezes one off from vintage 6-inch Highway Patrolman.

S&W Highway Patrolman, standard configuration, 6-inch barrel. Pinned barrel shows it was manufactured prior to 1982.

down model with all of the "go" and none of the "show." It is a genre that continues in today's firearms industry, on the long gun side as well as with handguns.

Pedigree

Despite its significant size and weight, the large frame Highway Patrolman was a popular law enforcement weapon. Many state troopers carried what was for them an eponymous gun; the Highway Patrolman was purchased in varying quantities by the state police departments of Texas and New York, among others. Columbia, Missouri, whose city cops were famous in the Midwest for their combat shooting skill, were issued this big Smith .357. The Highway Patrolman was the choice of Ed Nowicki, a Chicago copper who would go on to become a police chief, a judge, and, today, one of America's most respected police trainers. Ed used his

Highway Patrolman in the first of his six gunfights.

As per Chicago PD requirements, it was loaded with .38 Special ammo at the time.

Gun experts appreciated the big Smith. It was interesting to see who preferred it and who chose its arch-rival in the marketplace, the Colt "357" that later was re-named the Trooper in keeping with its .22 and .38 caliber near-twins, which had been called that since their inception. Jeff Cooper, whose preference in revolvers generally seemed to run toward the S&W, expressed his partiality to the Colt in this comparison. Speaking of trail guns, he wrote, "...the Colt can be had with the 6-inch barrel at 39 ounces, making it the lightest long-barreled pistol in the high-power class. As a compromise between weight, power, trajectory, and long sight radius, the Colt stands out."[1] At about the same time, handgun guru Chic Gaylord, normally a Colt man through and through,

wrote: "My feeling is that as a hunting weapon, Smith & Wesson's Magnums have a slight edge over the standard Colt .357 in current production."[2] Go figure.

Later gun writers appreciated the Highway Patrolman, almost always listing it in articles about "best buys." In the '70s, Gene West at *GUNsport* often sang the praises of his. By then the guns were becoming known by the numeric model system S&W introduced in 1957. The original deluxe heavy-frame ".357 Magnum" was designated the Model 27, and the Highway Patrolman, the Model 28. Charlie "Skeeter" Skelton was personally partial to the Model 27, particularly in the uncommon 5-inch barrel length that he did much to re-popularize. However, he found the plain-Jane Model 28 came into its own as the basis of a custom handgun rechambered for a big bore cartridge such as the .44 Special or .45 Colt in a time when those calibers were not available on order

from the Smith & Wesson factory.

On the other hand, gun expert Joe Rychetnik, an Alaska State Trooper during that period, went with the Colt "357" in the 6-inch length over the department-issued S&W .38. The weight factor in favor of the Colt would have been as much appreciated by Rychetnik as by Cooper given the "Bush Cop's" far-ranging duties in the wilderness, but the late, great trooper was also a man who appreciated accuracy. As we shall discuss further, the Colt very slightly edged out the S&W in this regard.

It may have been contemporary writer Stan Trzoniec who told the Model 28's story the simplest, the starkest, the best, in 1981. He said, "Since the Model 27 was a super deluxe pistol and not readily available to police officers who wanted a truly rugged handgun, plans were made under the supervision of C. R. Hellstrom to bring down the cost of this gun. Enter the Model 28, or Highway Patrol-

4-inch Model 28 was highly popular among police.

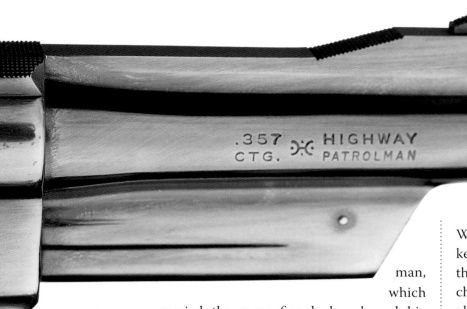

.357 CTG. :C: HIGHWAY PATROLMAN

Highway Patrolman was one of the few S&W models to have its name inscribed on the barrel.

man, which carried the same fine lockwork and big frame of its brother, the 27. Even though S&W deleted such fancy frills as the checkered top strap and the bright blue finish, this is still one of the best .357s made for law enforcement work. A bit heavy, but one tough gun."[3]

These guns found huge favor with hunters. Elgin Gates, the famed worldwide big game hunter, was once treed by an enraged Cape Buffalo and unable to reach his trademark Weatherby Magnum rifle. He killed the great beast, firing downward with armor piercing .357 Magnum slugs from the Highway Patrolman revolver he had been wise enough to carry for insurance in a belt holster.

Why did a wealthy connoisseur of firearms who favored top grade hunting rifles carry a budget grade revolver? It was a syndrome I saw again and again over the years in shooters whose heart was primarily with the long gun. Sparing no expense for the finest Perazzi shotgun or Rigby rifle, they often saw a handgun as a tool rather than a work of art and they treated its purchase in a matter of fact, frugal manner appropriate to something utilitarian rather than something in which they were emotionally invested. Visiting serious riflemen who only owned

the few sidearms they felt they really needed, I saw certain handguns over and over. Ruger single actions. Ruger .22 auto pistols. The S&W Highway Patrolman.

A Brief History

S&W had brought out the .357 Smith & Wesson Magnum in 1935, and had that market niche pretty much to itself ever since. In the pre-war years, only Colt had mounted challenges, and those, feeble ones: the Single Action Army and the big double action New Service guns had been offered in the Magnum chambering. Neither model had survived WWII, and in 1952, S&W's deluxe Magnum was the only game in town.

However, Colt announced its affordable .357 service revolver in 1953, at a price that would dramatically undersell the carriage trade S&W Magnum. Meanwhile, the Magnum had not by any means taken over the police market. Most departments still had .38s. New York State Police carried the big Colt New Service .45 revolver, and the only FBI agents who had .357s, even though the gun had been associated with their collective persona since the company presented the first one to J. Edgar Hoover, had bought them out of their own pockets. Only a few whole departments had said, "Hang the cost" and, like the New Hampshire State Police, outfitted the entire rank and file with S&W's prestigious .357.

We pick up now with official S&W historian Roy Jinks. "The .357 Magnum had created a strong and favorable impression on the law enforcement community, and many state and local agencies were interested in purchasing a revolver in this caliber. However, the Smith & Wesson .357 Magnum revolver was a deluxe handgun sold at a premium price. Inquiries from such agencies as the Texas Highway Patrol were directed to the possibility of manufacturing an inexpensive .357 Magnum handgun for use by law enforcement. C.R. Hellstrom discussed the problem with his engineers and it was determined that a revolver could be manufactured that had the smoothness of Smith & Wesson lockwork, but that would do away with the cosmetic beauty of the revolver. In January of 1954, the factory manufactured an N frame similar to the Model .357 Magnum except that it was a brush blue finish rather than the bright polish blue. The top strap of the frame and top rib of the barrel were given a matt finish rather than being checkered or serrated. With those changes, the factory could successfully reduce the cost of the handgun."

Continues Roy, "Samples were forwarded to the various agencies for evaluation. By March 1954, the factory had received enough favorable comments so that a production run could be planned. The first production revolvers completed were on April 15, 1954, beginning at serial number S103,500. The revolvers were listed to the Smith & Wesson catalog of January, 1955…

Sales for the first year were very strong, with the company producing 8,427 by the end of December 1954."[4]

S&W president Carl Hellstrom and his crew were onto something. Not only was there police demand for an affordable Magnum service revolver, which Colt would meet if Smith didn't: there was also the civilian market to think about. For 20 years hunters and shooters had heard the ballad of the Magnum, and only those with Abercrombie and Fitch level gun budgets had been able to answer that siren song. A Magnum for the masses, Hellstrom must have realized, would sell big time. Colt had come out of the closet with their affordable .357, and Hellstrom may well have been aware of Bill Ruger's plan to follow his hugely successful, low priced .22 auto pistol and single action revolver with a .357 Magnum.

He was doubtless also aware that the Colt 357, built on their intermediate .41 frame, would be lighter and more compact and therefore more desirable to many police than the huge .44 frame S&W. He saw a chance to hedge his bets in 1954 when famed Border Patrol gun expert and WWII combat vet Bill Jordan approached him with

Below: Simple grooves across back of sight and down backstrap were economy measures that allowed M/28 to be made more economically than M27. Note "scuffing" near upper edge of backstrap, which showed up more on flat finish than on finely blued deluxe guns. 10-groove backstrap serration pattern indicates late period of manufacture.

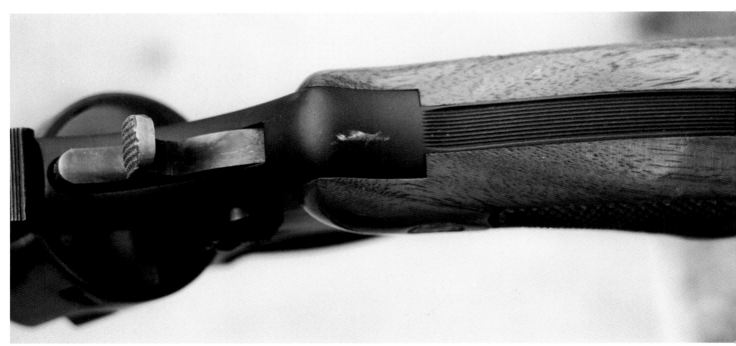

the suggestion that modern metallurgy would make possible a .357 Magnum on a .38 frame. Work on this gun, the .357 Combat Magnum, paralleled the Highway Patrolman project. The executive suite in Springfield had apparently decided that, having dominated the .357 market since conceiving it, they would cover all bases to protect and indeed expand that fiefdom.

Meanwhile, a name was needed for this new stripped-down blaster. According to gun historians Jim Supica and Richard Nahas, "...original test production (was) marked PATROLMAN. The name change was suggested by Mrs. Florence Van Orden of The Evaluators Ltd. to then president Carl Hellstrom."[5]

Time marched on. Beginning in the now-coveted five-screw configuration of old, the Highway Patrolman soon lost "screw #5" (at the upper juncture of frame and sideplate on the right, just below the rear sight), and the rest of the "pre-numerical models" were four screw Smiths. The fourth screw, at the front of the trigger guard, was deleted from S&Ws as a cost cutting step circa 1962, giving subsequent revolvers the three-screw

Above: Rugged as it was, even the massive N-frame could not withstand the hugely overcharged handload that blew up this Highway Patrolman. Gun was the uncommon original "five-screw" with fifth screw visible below where rear sight had been, helping to secure sideplate to frame.

format the firm has used ever since. Like its famous predecessor, the Model 28 (as it was known after 1957) had a counter-bored cylinder that enclosed the case heads. This was done away with in 1982 in another cost-cutting binge. The pin that helped hold the barrel level in the frame passed into history at the same time.

In keeping with its plain vanilla format, options were limited. The gun could be ordered from the factory with target hammer and trigger and stocks, but most came with standard components. 4- and 6-inch barrels were the staples, with one run of fewer than 100 getting out with 8-3/8-inch barrels. A smaller number were made with 5-inch barrels for the Florida Highway Patrol, which for the most part stayed with their Colt .357s until their subsequent adoption of the Beretta auto pistol. A small number were also produced with nickel finish.

S&W applied the Highway Patrolman concept to their deluxe Model 41 .22 target pistol, creating the top-value Model 46 with plain stocks and flat gray finish. The 46 lasted from 1959 to 1968. I was shooting bullseye at the time the Model 46 was dropped, and can tell you it was hugely popular in my part of the country. If I recall correctly, it was standard issue for the USAF pistol team.

The 28's popularity remained strong. During the third quarter of the 20th century, it was a staple on the display shelf of virtually every gun shop and sporting goods store. At the close of that quarter, in 1975, Roy Jinks would write, "To date, sales of the Model 28 have remained strong, since the revolver has met high acceptance from law enforcement personnel as well as the sportsman who is

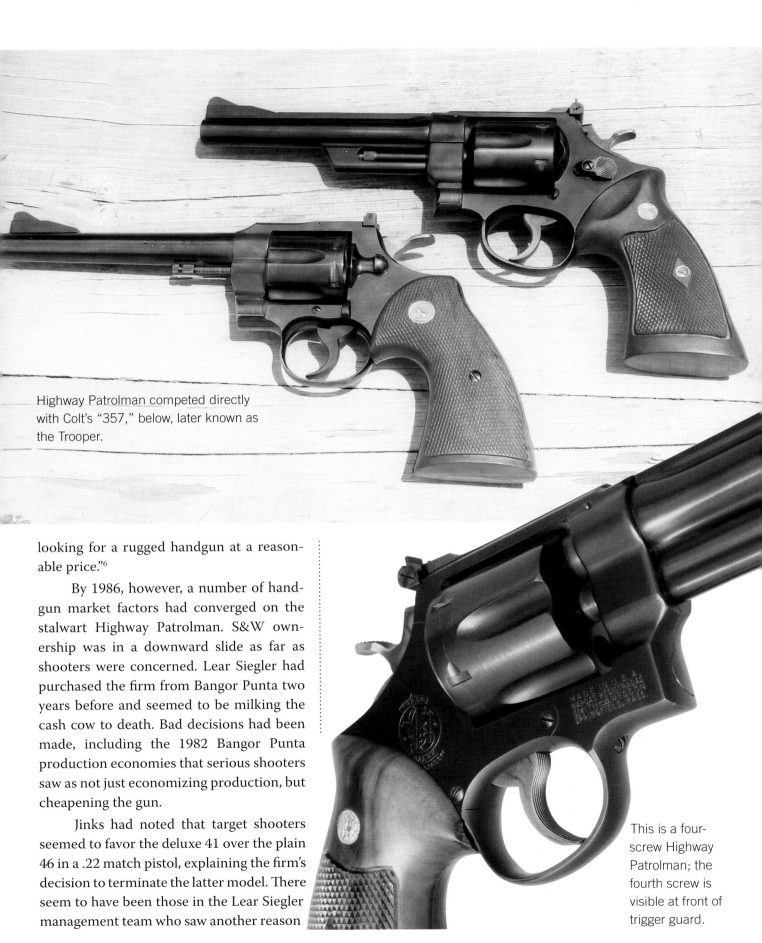

Highway Patrolman competed directly with Colt's "357," below, later known as the Trooper.

This is a four-screw Highway Patrolman; the fourth screw is visible at front of trigger guard.

looking for a rugged handgun at a reasonable price."[6]

By 1986, however, a number of handgun market factors had converged on the stalwart Highway Patrolman. S&W ownership was in a downward slide as far as shooters were concerned. Lear Siegler had purchased the firm from Bangor Punta two years before and seemed to be milking the cash cow to death. Bad decisions had been made, including the 1982 Bangor Punta production economies that serious shooters saw as not just economizing production, but cheapening the gun.

Jinks had noted that target shooters seemed to favor the deluxe 41 over the plain 46 in a .22 match pistol, explaining the firm's decision to terminate the latter model. There seem to have been those in the Lear Siegler management team who saw another reason not to have economy grade "value guns" in the catalog: the company made more money manufacturing and selling a top of the line handgun than a plain one.

By that point in time, the Model 28 had won against its arch-rival, the Colt Trooper. Colt had discontinued it in 1969, replacing it with the unpopular Mark III. Ruger had passed Colt in the police revolver market and was now in second place behind S&W, and closing fast.

The Highway Patrolman was facing more competition within its own family than from anywhere else. The Combat Magnum had become the dominant police service revolver in .357; cops everywhere appreciated its lighter weight and more "carryable" size. Moreover, in 1980, S&W had taken a page from Colt's playbook and finally built a .357 Magnum on a .41 frame. The Models 586, 686, 581, and 681 instantly vaulted to the forefront of the heavy-duty .357 service revolver market, soon dueling with the Ruger GP-100 introduced in 1986. With muzzle-heavy under-lugged barrels, these guns seemed to shoot better at high speed than the differently-balanced Highway Patrolman.

The S&W Model 28 Highway Patrolman was discontinued in 1986.

Shooting the Highway Patrolman

If you're familiar with modern Smith & Wesson revolvers, shooting a Model 28 will hold no surprises for you. Let's say it was 1970, exactly halfway through the period of the Highway Patrolman revolver. The Chevy dealer is showing you two brand-new models. The Impala Super Sport hardtop is gorgeous, but its sticker price is imposing. You choose the chromeless, stripped down Biscayne sedan with bench seats instead. If ordered with the same engine, suspension, tires, and steering and braking options, each car will handle exactly the same way. In just this fashion, shooting a Model 28 was absolutely like shooting a Model 27 of the same barrel length.

A perception floats about that the Model 27 got more attention from factory craftsmen and had a smoother action than its plainer sister. Can't prove it by me. In shooting a lot of both models during those decades, one was not consistently better than the other. The deluxe .357 hadn't been truly handcrafted since Smith & Wesson stopped the original "registered Magnum" program that had made the big gun so prestigious before WWI.

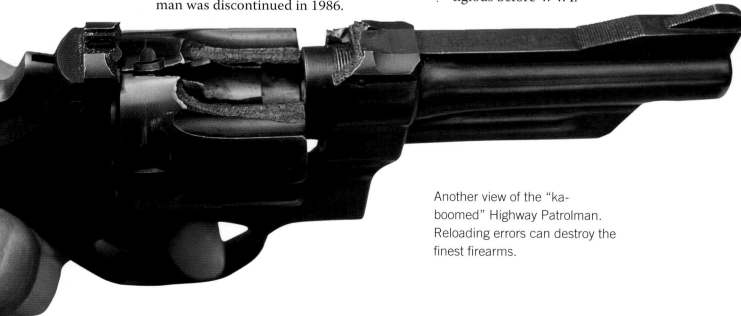

Another view of the "ka-boomed" Highway Patrolman. Reloading errors can destroy the finest firearms.

Above: Highway Patrolman remains in use today. This student uses one to shoot his way into "top five" in qualification at Ayoob's Lethal Force Institute.

Below: Flat, unadorned barrel rib and simple serrated sight distinguished Model 28 from the Model 27, which was exquisitely, and perhaps superfluously, checkered in these areas.

Above: M28s were test-fired with target ammo, represented here by Remington; hunting loads (American Eagle); and defensive rounds (Winchester USA).

Fired next to its baby brother the Combat Magnum and its upstart brother the L-frame, the 28 would come in a close but distinct third to them in controllability. Some nine ounces heavier than the smaller K-frame gun, the 44-ounce Model 28 absorbed more rearward kick and didn't come back into the hand as hard, but the big gun's deeper frame put its bore axis higher, giving it leverage against the shooter that created more muzzle jump. In other words, the Highway Patrolman was more comfortable to shoot than the Combat Magnum, but

we could keep the latter on target better in rapid fire. The L-frame split the difference, with a heft in the 40-ounce range but with more of the weight forward with its under-lugged barrel to tame the muzzle jump.

The conventional wisdom during the many years in which the similarly named S&W Highway Patrolman and Colt Trooper vied against each other was that the S&W definitely had the smoother double action trigger pull, while the Colt was a tad more accurate mechanically. To test this thesis, I sat down at the shooting bench with Brad

Eagle 158-grain semi-jacketed Magnum soft points, and Remington 148-grain mid-range .38 Special target wadcutters. Each of us shot each gun from 25 yards with each load, measuring the best group with each combination twice. The first measurement was all five shots, center to center; the second was the best three shots in each group. Experience, validated by a double blind test Charles Petty and I did circa 2002 for *American Handgunner*, has shown me that the "best three" measurement will give a pretty close prediction of what the same gun and load will do for all five shots out of a Ransom rest. Suffice to say that, in terms of accuracy, the conventional wisdom was right. The solid cylinder lockup at the instant of hammer fall afforded by the Colt's "double cylinder hand" system gave that brand an edge. So, across a broad range of bullet weights and velocities, did the Colt's 1:14 rifling twist compared to the Smith's 1:18-3/4 twist, a holdover from *fin de siecle* black powder days. Still, the Colt's accuracy advantage was not that huge. The Model 28s shot very well. Yes, guns S&W mass-produced many years ago were outclassed by a gun produced today by the craftsmen at their Performance Center with access to the latest equipment and knowledge. But, again, not by all that much....

In Summary

Its 32 years of continued production made the Highway Patrolman the longest lasting stripped down economy version of a pre-established top line firearm. It began a trend still seen today. S&W has returned to the concept with their "Value line" of conventional semiautomatic pistols in matte black and stainless such as the Model 457 and the Model 410S, and also with a low-end offering in their polymer line, the Sigma. Colt has been successful for years with

Lewis. Brad runs Lewis Arms in Bow, New Hampshire, a plush gun shop whose spacious layout evokes Abercrombie & Fitch at mid-20th century, but without the upscale prices. In addition to top quality new guns, Brad has a large stock of the classics. He took from the used gun shelves Model 28s in 4- and 6-inch lengths, and an early 6-inch Colt "357." All three were cherry. Brad tossed in a late model S&W Performance Center .357 competition revolver. We headed to the range with 110-grain Winchester USA .357 hollow points, Federal American

25 YARD BENCH TESTING

S&W Model 28, 4-inch Barrel

AMMO BRAND	LOAD	5-SHOT GROUP (")	BEST 3 SHOTS (")
Remington	.38 148gr WC	1-11/16	1-1/16
Winchester USA	.357 110-gr SJHP	3-1/8	1-5/8
Federal American Eagle	.357 158-gr SJSP	1-15/16	13/16

S&W Model 28, 6" Barrel

AMMO BRAND	LOAD	5-SHOT GROUP (")	BEST 3 SHOTS (")
Remington	.38 148-gr WC	2-1/16	11/16
Winchester USA	.357 110-gr SJHP	1-5/16	1.00
Federal American Eagle	.357 158-gr SJSP	1-3/4	1-1/4

S&W Performance Center Model 627, 6-inch Barrel

AMMO BRAND	LOAD	5-SHOT GROUP (")	BEST 3 SHOTS (")
Remington	.38 148-gr WC	1-1/4	3/8
Winchester USA	.357 110-gr SJHP	2-3/4	9/16
Federal American Eagle	.357 158-gr SJSP	1-1/2	1/2

Colt "357," 6-inch Barrel

AMMO BRAND	LOAD	5-SHOT GROUP (")	BEST 3 SHOTS (")
Remington	.38 148-gr WC	1-3/8	1/2*
Winchester USA	.357 110-gr SJHP	1-9/16	1.00
Federal American Eagle	.357 110-gr SJSP	1-1/2	1-1/8

*4 of 5 shots in 11/16" nch

their similar treatment of the 1911 pistol, the Colt 1991A1.

The concept extended to long guns as well. Every rifleman who ever saved a pretty penny by purchasing the no-frills Ranger version of the Winchester Model 70, and every shotgunner who got a bargain with the Express grade Remington Model 870, owes a part of that saving to the firearm that began this particular value concept: the Smith & Wesson Highway Patrolman revolver.

Notes

[1]Cooper, Jeff, *The Complete Book of Modern Handgunning*, Englewood Cliffs, NJ: Prentice-Hall, 1961, p. 57.

[2]Gaylord, Chic, *Handgunner's Guide*, New York City: Hastings House, 1960, p. 60.

[3]Trzoniec, Stanley, *Modern Centerfire Handguns*, Tulsa: Winchester Press, 1981, p. 37 .

[4]Jinks, Roy G., *History of Smith & Wesson*, North Hollywood, CA: Beinfeld Publishing, 1977, pp. 216-217.

[5]Supica, Jim, and Nahas, Richard, *Standard Catalog of Smith & Wesson*, Second Edition, Iola, WI: Krause Publications, 2001, p. 144.

[6]Jinks, *op.cit.*, p. 217.

Smith & Wesson's .44 Magnum

CHAPTER 20

1955 It's a time when the world celebrates American ingenuity, American influence, American strength. Cars, televisions, and appliances are all growing bigger and more powerful. It is a year when Ford will introduce the sleekest family automobile in their history, when Walt Disney will introduce the Mickey Mouse Club, when Smith & Wesson will introduce the .44 Magnum revolver.

More than half a century later, only one of those symbols of American progress will have survived and flourished. It won't be the '55 Ford or the Mouseketeer.

Introduced mid-20th century, the S&W Model 29 raised the bar for handgun potency, and in the hands of icons from Elmer Keith to Jeff Cooper to "Dirty Harry" became a symbol of Americans' strength.

Below: This is the remarkably accurate 4-inch 629 Ayoob carried on his first African safari. It wears Hogue grips in this photo.

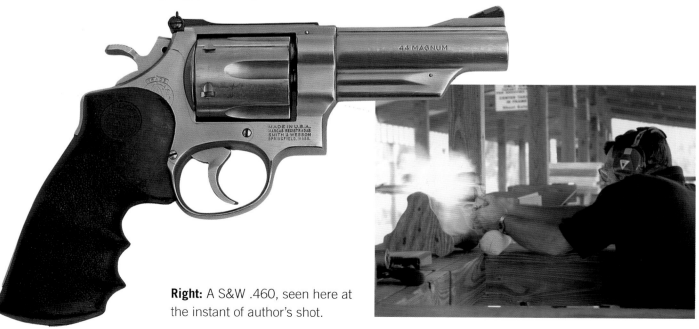

Right: A S&W .460, seen here at the instant of author's shot.

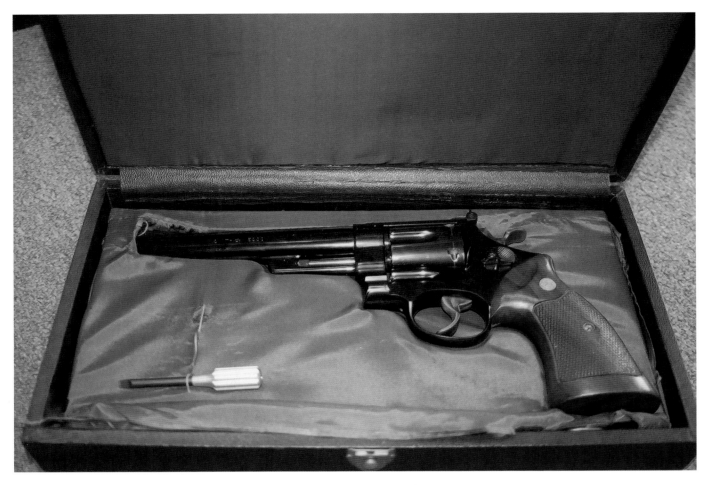

Icon of handgun power: the Smith & Wesson Model 29 with 6-inch barrel in its early, classic configuration. This one is from first year of production.

Pedigree

The Smith & Wesson .44 Magnum revolver has been a staple on the American handgunning scene since its introduction, a couple of years after which it was dubbed the Model 29. *Guns & Ammo* publisher Tom Siatos criss-crossed the world shooting all manner of big game with it. Jeff Cooper insisted that the 8-3/8-inch barrel version was deadlier on deer-size animals at 100 yards than a .30-30 rifle. The .44 Mag's prime mover, Elmer Keith, sang its praises of course, but so did virtually every other gun expert of the time, and since. Ross Seyfried, who in many ways would follow in Keith's footsteps, became the second American to win the world IPSC championship. He used a Pachmayr Custom Colt .45 auto for that, but his daily carry gun as a working cattleman was a 4-inch Model 29.

John Milius armed the protagonist with a Model 29 when he wrote the screenplay for *Dirty Harry*. Milius told me that its raw power and its individuality complemented the character of a righteous cop who acted on the edge of the law, and Clint Eastwood understood that and played it up as the title character. Never before nor since did a movie sell so many guns: for years after the 1971 debut of *Dirty Harry*, Model 29s were so much in demand that they brought scalper's prices. Indeed, they'd been hard to come by before: rumor persists that in the movie, Eastwood actually wielded a Model 57 .41 Magnum because the prop masters couldn't find a genuine Model 29. Milius, however, insists that they filmed with the real deal.

A rugged minority of gun-wise real cops liked the gun. It was especially popular in Texas and in Detroit, where many officers thought its raw power might make up

Presented to him by Smith & Wesson when he was named Outstanding American Handgunner of the Year in 1998...

for the fact that they were forbidden to use expanding bullets. Detective Denny Reichard, the brawny pistol champion and revolversmith, carried one or another Smith .44 Mag on his hip for most of his career, and often one on each hip. Such famous modern police trainers as Clint Smith and Jerry Lane carried 4-inch Model 29s to work as young patrolmen. Addison Clark wore one as a Kalispell cop, where he rose to Chief before retirement, and used a full-loaded Model 29 with 8-3/8-inch barrel, custom vent rib, and Magna-Port to win the Laramie Shoot for Loot and the Second Chance Shoot. His victories made him the first big money winner in the early days of the "handgun competition pro tour."

A Brief History

1956 is often listed as the year the .44 Magnum was introduced, but that is incorrect. S&W historian Roy Jinks confirms that the first production model came off the line in December of 1955, and one or more prototypes were in Elmer Keith's hands throughout that middle year of the Fabulous Fifties. In fact, he had received one prototype in February 1954, according to his autobiography *Hell,*

I Was There.[1] This gun, with 6-1/2-inch barrel, was the one he used for his controversial kill of a rifle-wounded deer at 600 yards. Keith wrote that he had convinced Carl Hellstrom at S&W to make the gun, and his friends at Remington to create the cartridge, in the latter part of 1953.

Keith had for decades experimented with handgun rounds of increased power, focusing on heavy handloads in the .44 Special cartridge. He knew that shell's old "balloon head" case was a weak spot, and he knew that the graceful S&W .44 Special revolver would have to be beefed up to withstand the power level he sought. Thus, the need for a new gun...and time for a new cartridge, its case a tenth of an inch longer than a .44 Special's chamber so it couldn't be fired in an older revolver, which could have had disastrous results.

...Ayoob favors the 4-inch .44, and cherishes this particular 629.

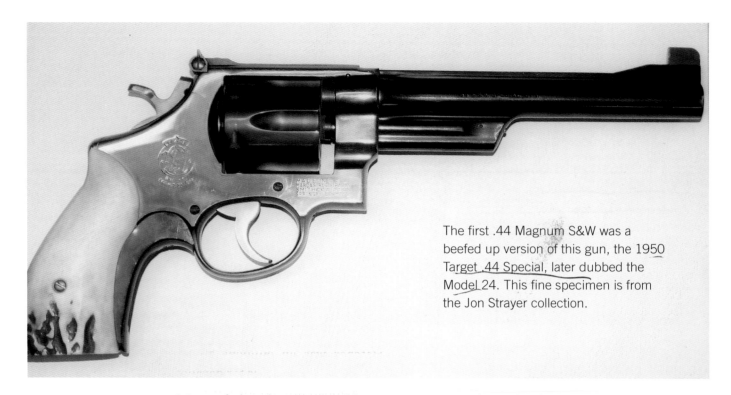

The first .44 Magnum S&W was a beefed up version of this gun, the 1950 Target .44 Special, later dubbed the Model 24. This fine specimen is from the Jon Strayer collection.

Most of the shooting world was introduced to the S&W .44 Magnum by the March, 1956 issue of *American Rifleman*, in an article titled "The Most Powerful Handgun" by Major General (Ret.) Julian S. Hatcher. The new .44 Remington Magnum round was loaded with a 240-grain semi-wadcutter bullet at 1400 foot-seconds velocity, and Hatcher well understood why it had to be the strongest revolver S&W had yet produced. He explained exactly how the dimensions of the new gun had been

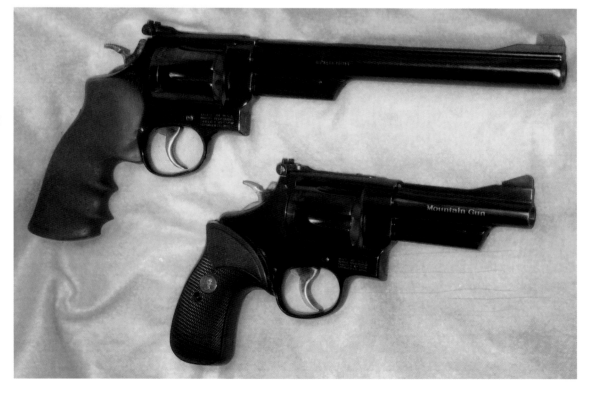

Right: Author finds uses for his 8-3/8-inch Model 29, top, but finds the Mountain Gun version in 4-inch, below, more useful for his needs all around.

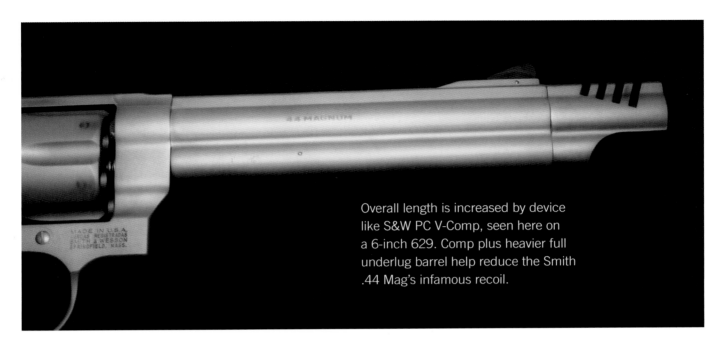

Overall length is increased by device like S&W PC V-Comp, seen here on a 6-inch 629. Comp plus heavier full underlug barrel help reduce the Smith .44 Mag's infamous recoil.

enhanced over those of the 1950 Target .44 Special on which it was based:

Comparison of 6.5"	.44 Special v.	.44 Magnum
Bbl. Diameter @ muzzle	0.60"	0.75"
Cyl. Length	1.57"	1.75"
Wt.	2 lb 9 oz	3 lb[2]

Hatcher was an eminent gun expert and had enjoyed that status for decades, and there was apparently no love lost between him and Keith. Animosity toward the .44 Magnum's already-acknowledged godfather seethed in Hatcher's review. He wrote, "No doubt, as happened in the case of the .357 S&W Magnum revolver, there will be shooters and gun writers who for years to come will stoutly claim the credit for this develop-

Left: Early cylinder latch, left, tended to cut right-handed shooter's thumbs with heavy recoil. Later redesign, right, seems to have eliminated the problem.

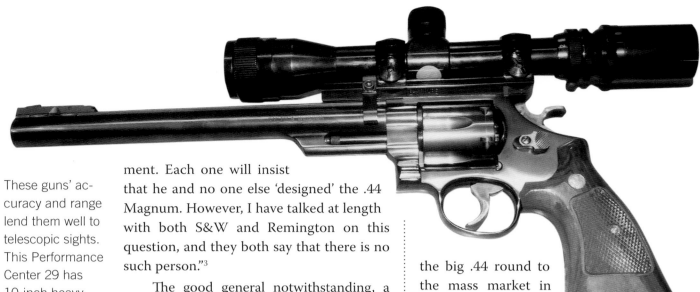

These guns' accuracy and range lend them well to telescopic sights. This Performance Center 29 has 10-inch heavy barrel and iron sights designed for metallic silhouette competition.

ment. Each one will insist that he and no one else 'designed' the .44 Magnum. However, I have talked at length with both S&W and Remington on this question, and they both say that there is no such person."[3]

The good general notwithstanding, a majority of gun historians today agree that we have Elmer Keith to thank for the .44 Magnum. This deluxe Smith & Wesson became the Model 29 when S&W went to numeric product designations in the late 1950s.

It became apparent almost from the outset that the Model 29 was not a long-lived gun when used constantly with full power ammunition. One early test-to-destruction showed that the Ruger single action in the same caliber would endure more massive overloads before blowing up. No sane shooter loaded their ammo that hot, but the cumulative battering of the gun's savage recoil even with factory ammo would quickly knock the S&W "out of time," and shooters noticed that the bolt would sometimes slip and allow the cylinder to rotate back a notch. This left the hammer falling on a spent, just-fired primer instead of the next live round. No such problems were noted with the single action Ruger, which also undersold the S&W. A pattern emerged: most pure outdoorsmen chose the Frontier-style Ruger, and only those who wanted fast shooting capability felt an absolute need for the Smith with its double action mechanism and swing-out cylinder. In a marketing coup, Bill Ruger had gotten hold of some proto-type Remington .44 Mag ammo, and built a flat-top Blackhawk revolver that brought the big .44 round to the mass market in quantity before S&W could do so. With input from Keith, Ruger soon followed that first Blackhawk with the heavier-duty Super Blackhawk, immensely popular to this day. Keith referred to that gun as the "Ruger Dragoon" because of its distinctive flat-back trigger guard and unfluted cylinder, which harkened back to the Colt percussion cavalry revolvers of the mid-19th century.

By the time the .44 Mag was produced in stainless as the Model 629, S&W had learned from the problems they'd had with the .357 Combat Magnums with stainless heating and expanding more rapidly than chrome-molybdenum ordnance gunsteel. The 629 earned a good reputation. Its reduced vulnerability to corrosion (not for nothing do the Germans call stainless steel *rostfrei*) made it much more appealing to outdoorsmen than the rust-prone blue or garish nickel of the 29. The 629 outsold the Model 29 so badly as to obsolete it, and soon only the stainless model was leaving the factory, unless a special order came in from a major distributor such as Lew Horton for a short run of blue Model 29s, like the M/29 Mountain Gun of 2003.

Perhaps the most important change came quietly, on little cat feet, in the late

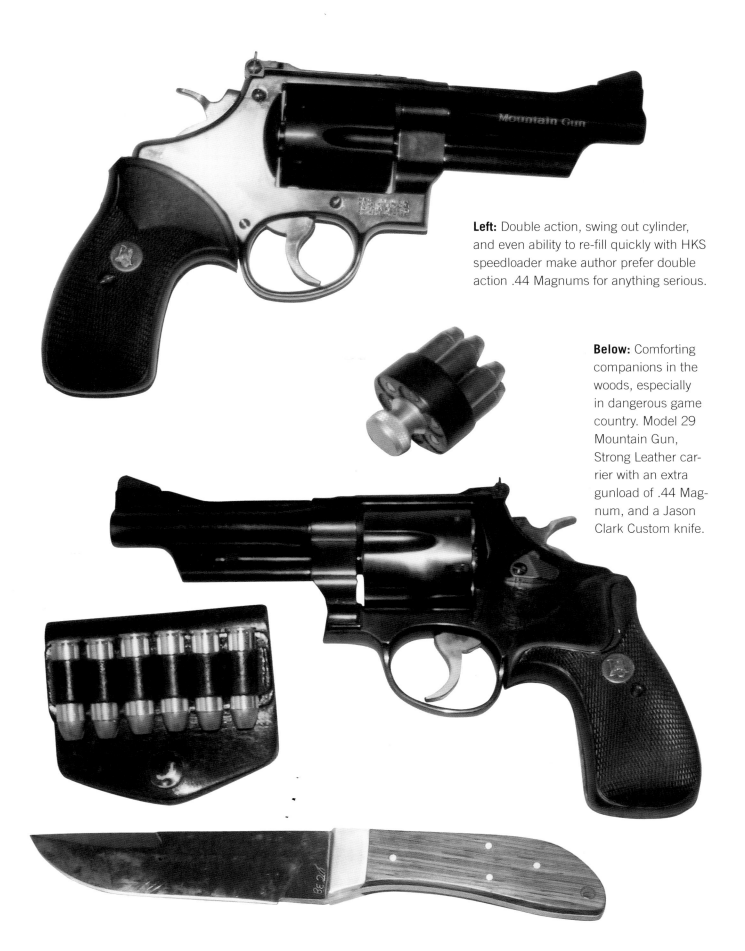

Left: Double action, swing out cylinder, and even ability to re-fill quickly with HKS speedloader make author prefer double action .44 Magnums for anything serious.

Below: Comforting companions in the woods, especially in dangerous game country. Model 29 Mountain Gun, Strong Leather carrier with an extra gunload of .44 Magnum, and a Jason Clark Custom knife.

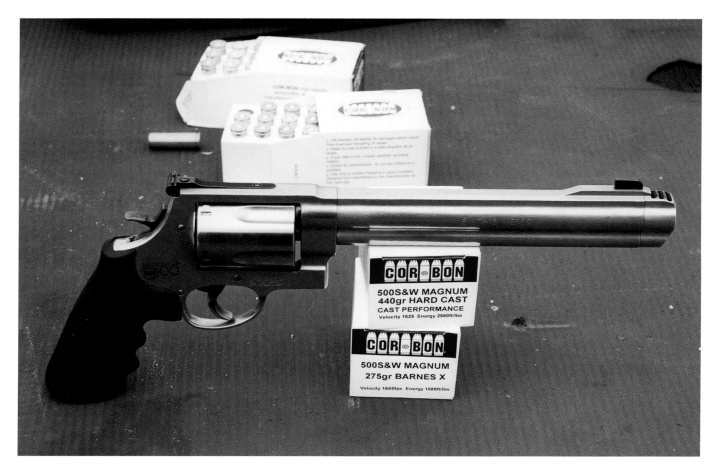

.44 Magnum lost its "most powerful handgun" title long ago. It is dwarfed by the power of this S&W .500 Magnum

1980s. Without fanfare that might have called attention to previous product weakness, S&W redesigned the innards of the .44 Magnum revolvers. Stronger pins and other subtle changes solved the problems of premature timing loss and cylinder slippage. For the first time, a heavily used Smith & Wesson .44 Magnum was now truly reliable for long periods.

By now, the .44 Magnum was no longer "the world's most powerful handgun" as pronounced by General Hatcher in real life and Dirty Harry in reel life, but it remained hugely popular. The cartridge had elevated handgun hunting from a stunt performed by a few gun experts into a legitimate and increasingly popular outdoor sport. In 2003, stimulated by the success of their super-light Scandium and Titanium revolvers in lighter calibers, S&W introduced the Model 329 .44 Magnum, which weighed less than 27 ounces. It was stirred out of

a *bouillabaise* of steel, Scandium, and Titanium, and its recoil was more savage than that of the .45/70-like, 4-1/2-pound .500 Magnum introduced along with it. Here, truly, was the epitome of what Jeff Cooper had once called "a gun designed to be carried much and shot seldom." I can't personally recommend it for serious work, though. I'm aware of instances where the violent recoil into the small parts of the currently-produced internal lock caused the lock mechanism to fail, rendering the gun unshootable.

The standard barrel lengths for S&W .44 Mags have always been 4, 6 and 6.5 inches, and the company's trademark 8-3/8-inch length, a dimension developed to bring the gun into compliance with the ten-inch sight radius demanded in revolver competition in the early 20th century. However, over the years S&W produced .44 Magnums with barrels ranging from 2-

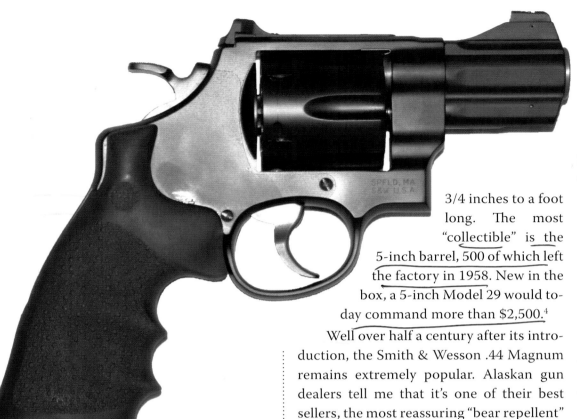

Left: The 329 Night Guard, the lightest .44 Magnum S&W has made yet.

Below: Tapered barrel of this Model 624 .44 Special give it a classic grace, but author prefers .44 Mountain Gun with the same profile, and .44 Magnum versatility.

3/4 inches to a foot long. The most "collectible" is the 5-inch barrel, 500 of which left the factory in 1958. New in the box, a 5-inch Model 29 would today command more than $2,500.[4]

Well over half a century after its introduction, the Smith & Wesson .44 Magnum remains extremely popular. Alaskan gun dealers tell me that it's one of their best sellers, the most reassuring "bear repellent" most of their customers can think of.

Shooting the Smith & Wesson .44 Magnum

Modern gun lore is replete with tales of S&W .44s that would show up on the second hand shelves of gun shops, along with a box of Remington .44 Magnum ammo that contained six empty casings. These aren't tall tales. I remember seeing them on those shelves as a kid who haunted the gun shops. In the 1950s, people simply didn't know how to master and comfortably shoot extremely powerful handguns. Said General Hatcher in his seminal *Rifleman* article, "In shooting the .44 Magnum, we found it advisable to use gloves, as the recoil can only be described as severe. Without gloves, the checkering hurts the hand and the sharp edges of the hammer and cylinder are almost certain to shave off bits of skin."[5]

Edges of the cylinder? Hatcher must have been firing in the old bullseye grasp, with the thumb resting lightly on the recoil shield. Photos exist of master shooters of the period, like former national pistol champ Col. Charles Askins, Jr. firing what was then called "the big Maggie" one-handed, and the recoil lifting the gun higher than the crown of his skull. Askins is believed to have been the first person to kill a man with the .44 Mag – an armed guerrilla he encountered in the Vietnamese jungle while working as a military advisor. Charlie related, "Instead of shooting this Viet Minh with the service rifle I shifted the gun to my right hand and pulled out the big .44 Magnum. I let this ambusher have the first 240 grain slug right through the ribs on the left side. It was probably the first man ever killed with the .44 because it was quite new in those days. The effect of

Left, recent production S&W .44 Mag with flat-face hammer and integral lock. Right, the original firing pin/hammer design on an older Model 29.

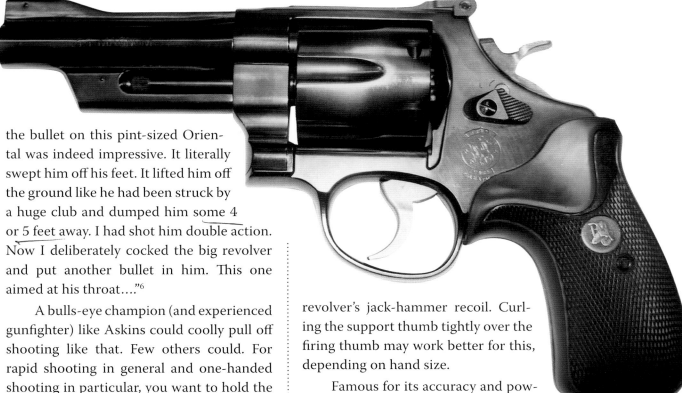

the bullet on this pint-sized Oriental was indeed impressive. It literally swept him off his feet. It lifted him off the ground like he had been struck by a huge club and dumped him some 4 or 5 feet away. I had shot him double action. Now I deliberately cocked the big revolver and put another bullet in him. This one aimed at his throat....."[6]

A bulls-eye champion (and experienced gunfighter) like Askins could coolly pull off shooting like that. Few others could. For rapid shooting in general and one-handed shooting in particular, you want to hold the .44 Magnum in a crush grip and get your entire body weight driving toward the gun. A grasp with the thumb curled down will be strongest, and will keep that digit out of the way of the sharp cylinder edge that apparently abraded General Hatcher. However, if you're right handed that will now put the proximal joint of the thumb directly in line to be lacerated by the old-fashioned square cylinder latch of the S&W revolver. We learned over the years to round off this part with a Dremel Moto-Tool, or cut it away entirely to prevent that from happening. S&W followed the latter path with their now pain-free redesign of their cylinder latches in the mid-1990s.

For a two-hand hold, forget the old "cup and saucer." Upon recoil, your .44 Magnum "cup" will lift right out of the "saucer." Let the fingers of the support hand lock into the grooves formed between the fingers of the firing hand. Crossing the thumb of the support hand over the back of the shooting hand, normally a bad idea, can help keep the hands from separating under this particular revolver's jack-hammer recoil. Curling the support thumb tightly over the firing thumb may work better for this, depending on hand size.

Famous for its accuracy and power, the S&W .44 Magnum is infamous for its rearward kick and its muzzle jump. Any recoil reducing device of proven worth will help. MagnaPorting will help hold the front end down. A heavy slabbed barrel is useful, as is an integral expansion chamber compensator (a custom job) or a removable one (as offered by S&W Performance Center).

Proper stocks will take much of the discomfort away. In the early days, broad-backed wooden stocks like Herrett's were seen as the ticket, but for maximum cushioning, you want "rubber." The softest Hogues (with cushioned back, not open back that still puts steel against the web of the hand), and Pachmayr Decelerators are excellent choices. Trausch grips, with a recoil shield like an auto pistol's grip tang that goes over the web of your hand, will minimize gun movement within your grasp, but the deep cushioning pushes the web of the hand back from the trigger and shortens trigger reach too much for good double action work unless you have unusually long fingers. My

Author's favorite S&W .44 Magnum is the Mountain Gun, designed by Tom Campbell. Note tapered barrel, radiused front of cylinder, rounded butt. This specimen is the rare blue M29 version produced for Lew Horton Distributors in 2003.

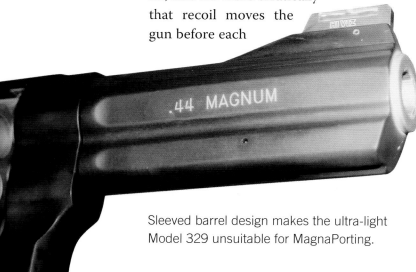

Sub-27 oz. weight, and Ahrends grips, make the recent Scandium Model 329 the hardest kicking of the S&W .44 Magnums, though certainly the most portable.

Sleeved barrel design makes the ultra-light Model 329 unsuitable for MagnaPorting.

personal favorite is the K-frame round butt Pachmayr Compac, which fits on the Smith .44s made for the last decade since they all have round grip frames. It seems counterintuitive that such a small grip could absorb recoil so well, but the secret is in its shape: broad across the back, it distributes recoil across the hand better than anything else I've tried, and its size makes it supremely practical for all-day carry.

With hard-kicking guns, consistency of hold is necessary if one bullet is going to impact on top of the next. Recoil is beginning while the bullet is still in the barrel, and the more erratically that recoil moves the gun before each

bullet clears the muzzle, the wider its groups will be. This is what Roger Clouser appeared to be addressing when he refers to "riding the recoil tango" in his enjoyable series in *The Accurate Rifle* magazine, "1,000 Yard Revolver Shooting." In terms of grasp, there are only two ways you can expect to be really consistent: a very light hold, or a very firm one.

The light hold will work for accuracy, if you don't need a fast follow-up, and if you're experienced enough to keep the gun far enough extended that it won't smack you in the head upon recoil. I've seen a .44 Mag held too close and too light open a shooter's forehead. On the other hand, holding as hard as you can, with your weight forward and into the gun, will give consistent recoil management and therefore consistent grouping, with the bonus of maximum recovery speed for follow-up shots.

Personal Experience

My first .44 Magnum was a Ruger flat-top Blackhawk at age 14, and I didn't get my own first 29 until my twenties, but the ones I shot pounded my hand more than the Ruger. The cowboy-style plow-handle grip of the Ruger let it roll up in your hand on recoil, while the flared horn at the top of the Smith's backstrap vectored all the recoil right into the hand. I soon discovered the joy of Pachmayrs.

I went through a series of stock and customized S&W .44 Magnums. One was a sweet 4-inch 629 that had left the factory with just superb accuracy, like the old Winchester "1 of 1000" selected rifles. It went along on my first African safari. The custom in South Africa is

to shoot "doubles" instead of three- or five-shot groups to confirm sight adjustment, in the interest of conserving ammunition that is so expensive there. From 100 yards, this sweet six-gun put a pair of 320-grain SSK hard-cast flat-points into snake eyes. The next day, firing double action at 117 yards, it dropped an impala with a spine shot. (My 10-year-old daughter gasped, "Dad! You hit it!")

Those superb 320-grain SSK bullets were loaded to a red-line velocity of over 1200 feet per second and would batter a Smith & Wesson of the period out of time in fewer than a hundred rounds. That particular 629 had been re-timed by armorer Rick Devoid just before I left for the hunt. I had always found the 4-inch to be the most useful of the big Smiths – I thought of them as "4X.44s" – and circa 1990, S&W came out with my very favorite. Designed in-house by handgun genius Tom Campbell for his friend and IPSC US National Team-mate Ross Seyfried, the Mountain Gun had the old, tapered 4-inch barrel of the .44 Special. It balanced beautifully. The barrel configuration and rounded front edges of the cylinder took a little weight off, but these features also helped the gun slip much more easily back into the holster. Accuracy was fine, controllability was superb with those round-butt Pachmayr Compacs, and best of all, it was among the first to get the new beefed up "guts" that S&W's engineers had come up with.

This particular gun became my favorite teaching revolver. I used it to demonstrate re-

Bottom: Strangely enough, author found round-butt K-frame Pachmayr Compacs dampened kick best of all…

Top: …shape of backstrap was the reason, and compactness was frosting on the cake.

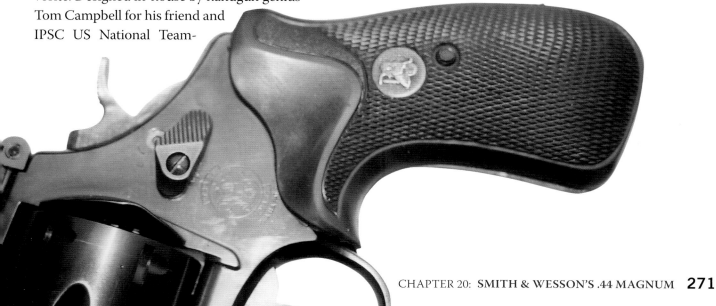

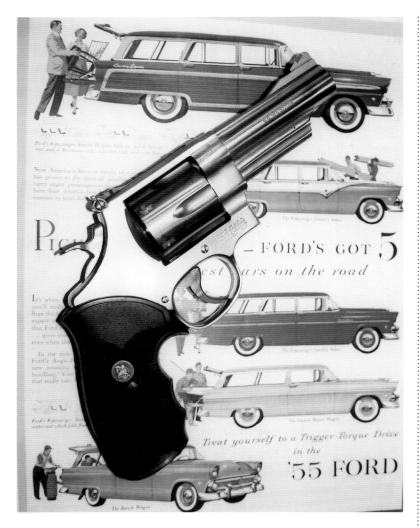

Streamlined Fords and powerful S&W .44 Magnum both debuted in 1955. The latter survived, seen here in Model 629 configuration with Pachmayr grips.

coil control in one- and two-handed stances, firing Federal's fierce 180-grain SJHP, which was loaded to an honest 1600 foot-seconds and delivered over a thousand foot-pounds of energy at the muzzle. Not until nearly 3,000 of these brutal rounds went through my Mountain 629 did it need a minor re-timing. S&W's fix had worked!

One day in 1990, I was teaching a class on the range in Connecticut that was hosting the New England Regional Championship in bowling pin shooting. The aggregate was made up of scores with three guns: auto pistol, revolver, and oddly enough, slide action shotgun. The steel pin tables had been left out over the winter and were covered with rust; it was like shooting pins off coarse sandpaper. With our .45 autos and loads that usually took a pin clean off with one hit, it was taking

a full magazine to get all five pins off the table and stop the time. I placed around fourth in that stage with a custom 1911 and +P .45 ACP hollow points. My borrowed shotgun, a Mossberg 500, felt as if it had sand in the action, and I placed about seventh there. It was looking grim. Revolver scores were turning up hopeless: .357 Magnums and .45s alike were requiring so many multiple hits on the recalcitrant pins that everyone was having to reload, ruining their times.

I remembered that I had my new Mountain Gun in the trunk of my car, along with a couple of boxes of that Federal 180-grain .44 Magnum, and went for it. Each time I fired that slim-barrel 629, there was a giant fireball and one fewer bowling pin. After several strings of one shot/one pin, I had won the revolver segment by large enough a margin to capture the overall aggregate title of New England Regional Champion.

I should have lit a candle to the memory of Elmer Keith. It was a moment that proved he was right in working so hard to create the Smith & Wesson .44 Magnum revolver, a convenient-size powerhouse that would come in handy at the most unexpected moments.

There are a lot of stories like that out there, and that's one reason that Smith's .44 Mag is one of the enduring, all-time classics of the handgunning world, appreciated by pistoleros and riflemen alike.

Notes

[1]Keith, Elmer, *Hell, I Was There*, Los Angeles: Petersen Publishing Company, 1979, p. 198.

[2]"The Most Powerful Handgun" by Maj. Gen. J.S. Hatcher, *American Rifleman* magazine, March, 1956, p. 24.

[3]*Ibid.*, P. 26.

[4]Schwing, Ned, 2004 *Standard Catalog of Firearms*, Iola, WI: Krause Publications, 2003, p. 1026.

[5]Hatcher, *op.cit.*, P. 26.

[6]Askins, Col. Charles Jr., *Unrepentant Sinner*, San Antonio, TX: Tejano Press, 1985, p. 245.

Smith & Wesson's Landmark Service Pistols

For most of the 20th century, American handgun connoisseurs tended toward Smith & Wesson for revolvers, and Colts for semiautomatic pistols. S&W's first foray into the semiautomatic pistol market had not gone well. Joseph Wesson, son of one of the founders, had bought the rights to the Belgian Clement .25 auto pistol around 1910. S&W tweaked its design, which had the recoil spring above and the barrel below, adding among other things a grip safety which worked from the front of the grip-frame instead of its usual place on the backstrap. Chambered for a proprietary new cartridge, the .35 Smith & Wesson Automatic, the gun debuted in 1913.

The first of America's double action "service automatics," these guns went from imperfect to close to ideal over the course of three generations of manufacture.

Perhaps the finest of S&W service autos, the author's Performance Center 5906.

The distinctive lines of the original Model 39 were preserved in the second generation. This is a Model 539, all steel and nickel, from author's collection.

Despite its beautiful fit and finish, it was a clunky-looking thing compared to the sleek Colt, which had been on the market since 1903, and the odd cartridge was hard to come by. The .35 sold poorly and was discontinued in 1922, replaced by a somewhat updated variation in the common .32 ACP chambering. It too was beautifully made, but so was the Colt Pocket Model in .32 and .380. The Colt was a simpler, cleaner design and sold for two-thirds the price of the equivalent quality S&W. Sales of the S&W .32 were even more dismal than those of its .35, and it was dropped from the catalog long before WWII.

After the war, Smith & Wesson dipped its toe in the centerfire auto pistol market again. This time, more thought went into the design beforehand. The result was the pistol we know today as the Model 39, and it paved the way for S&W's successful entry into the auto pistol market.

Pedigree

In mid-century, Henry M. Stebbins wrote of the Model 39, "The S&W is compact. It's thin, and for a powerful autoloader it's easily carried. The grip is built around a short, thin cartridge, doesn't have to hold a supply of .45s. The slide tapers from front to rear, adding to appearance and reducing bulk. It isn't a tiny gun, but it's small enough for a rather small hand, and the short trigger reach – short for an automatic – is a definite help. The grip slants well to the rear, assisting toward the so-called instinctive pointing that really comes from long conscientious practice, with any gun. It flares forward at the lower front to position the hand, and it flares back at the upper rear to save the web of the hand from being chewed by the hammer spur when the slide flies back in recoil."[1]

Tim Mullen would comment, much later, "They're not designed as a match-shooter's gun, but rather as a serious weapon for combat or military use. Although I prefer the Glock 17 in 9mm or the SIG P225 in 9mm, the Model 39 has to rank up there with one of the top 9mm double-action pistols in the world."[2]

At the time of the Model 39's introduction, two of the most influential handgun experts in the USA were Col. Charles Askins,

Jr. and Major George C. Nonte, both Army men. Each took the Model 39 as a personal favorite. Charlie carried his often. A southpaw, he wore it with the hammer down on a live round and the safety off, since it's safety-decock lever did not then come in an ambidextrous form. He wrote that his son Bill took one to Vietnam with him at Charlie's urging.

The Model 39 became even more of a trademark gun to Nonte, who had strong credentials in gunsmithing. Nonte did some of the first, perhaps the first, "chopping and channeling" to make a pocket gun out of the Model 39. He is credited with having assembled many of the popular ASP pistols that were offered in this form by Paris Theodore. I knew Nonte late in his too-short life, and he told me then that the Model 39 was still one of his all- time favorites.

he made a commitment to improve production facilities and develop new models. One of the new models he wanted developed was a 9mm semi-automatic pistol featuring the double action first shot design. This type of pistol was manufactured by Walther in Europe prior to World War II. The assignment of this task fell to Joe Norman, Smith & Wesson's chief designer. On October 28, 1948, Joe Norman completed a prototype pistol serial numbered X-46.... In 1954, the decision was made to place the 9mm double action into production as a lightweight alloy-frame pistol.... Since interest was shown in both models, the January 1956 Smith & Wesson catalog carried illustrations of the 9mm single action, priced at $65 and of the double action, priced at $70."[3]

While initial development had been with military purchases in

The legendary "feel" of the Model 39 grip format. Note good trigger reach. Thumb is placed to verify off-safe position of lever in firing.

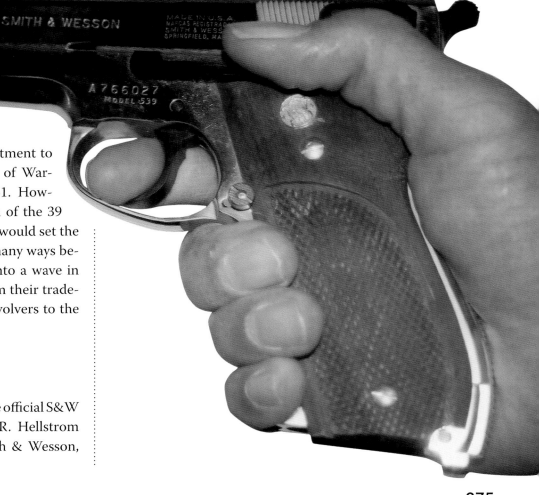

According to Mullen's research, the first police department to adopt the Model 39 was that of Warwick, Rhode Island circa 1961. However, it would be the adoption of the 39 by the Illinois State Police that would set the gun on its way, and would in many ways become the ripple that turned into a wave in changing American police from their trademark double action service revolvers to the semiautomatic pistol.

A Brief History

According to Roy Jinks, the official S&W Historian, "In 1946, after C. R. Hellstrom was elected president of Smith & Wesson,

A single action auto, the Model 952 is carried cocked and locked as shown, a descendant of the super-rare original Model 44 of the 1950s.

The Performance Center 952.

Firing the 952. Thumb has "wiped off" safety with 45-degree angle thrust, finger is deep into trigger for better control in extreme rapid fire.

mind, the US Government had decided to hold off on buying new service pistols as it had ample stocks of 1911 .45s on hand. To recoup investment cost in research and development of lightweight service pistols going back to the almost immediate post-war years, both Colt and S&W decided to offer their aluminum frame autos on the commercial market. Colt was far ahead of Smith & Wesson on this, introducing their lightweight Commander in 1950 in calibers 9mm Luger, .38 Super, and .45 ACP.

The single and double action S&W's Roy Jinks alluded to in the above quote became the Models 44 and 39 respectively under the numeric model designation system the company adopted in 1957. Very, very few Model 44s left the factory, and probably none were marked as such, making them

the ultimate "holy grail" of Smith & Wesson auto pistol collectors today. The Model 39 found more favor.

The Model 39s received a significant sales boost when the gun was adopted as standard issue by the Illinois State Police in 1967. For decades, Illinois troopers had carried .38 or .357 Colt or S&W revolvers in their cross-draw duty holsters, and snub-nose .38s by the same makers off-duty. Qualification scores on the range with the latter had been dismal, and it occurred to Sgt. Louis Seman, head of the ISP Ordnance Section in Springfield, IL that the Model 39 was flat and compact and light enough for plainclothes and off-duty troopers to carry concealed, but far more "shootable" both on the range and if needed for its intended pur-pose. Initial regulations after the adoption

A Performance Center match grade single action auto, built for the splendid but short-lived .356 TSW cartridge, which fired a 125 grain bullet at 1450 feet per second.

limited troopers to the 39 as the sole weapon they could carry on or off duty, though rules would later be relaxed on that, in part to encourage carrying small backup handguns.

It was the first large police department (over 1500 sworn at the time) to adopt a semiautomatic pistol as standard issue. Always an innovative agency, ISP grabbed the attention of both the police professional journals and the gun magazines with the adoption. Other state police organizations, and major departments, stood back for the most part and gave it time to see if this radical new concept would work. The late 1960s were a time when it was becoming popular to cry "police brutality!" at any use of force. Chiefs were hesitant to adopt the better-performing hollow point ammunition popularized by Lee Jurras and his new ammo factory Super Vel, because ACLU and other groups were raising loud rants about "dum-dum bullets." In many communities, and in the headquarters of many large police departments, the powers that be just weren't ready to trade in their traditional six-shooters for "automatics" with "more firepower."

The ISP thus became an intensely studied test-bed of the use of the semiautomatic pistol in police service. Using full metal jacket ammunition for the first several years (a 100-grain bullet at high velocity, made for them by Winchester), the department soon discovered that predictions of stopping power failure with their 9mms were coming true. In the 1970s, I became feature editor of *Trooper*, a regional police publication that had an Illinois edition, affiliated with the Troopers Lodge #41 of the Fraternal Order of Police. This was the organization that represented the troopers. Depending on what superintendent was in charge at a given period, the labor organization was often able to work hand in hand with department brass to the benefit of both the agency and

One of the author's old service pistols, a "transitional" 4506 from 1988 stamped "645." Note square trigger guard. This .45 has just completed a qualification with 58 of 60 shots in the same hole.

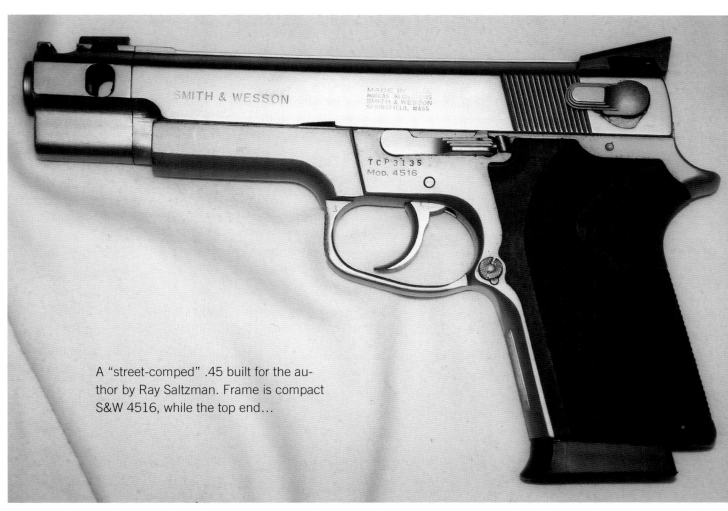

A "street-comped" .45 built for the author by Ray Saltzman. Frame is compact S&W 4516, while the top end…

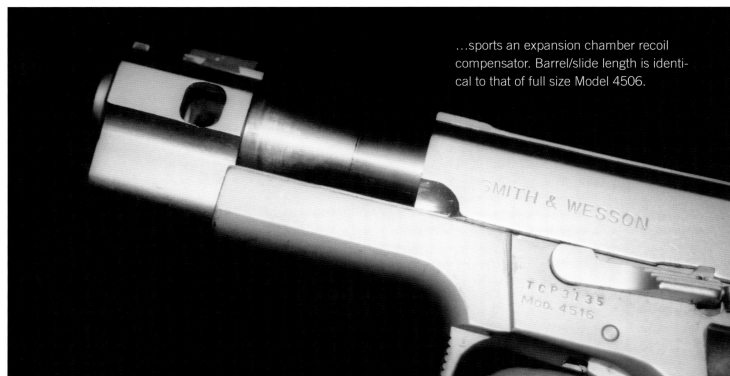

…sports an expansion chamber recoil compensator. Barrel/slide length is identical to that of full size Model 4506.

the personnel on the street. During this period, the Illinois State Police gave me carte blanche to look at their records on the Model 39 and how it had performed in the last decade and more. Through the Troopers' Lodge, I also had access to the rank and file, who were able to speak frankly since they weren't acting as department spokesmen.

Louis Seman was still alive, and I was able to extensively interview him and his successors, and also the superintendent who had signed off on the original adoption of the S&W Model 39.

Through those sources, I learned things that both supported the adoption of the Model 39, and showed that it was a flawed weapon.

On the one hand, review of the records showed that the pistol had worked out remarkably well in gunfights, despite the perceived inadequacy of the 9mm cartridge. I identified some 13 men in a 10-year period who had survived murder attempts while armed with a Model 39 who almost certainly would have been killed had they been armed with the service revolver that preceded it. Four of those could be categorized as "firepower saves." In two separate shootouts, Ken Kaas and Les Davis shot down men who were charging at them with shotguns. Trooper Kass dropped his man with his seventh shot, and Davis killed his antagonist with either the seventh or eighth shot, from their Model 39s. Each had fired six shots without stopping the assailant, and neither would have had time to reload a revolver and stop the attack before they would have been killed. In a gunfight with an outlaw biker armed with two guns, Troopers Lloyd Burchette and Bob Kolowski used their Model 39s to sustain a drumbeat of gunfire into him – with Kolowski reloading and sustaining fire – until the perp slumped and died with a total of 13 gunshot wounds. None of these troopers were wounded themselves.

Of the remaining nine survivors, a few

The Model 4040 was a superb pistol, with Scandium frame for light weight and no bigger than S&W's smallest 9mm, the 3913, but chambered for .40 S&W.

Aluminum frame Model 457 has "plain Jane" finish and machining to reduce price, but performs superbly. Author rates his a "best buy" value in a concealed carry .45.

survived because as a perp was struggling for their pistol and they felt it slipping out of their grasp, they pressed their magazine release buttons. The Model 39 had a magazine disconnector safety, and with the magazine not locked in the pistol would not fire the remaining chambered round. In each case the man who successfully disarmed the officer tried to shoot him with his own gun, and in each case, failed to do so because of this feature.

The remainder of the "Model 39 saves," the single largest category, were troopers whose guns were taken from them by offenders and used against them. None succeeded because in each case the Model 39 in question was on-safe. The 39 had a Walther-like lever on the slide that acted as a combination de-cocking lever and manual safety. For most of the time the 39 was carried by ISP, troopers had the option of carrying it on or off safe. In one of these cases, the sus-

pect pointed a trooper's snatched weapon at both a trooper and his sergeant, and pulled the trigger. The gun, on-safe, did not go off. The sergeant, who damn sure knew how to operate *his* Model 39, instantly dropped the would-be cop-killer with a fatal muzzle contact shot to the liver.

To the best of my knowledge, no Illinois State Trooper was ever shot by an offender with his own Model 39. Nor did I ever find a case of a trooper being killed or even wounded in the line of duty while armed with a Model 39, where it would have turned out differently had he been armed with a revolver.

On the other hand, there were facets of the Model 39 that the troops were not happy about. Circa 1977, Lodge 41 allowed me to poll its members on how they felt about their service gun. Response was strong, and an amazing 87% voted somewhere between "less than totally confident" and "totally insecure and unsafe" with the Model 39. This stemmed largely from perceived reliability problems. The early 39s had had a two-step feed ramp, which was not conducive to good feeding. Many troopers didn't realize that their guns were pretty much customized by top hands at the Ordnance Unit such as Bob Cappelli, who succeeded Seman as head of the unit, and Sebastian Ulrich, to get them to feed with factory ammo. Memories of malfunctions early in training, often with reloads that the department made itself to save money, still undermined confidence to a significant degree. I was only able to find one case of a 39 ever jamming in an actual firefight. That trooper was already wounded when he returned fire weak-hand only, and may have limp-wristed the gun, which was also found to be completely dry when examined by the Ordnance Unit.

ISP found things wrong in the extractor mechanism and the lockup. While historically, the gun companies have taught the police departments about their guns through armorer's schools, folks at S&W at the time confirmed for me that the Model 39 was largely a case of S&W learning more about their own gun from the Illinois State Police than vice versa. By then, some 1700 troopers were shooting them regularly: it was the 39's first real shakedown cruise on large scale since its inception. The extraction and other problems were addressed, resulting in a new extractor system, an improved feed ramp, and a totality of tweaks that became the Model 39-2 in 1971. Though the 39 had always been advertised as having 8+1 round capacity, ISP had discovered early on that it worked best with only seven in the mag plus one in the chamber, and mandated that personnel carry them that way. This seemed to contribute to improved reliability.

That same year, S&W introduced the Model 59, a high capacity version with double stack magazine. It was S&W's first double-stack pistol, and that may have accounted for the fact that it seemed to malfunction more often than the 39-2. Nonetheless, it was the first high-capacity US auto pistol, and police departments began adopting it.

In 1982, S&W entered a second design generation with its three-digit model number series in both single and double stack pistols. The 39 and 59 had always been commercially sold as aluminum alloy framed guns, though all steel models had been made in tiny military quantities, but now they were offered in the catalog. Stainless came out too. A 439 would be the updated version of the original gun with the eight-shot magazine and aluminum frame; Model 539 was the same in all steel; and Model 639 was the designation for the same gun in all stainless.

Until then, the 39/59 series had been "drop-safe" only when carried with the manual safety engaged. With the gun off safe, it could fire from being dropped or struck. This was corrected in the three-digit second generation. Grip shapes remained the same. An ambidextrous safety was added but seemed an afterthought, held on the right side of the slide by a screw and often coming loose. Before the decade was out, the line would include the first compact, the "69" series called the Mini-Gun in 9mm. The second generation would also encompass S&W's first .45 automatic, the Model 645.

It should be noted here that, in the troopers' survey, distrust of the 9mm cartridge had been a huge source of the dissatisfaction expressed. Most of the respondents said they wanted to carry a .45 or a Magnum instead. Ordnance Unit personnel told me that during the years they'd had to carry full metal jacket ammo on the road, the only instant one-shot stops in gunfights had involved central nervous system hits. Soft-points such as the 95-grain load the sergeant used to kill the gun-snatcher at muzzle con-

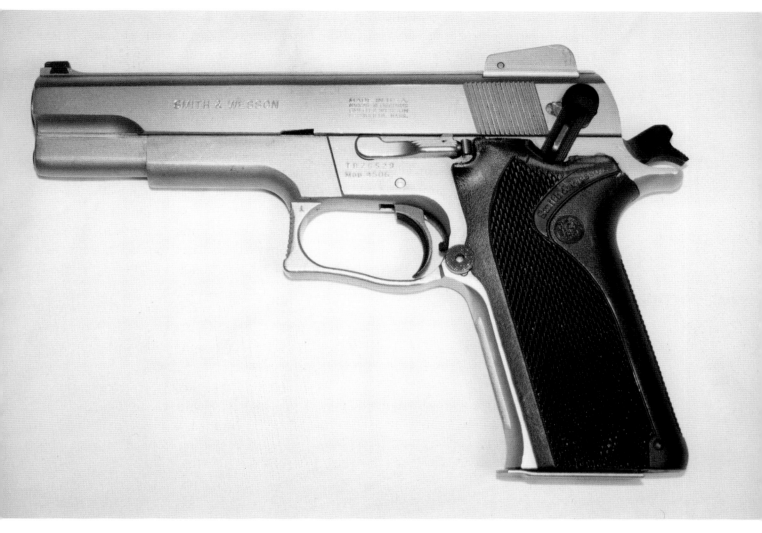

tact worked better, but short overall length led to feeding problems. The Winchester 115-grain Silvertip was the first hollow point adopted, but after it took 13 rounds for Kolowski and Burchette to drop the outlaw biker, the department looked elsewhere. Federal 115-grain 9BP worked better in the interim, but it was the department's subsequent adoption of 115 grain +P+ hollow points from Federal and Winchester that put the 9mm over the top in Illinois. At 1300 feet per second, this load proved devastating in gunfight after gunfight, restoring the troopers' confidence in the 9mm.

Over 1988 and '89, S&W transitioned into the third and final generation of its traditionally styled double action auto pistols. These had four digit serial numbers. The

ambi safety had been improved, and a six-figure study in ergonomics had been undertaken along with a computerized study of trigger pulls that included computer analysis of the pull stroke. The sleek grip lines of the Model 39 remained in the Model 3904 and 3906, but the square, boxy grip of the 645 and particularly the 59 series was considerably enhanced. The new Model 5906 felt for all the world like an all-steel SIG-Sauer, and indeed, some in the business referred to it as "the SmIG." The trigger pulls on these guns were the smoothest they had ever been.

The 10mm FBI gun, the Model 1076, was a third gen model, albeit with a side-mounted decocker demanded by the Bureau and apparently designed by committee. Reliability problems with this big 10mm forced it out of the FBI after a long internal battle. Another Gen Three S&W was the Model 3913, a flat, compact single-stack 9mm which many experts pronounced the ideal size for concealed carry. The third generation also included the double action only (DAO) series, such as the 5946 16-shot 9mm and the 3953, which was basically the 3913 in DAO. These two guns were adopted as standard by the RCMP, and approved by the NYPD.

1990 brought the Model 4006 and its .40 S&W cartridge, co-developed with Winchester with Tom Campbell, Paul Lieben-berg, and Ed Hobbe on the design team at the Springfield, Massachusetts, end. It was the right round at the right time, and the 4006 was instantly adopted by California Highway Patrol, which issues it to this day. There were many other models – S&W was going into its "gun of the month" period – and it takes the excellent *Standard Catalog of Smith & Wesson*, written by S&W authorities Jim Supica and Richard Nahas (Krause Publications) to chronicle them all.

However, the winds of change were upon these guns. No other state police agencies but Illinois adopted auto pistols

With the trigger of a Model 52 target pistol, this 4506 was converted to single action for competition shooting by Wayne Novak.

for almost 15 years, but then in the early '80s, Connecticut and North Carolina adopted the Beretta 92 and New Jersey the HK P7M8, and then the dominoes started to fall. S&W had been the leader of the then-small market for police autoloaders in the '60s and '70s, but news of the pending adoption of the Beretta by the US Government put that brand on top. Then, the easier decocking mechanism of the SIG, which made it easier to train officers with, put that brand ahead of Beretta. Meanwhile, Glock had come from nowhere and, by 1990, swamped them all and taken a lead in police sales. Interest in the conventional S&W service auto waned. The Illinois State Police, after switching from the 39 to a Gen Three 16-shot Smith, at the end of the 20th century switched to the Glock 22 in .40 S&W.

Today, S&W's flagship pistol for police is its polymer Military & Police series designed by Joe Bergeron and his in-house S&W team. At this writing, though, several of the Model 39's progeny remain in the line, usually with a "TSW" suffix that stands for "Tactical Smith & Wesson" and includes flashlight rails. One that doesn't is the S&W Performance Center's Model 952 series, a superb target pistol in 9mm that's much less finicky than its direct antecedent, the .38 wadcutter Model 52 that was introduced in 1961. Another choice specimen is the Model 457 from their "value series," which is reliable, accurate, and quite possibly the best buy available in a compact, conventional double action .45 auto for concealed carry.

As guns depreciate and departments buy new replacements, third generation S&W autos with limited wear and often in remarkably good condition come onto the market regularly. Seen as "old school," they sell for stunningly low prices, and are at this writing one of the best values available in the used firearms market in general.

Personal Experience

Like so many others, I loved the feel of the original Model 39. Legend has it that when Jim Hoag designed the first beavertail grip safety for the 1911, he cloned it from the Model 39. Its double action trigger was set perfectly for an average size hand like mine. I did find the accuracy spotty, particularly with the Model 59, which often wouldn't stay in the big "K-Zone" of a Colt silhouette target at 50 yards. Others found the same. Writes Mullen, "...I have seen one Model 39 that shot into 1-1/4 inches at 25 yards with good ammunition. I have seen others that could not shoot into 8 inches."[4]

This got better with time. Most of the third generation guns, I found, would do more like two, two and a half inches at that distance. I've broken an inch with both the Performance Center 5906 and the Model 952 at that distance, with 115-grain Federal 9BP and Winchester 147-grain subsonic ammo. The 952, of course, is a designated target pistol. The PC5906 differs from the standard 5906 in that it is fitted more tightly across the board, has a proprietary bushing, and is re-sprung to delay unlocking until the bullet has left the muzzle, guaranteeing consistent alignment of bore with sights for every shot.

In 1988, the police department I then served became the fourth in the country to adopt the S&W Model 4506. Ours functioned flawlessly with Speer 200-grain "flying ashtray" hollow points, the best .45 ACP load of the time. (Interestingly, they would occasionally fail to extract Remington brass. Mindful of the loss of confidence ISP troopers had experienced with malfunctioning 9mms in training, I was meticulous to cull all Remington headstamps out of the practice ammo when the budget forced us to train with commercial reloads. Later, both Remington and S&W fixed the incompatibility, and it does not exist with current S&W .45s

Former IDPA National Champion Tom Yost shot his way to fame with third generation S&W autos, this one in 9mm.

nor current Remington .45 ammo.) A couple of years later I joined another PD, and found myself often carrying the 4506 by choice until that agency adopted another brand of .45 auto as standard issue.

Taking thirty or so years to get it right, S&W wound up with a truly fine service pistol in its third generation guns. For the person concerned with losing their weapon to a criminal in a struggle, the combination of workable manual safety and magazine disconnector feature has proven itself many times over to be a life-saver. These guns re-

main excellent choices today for law enforcement, professional security, or home defense and personal concealed carry needs.

Notes

[1]Stebbins, Henry M., *Pistols: A Modern Encyclopedia*, Harrisburg, PA: Stackpole, 1961, p. 24.

[2]Mullen, Timothy J., *The 100 Greatest Combat Pistols*, Boulder, CO: Paladin Press, 1994, p. 368.

[3]Jinks, Roy G., *The History of Smith & Wesson*, North Hollywood, CA: Beinfeld Publishing, 1977, pp. 241-242.

[4]Mullen, *op. cit.*, p. 368.

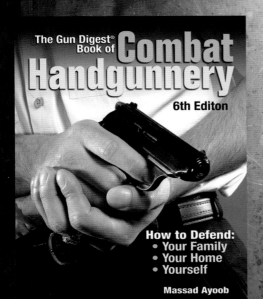

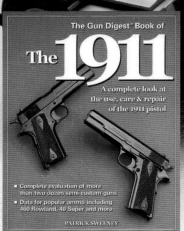
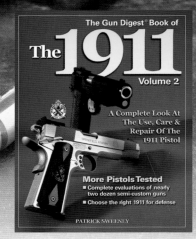
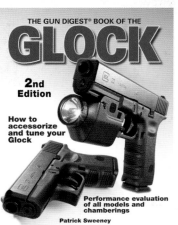
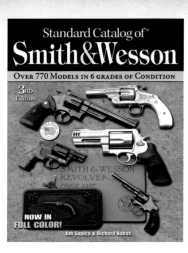